French Moves

Oxford Studies in Dance Theory

MARK FRANKO, Series Editor

French Moves: The Cultural Politics of le hip hop
Felicia McCarren

FRENCH MOVES

The Cultural Politics of le hip hop

Felicia McCarren

OXFORD
UNIVERSITY PRESS

UNIVERSITY PRESS

Oxford University Press is a department of the University of Oxford.
It furthers the University's objective of excellence in research, scholarship,
and education by publishing worldwide.

Oxford   New York
Auckland   Cape Town   Dar es Salaam   Hong Kong   Karachi
Kuala Lumpur   Madrid   Melbourne   Mexico City   Nairobi
New Delhi   Shanghai   Taipei   Toronto

With offices in
Argentina   Austria   Brazil   Chile   Czech Republic   France   Greece
Guatemala   Hungary   Italy   Japan   Poland   Portugal   Singapore
South Korea   Switzerland   Thailand   Turkey   Ukraine   Vietnam

Oxford is a registered trademark of Oxford University Press
in the UK and certain other countries.

Published in the United States of America by
Oxford University Press
198 Madison Avenue, New York, NY 10016

Library of Congress Cataloging-in-Publication Data
McCarren, Felicia M.
French moves : the cultural politics of le hip hop / Felicia McCarren.
    p. cm.—(Oxford studies in dance theory)
Includes bibliographical references and index.
ISBN 978-0-19-993995-4 (alk. paper)—ISBN 978-0-19-993997-8 (alk. paper)
1. Hip-hop dance—France.   2. Hip-hop—Social aspects—France.
3. Hip-hop—Political aspects—France.   4. France—Social life and customs.   I. Title.
GV1796.H57M43 2013
793.3—dc23   2012034147

For Adil Amedeo, my hip hope.

CONTENTS

ACKNOWLEDGMENTS

My thanks go to all the dancers and choreographers, managers and cultural agents, and my colleagues in research, in particular Roberta Shapiro and Isabelle Kauffmann, in the world of French hip hop. Claire Bustarret and Anne H. Bustarret were excellent companions at performances and I thank them for their insights.

Research on this book was facilitated by a grant from the Ministère de la Culture et de la Communication (2000–2001) and by a Tulane University Research Enhancement Fellowship (2007–2008).

A portion of chapter 2 appeared in an article "Monsieur Hip-Hop," in *Blackening Europe: The African American Presence*, edited by Heike Raphael-Hernandez (Routledge, 2004), pp. 157–169. A French version of part of chapter 3 was published as "Le hip-hop. Une autre revolution," trans. Christine Langlois, in *Terrain 44. Imitation et Anthropologie* (March 2005), edited by Nelia Dias, pp. 57–70. I am grateful to the editors of these two collections for their comments. All errors and omissions remain my own.

The opening section of chapter 5, on Cixous, was presented at a conference in Stockholm, Sweden, organized by Cristina Caprioli of CCap Dance, in October 2000. A condensed version of chapter 1 was presented at the invitation of Professor Carrie Noland, at UC Irvine, in March 2012. Professor Etienne Balibar, UC Irvine, responded. I am grateful to all for their engagement with my work.

My title is borrowed from a conference held at Columbia University in 2004: *French Moves: Performance, Language, and Identity in the Francophone World,* organized by Professor Madeleine Dobie, and to which I contributed the "…Moves." My thanks to the conference organizer and participants responding to my paper, "Hip Hop and *le patrimoine*."

During the difficult fall of 2005, after the evacuation of New Orleans, I was honored to be named a Visiting Katrina Fellow in the Department of Comparative Literature at Princeton University. I thank in particular

Professor Eileen Reeves, who managed to find me in the diaspora and bring this opportunity to my attention, and the then-chair of Comp Lit, Professor Sandra Berman, for shepherding me and my family. The time spent at Princeton proved crucial to the elaboration of my thinking about this and other publication projects.

With support from the office of Tulane University's Provost Michael Bernstein, my undergraduate student Ann Calvin researched the bibliography of global hip hop and made the topic her own. Johannah White was the best librarian one could hope to work with. At Tulane, I am also grateful for support from the School of the Liberal Arts and Dean Carole Haber; for the ongoing support of Newcomb College Institute and its head, Professor Sally Kenney; for tech support from the Innovative Learning Center and FLITE (Foreign Language Instructional Technology), especially John (Curry) O'Day; and for support from my colleagues at Tulane.

During their mission in New Orleans, 2007–2011, the Consul General of France, Olivier Brochenin, and Rina Brochenin turned the official residence into a welcoming home for local and global francophone cultures. Connie Balides and François Brunet pointed me toward important work that enriched the book. My colleagues and students at EDUCO, our Paris program, provided me with the best work environment for laboring over the final manuscript while serving as présidente of the association in 2012–2013.

At OUP, Norm Hirschy has been everything one could wish for in an editor. I am delighted that this book launches OUP's new series in dance theory under the stewardship of Mark Franko. Kate Nunn and Lisbeth Redfield were attentive to the author and the manuscript, and everyone who contributed to the book's design and production is hereby thanked.

Many friends read all or portions of the manuscript as it evolved, and many discussed with me its contexts. I am grateful to Julie Hernandez, Olivier Bourderionnet, Victorine Mbengue, and Myriam Ferdjani for bringing to our garden in Faubourg St. John in New Orleans their understanding of what was going on in France. Shana Sassoon brought her fine insight into global hip hop culture and Abram Himmelstein and Rachel Breunlin of the Neighborhood Story Project inspired me to remember my community arts roots. My husband, Ali, built me a room of my own in which I was able to finish the manuscript. His fellowship and that of our son have sustained me during the writing at home and abroad. Although I began this work before he was born, in ten years my son has become a hip hop dancer without any instruction from me, and although I wrote the book, he now outdances me entirely.

INTRODUCTION: "FRENCH"? CIRCULATION, IMMIGRATION, AND ASSIMILATION

I am walking up the street in a suburb of Paris: Montreuil, Mali's second biggest city. After Bamako, there are more Malians living here than in any other city in the world. Today, a Saturday morning, more are heading up the slope coming from the metro terminus than going down to work. In front of the foyer (Montreuil's principal residence for single workers whose families are not living here in France) that houses a good number of Malian and Senegalese men, some of them, wearing the *gandoura* and sandals, are loading or unloading foodstuffs, bags of goods wrapped in plastic; others are working on their cars; and still others are crossing the street to use the phone booth or heading over to the post office a few blocks away.

Having recently returned from a year in North Africa, I understand for the first time how these men are Malian yet living in France; even residing and working in France, they remain Malian. They bring their culture with them and will some day probably take it back to Mali with them. This is an alternate model of migration to the one that has been discussed under the banner of integration in France over the last forty years. When, on another day, a Friday shortly before the beginning of Ramadan, I see the residents of the foyer butchering two lambs in the courtyard, I think I see why stereotypes about Muslim immigrants and religious practices have endured in France, in spite of long-term assimilation and the very different experience of second- and third-generation immigrants born in France. I understand better than before one Parisian student, who came to Montreuil to take a hip hop dance class, telling me that she cannot tell her Malian family, who lives across Paris, that she dances, and that her father has one family here but another wife, another family in Mali. To her hip hop she brings this rich cultural background and in her hip hop she seems to escape from it or from her family, joining a youth movement and a performance community unknown to her family, one that allows her to dance "French."

Later the same day, I am walking down a street next to the Bastille and am drawn by some drumming; in fact, it is not a strike or demonstration but a carnival, a long parade of groups of musicians and dancers representing the various DOMs and TOMs, French overseas *départments* and territories, and some former colonies. Most of these groups are wearing the garb representing the Antillean island they call home; there is also an Indonesian group, one from Trinidad, and several from Guyana, as well as the Antillian groups, dancing African-style dances and wearing historic French costumes, African tribal costumes, or Indian saris. Many of the young people accompanying the parade wear hip hop clothes—a style called *baggies-baskets* in French—and I realize that in their dancing the *hip hoppeurs* have incorporated not only dance forms visible on Paris stages but also the moves of their dance cultures. These cultures parading down the street are dance cultures, and all of these Parisians representing some country they consider their other home know how to dance to the Caribbean rhythms being played.

Hip hop dance forms arrived in France in the early 1980s and were taken up first in suburban and immigrant communities, becoming a forum for debate on assimilation and multiculturalism. Break dancing and the various styles referred to as *la danse debout* were practiced in and associated with mixed immigrant communities and had to negotiate local cultural practices often (also) brought from abroad: Islam and its practice in France; Antillean carnival culture; traditional dance forms surviving in communities in exile.

The Tunisian-born head of a French *association* for immigrant mothers with French children tells me that immigrants do not return home; she is working from the now generalized model of immigration from francophone Africa and North Africa. Her organization makes possible "intergenerational" voyages within France that educate the mothers about the country that is their children's if not their own and discourages the great expense of returning whenever possible to the *bled*. One can only conclude that there are many layers of immigration in France: some staying and others returning. Some cultures integrate and other cultures remain distinct; some are performance cultures and others are ostensibly opposed to certain kinds of performance. The cases explored in this book consider hip hop dance developing in the context of the particularities of these groups, sometimes referred to in French as *groupuscules*, coming to terms with the state's *universalism* that does not recognize minority groups. I work through this question through what might be called the "universalism" of dance performance in France, dance's civic status, strategically deployed in the socialist choice to use this dance as part of a *politique culturelle*, and its choreographic language.

A decade-long project, my work on hip hop dance in France was at first inspired by the French revolutionary rhetoric, and modern practice, of universalism: I have seen hip hop as a practice of inclusion, with the early motto of solidarity *black blanc beur* and of valorization of a popular form even while developing an aesthetic as *la danse urbaine*. This was how *le hip hop* was promoted by politicians, *fonctionnaires,* and cultural agents at the national, regional, and local levels in France, with the goal of using culture to address social problems: with funding, and in sync with dance institutions (state and local festivals, regional centers for choreography and dance training, national and city stages), hip hop developed into a form of concert dance, *la danse urbaine*, recognized globally as French (or European). I have emphasized, under the rubric of a particularly French universalism-in-dance, that hip hop there, because of such state funding and support, developed differently from its US predecessor. But the universal, humanistic values expressed in this dance form, not unlike other forms of hip hop worldwide, respond in France to a legacy of universalism that is now acknowledged as problematic. Coming into these communities in France, hip hop became part of the discussion about identity, postcoloniality, and globalization: it was a mode through which the discussion about multiculturalism and minorities took place, using performance first to remark on social differences and, eventually, to posit a broader equality moving beyond social status or difference, arrived at through acknowledgment and understanding of such differences, largely ignored in the universalist rhetoric of the French Republic.

By noticing that these men from Mali cling, in Paris, to some of their Malian-ness even as the Malian-born Parisian student seeks to escape her family via hip hop; by seeing the cultural links to dance present for people of many cultures living in Paris; and by understanding that hip hop did not arrive into a vacuum, my analysis participates in the theory of the circulation of cultures, from acculturation to transculturation. But in this context, my analysis also explores how a discourse of difference in France is an acknowledgment that the "universal" ideal of *égalité* has not created equality, although my Tunisian-born French friend who is helping her fellow immigrants integrate clearly believes it can still be achieved. Hip hop dance, I argue, suggests that it can only come through acknowledgment and valorization of difference rather than culture-blind assimilation. This idea is often described as an "Anglo-Saxon" model of particularism and associated with US identity politics. (See Figure 0.1) I now understand many French hip hoppers' choice to identify with US black culture as a way to bring attention to their inequality, a difference that has not otherwise found expression in the universalist rhetoric that denies the existence of

FEEDBACK

Please spare a couple of minutes to help us with these questions. Your answers will assist us in planning and fundraising for future festivals and events. Simply complete and return to the FREEPOST address overleaf (no stamp is required).

1 Which event did you attend? _____

2 What is your postcode? ☐ ☐ ☐ ☐ ■ ☐ ☐ ☐

3 London residents only. Which borough do you live in? _____

4 Do you consider yourself to be disabled?   Yes ☐   No ☐

5 Are you   Male ☐   Female ☐

6 Please tick the box that applies to your background

Asian Bangladeshi	☐	Black British	☐
Asian Indian	☐	Any other Black background	☐
Asian Pakistani	☐	Chinese/Vietnamese	☐
Any other Asian background	☐	White	☐
Black African	☐	Other group	☐
Black Caribbean	☐		

7 How did you hear about this event?

GDIF brochure/leaflet	☐	'The Greenwich Festivals'	☐
Eflyer/Website	☐	Greenwich Dances	☐
Press/Radio/TV	☐	Friend/Word of Mouth	☐
Advertisement	☐	Other - please secify	☐

8 To join the free GDIF mailing list, please provide your name and address here:
(we won't share your information with anyone else)

_____

_____ email _____

7 Please write here any comments about the event you attended:

_____
_____
_____
_____

Figure 0.1
The "Anglo-Saxon" model of particularism.
"Feedback" form distributed to the public at the Greenwich Dance Festival, London, summer 2011.

race, even as racism, sadly, shapes and limits their daily lives. While cultures may circulate globally, locally—in the French suburbs—access to certain kinds of culture remains an issue. While French hip hop values inclusiveness, hip hoppers have themselves been excluded. While French socialist governments remade French social space with high-tech architecture and infrastructure, *banlieusards* were largely left out. As Amizagh Kateb, the son of Algerian French writer Kateb Yacine, sings (in English) with his (French) band Gnawa Diffusion on their album *Algeria*: "I live in the *banlieue* without . . . information."

While hip hop is a global form, imitated worldwide via the media, as well as through contact and live performance, its specific development in France into a form of concert dance, facilitated by an omnipresent dance culture and the financial support of a *politique culturelle*, also suggests a counterexample: the aestheticization, rather than mainstreaming and marketing, of this form, adopted from the US . Sociologist Roberta Shapiro describes this process surrounding French hip hop as part of a general phenomenon of "artification," or valorizing a practice as art.[1] This was my study's opening paradox. Invited by Shapiro to join a group of researchers working on hip hop dance in France in 2000, I found a divide: on the one hand, a popular form, almost a sport, linked to parties, battles, the *banlieue*; on the other hand, a new influence in choreography and concert dance, with master classes given in state-funded dance centers, performances on big "national stages," and companies touring in France and overseas. While this team of sociologists was studying how "hip hop dancer" became a *statut civil*, a job description entitling *intermittants du spectacle* to unemployment compensation, and how the form is transmitted and how it is aestheticized particularly by dance reviewers in the press, less attention was being paid to the choreographies themselves. This became my focus: the development of hip hop concert dance in France.

In fall 2000, at a lunch for cultural actors in the hip hop community ("urban cultures") at the la Villette festival, I described hip hop as borrowed from the United States, and the response from French participants was: "ah, for you it is a question of acculturation," because they did not see it that way. The festival itself consecrates the "founders" and the "old school" and screens films on dance history and the civil rights movement in the United States; however, it is not focused on US culture or cultural domination but rather on the immigrant communities in France. The leading sociologists argue that the multicultural margins of French cities and French society do not resemble the US inner cities identified as the place where hip hop was first mixed. But at my hip hop dance class in the suburbs of Paris, my teachers say "this dance comes from there. . . ." Yet they do not understand why its founders are not famous and they do not understand the lyrics to the rap songs they like. At the round tables, too, I find that people do not know that much about the United States and don't really understand how things work—or haven't worked—there. So the United States is there at the "beginning" of the story, but it is not the only reference, is not the only language, and, in fact, is less than ever the foundational point or reference against which hip hop dancing in France is measured. Presenting my work in California in 2012, I found that the break dancers in the audience know the French hip hop "champions" now respected all over the world.

Readers may find it strange that my investigation of the global form of hip hop focuses on a nation and a national choreographic specificity. In emphasizing the special case of France, I do not want to suggest that US hip hop, or global hip hop, is less complex or less interesting, nor do I assume that, when state-supported French hip hop is sent on cultural embassy to other places, for example, the United States or the Caribbean, it is received unproblematically as "French." But the French model of state "recuperation" of the form is both unique and groundbreaking and—along with European but also especially Belgian cultural institutions—has led the way for its choreographic and even national development in other countries and other contexts. With hip hop dance companies rising up all over the world, a French influence is evident—for example, in the Laotian company Lao Bang Fei, following a French model while incorporating local (national or ethnic) movement traditions, representing a new opening (in Laos) to Western music and influence but also, significantly unlike the French model, danced by a middle-class or upper-class elite. In a recent report by French television, TV5MONDE, the young Laotian dancers' discourse sounds like the French one of the past twenty years: solidarity across the group and individual self-expression using the entire body.[2]

In France, *le hip hop* has not been about gangs and guns. It refers to US culture without reproducing it in any simple way. Nor has it been about "bling." As I turn the pages of *Hip Hop Weekly*, a glossy magazine produced in Miami reproducing "iconic images" by photographer Chi Modu of music stars from 1980 to 2010 and advertising the First Annual Hip Hop Weekly Music Awards (to be held in 2011), I see again how far what we call "hip hop" in the United States is from what is called *le hip hop* in France. Fans of US hip hop music may be disappointed by what they find here: this book is not about how the French public has embraced rap music or hip hop culture in general. It is not analyzing *Hip Hop Weekly*-style accounts of the music industry and the private and performing lives of its stars. Nor does it say anything about US inner-city histories or realities, except as they are imagined or represented at French hip hop festivals.

The French word *hip hop* refers *primarily* to dance. It refers to the African American dance idioms incorporated in it, as well as the pan-African dance forms represented by French dancers' culture, training, and exposure to the myriad forms of African and other dance accessible in France. This dance was, as I will discuss here, "protected" from the commercialization that has marked hip hop in the United States. In France, its potential countercultural force was channeled by the state, and by local educational and social structures, toward the realm of noncommercialized artistic expression. The moves themselves remain radical, but they are produced, taught, and consumed in a very different way in France.

At the same time, France is a heavily mediatized nation, with rapid expansion of media and broad access to telecommunications, television, and Internet across the same decades that brought hip hop. Although high-tech modernization did not "trickle down" to the suburbs as planned, most French hip hop dancers have now moved into the information age and use digital video, YouTube, and social networking as part of their art. The "global" accessibility and diffusion of moves on the Internet, the opportunities for the promotion of one's choreography or music, and the global reach of the online community are also significant factors in the development of a specifically "French" hip hop even as it focuses on local communities and national problems through the structures called *associations*—not-for-profit, often neighborhood-based groups.

What are these "French moves" and what is the so-called *mouv'*—the social movement they give legs to?

In the first part of this book, I focus on choreographies that manifest new identities for their dancers through the poetics of dance's figural language. I argue that in the choice and elaboration of this language, dancers are enacting new roles for minorities, changing the discourse and terms for discussion of race and identity in France: first, through reference to US culture and second, through a specifically "French" choreographic language. In the second part, I consider choreographies (and their conditions for creation in classes and studios) that elaborate these identities via new technologies as well as new dance figures. In these choreographies, there are references not only to the US origin of the forms and the European *politique culturelle* that developed them but also to the global culture and global media that have influenced them. In these examples we see dance poetics as *poesis*, creation, responding to an idea of *techne* not based in a tool but in the gesture of its use and an idea of technique that can include dancers as well as engineers. Simultaneously "high tech" and "low tech," featuring the dance technique that is a form of bodily knowledge or practice and in some cases the use of image technologies for choreography, these choreographies stage the fascination and fear that technologies generate, as well as their proposed new possibilities for bodies.

From my perspective as a US-trained dancer and academic, the French embrace of US black culture seemed at once both refreshing and patronizing. While African American music and dance forms contributed to our American uniqueness in France—in line with a long performance history—the French perspective seemed to me at times confused. First, the dance form seemed closer to funk music and to jazz dance forms than to a specific well-defined category of US hip hop; second, it was already mixing with modern dance choreography and being performed on dance stages for a dance public. Nobody was talking about dancing "in the break," which dancers in New York still used to define the basics of "break dance."[3] Finally, it was being funded by the Ministry of Culture and *studied* and taken seriously by dance critics, sociologists, and other academics.

When I took up this work in 2000, I was amazed to find, in the hip hop dance world in France, many of the moves and beats familiar to me from modern jazz dance in Chicago in the 1970s and 1980s. This hip hop built, in the dance studio, solidly on a jazz dance vocabulary. Many of its teachers in France now have that background and receive diplomas in that form, one that has become standard "show dancing" in many genres of entertainment. Although breaking and head spinning were not things I had done before in jazz, I had learned elements crucial to them in modern dance, contact improv, and gymnastic Pilobolus-inspired group work. In many ways, nothing here was new to me.

In the United States, I felt that I knew nothing about hip hop: I was far from the music, and I began by reading Nelson George and bell hooks; but in France, somehow, I was completely at home in the form and found its ownership being projected onto me. I approached my work as a comparatist and dance writer and, perhaps most importantly, as a dancer. French hip hoppers, finding out I was American, would spontaneously utter a few words of English, take me under their wing, and recognize some immediate kinship. From their perspective, this had to be "my" dance. Whereas in the United States I am a professor in a discipline that takes no account of my dance training, in France, the fact that I was white or an academic was secondary to my being American and a dancer. My response to those dancing hip hop in France then ranged from feeling a sense of inclusion to feeling a sense of proprietary defense of a US culture that in no way belonged to me.

French hip hop is homage to African American popular culture, but it is also a *displacement* onto the United States of the nondialogue with peoples of African descent within France. Because there has not been historically any significant discourse about the postcolonial status of immigrants from former African colonies into France or of Antillian French citizens of African descent, Pap N'Diaye has argued, this discourse took shape using the United States as an example.[4] The use of the word *black* (rather than *noir* or *les noirs*) in this discourse in French, adopted from English, reveals the arc of this displacement. Yet in spite of this evident homage to US black culture, more than a simple gravitation toward the prevalence of global popular culture, it has always seemed to me that the French are somehow missing the point of the American sources and sites of hip hop dance. The history of the development of hip hop in France suggests that the United States was never really the point; it was a *politique culturelle* aimed at the specifically "French" mix of multicultural immigrant (or immigrant background) populations in the suburbs. The state's cultural and social structures seized on this interest in US black culture to encourage art, addressing economic and social inequality in France, displacing the form into the French context, and developing it as state-funded art—seemingly at the antipodes of the US form. And yet ultimately, because the state cannot control the choreographies it was producing, the hip hoppers have gone beyond this mandate and have made works that work metaphorically, transformationally, and transcendentally. If French hip hoppers relate to the gangs at the root of a US counterculture, the dance form early on left aside the terrain of gangs. For the most part, hip hop in France has not been about violence or commercialism but about cultural production as a vehicle to a different, better civic engagement. Only recently has the term *violence inter-communautaire* been used to call attention to the internal violence in *banlieue* communities.

During my research, I was shocked to arrive in dance class in a suburban housing project, announce to the teachers that I was on a mission from the Ministry of Culture, and find that such an announcement created little stir. I was equally shocked that dancers who didn't understand the words could dance to hard-core rap songs, interpreting them musically with no concern whatsoever about the meaning or content of the lyrics. I couldn't believe children's hip hop dance classes were also accompanied by such songs. I was convinced that the situation in the French suburbs had nothing to do with America and that it was a paradise of arts funding, social security, and *multiculturalisme*. The events of 2005 forced me to rethink this perspective.

THE MOVES AND *LE MOUV'*

In the beginning, there was the rage needed to dance this dance—"il faut avoir la rage pour danser"—said the Lyon-based Company Käfig founder, dancer/choreographer Mourad Merzouki, in an interview on film in 1995. There was the rage over the stories this dance form had to tell—about civil rights (a concept that, I am told, is untranslatable in French), political disenfranchisement, technological-industrial disempowerment, and the events leading to emigration. There was rage about the invisibility, unrepresentability, or incommunicability of the situation of immigrants in

France, often second-generation immigrants seeking the language in which to speak about the failures of decolonization, integration, and assimilation. How did this dance form come to "speak" French, to speak of the French version of these global ills—the legacies of colonialism, the impossibility of "minority" discourse in the face of the rhetoric of universalism? How did it come, above all, to speak *differently* even in a culture that has emphasized universalism over difference, and to represent a kind of freedom often traded in for the acknowledgment of difference in the French Republic?

In the case studies this book considers, hip hop is a figure for the rage of those still referred to as *issus de l'immigration*, a figure for the madness of colonization and the continuing effects of European racism for so-called postcolonial minorities. It is also a figure for the expression made possible in French, by a European forum, for debate about colonial histories and their neocolonial aftermaths. If this book argues for French urban dance as a particular language within a global movement, it is because the rage that sparks it does not entirely characterize it. If *le hip hop* is dancing out rage, it is also a dance of catharsis, which has staged but not solved the social problems to which it gives expression. Raising the problem of disempowerment and bringing to view what hadn't been discussed, at first, the subject of French urban dance was unquestionably the problems in the *cités*. But in elaborating a movement vocabulary, in the past decade, this dance has come to speak about other things: to figure its dancers as something or someone else, to include dance forms from other cultures, to travel—metaphorically, to speak about global culture and global movement of people and information.

US journalists reviewing early French hip hop choreographies on tour in the US saw both similarities and differences with American black culture. The "French-Algerians" of Compagnie Käfig, for example, had not only funding, but also a recognizable style that made them different. Yet their *situation* as immigrants and minorities in France is understood as comparable to that of the originators of hip hop.

As early as 1999 Shayna Samuels pointed out, in *The New York Times*, that European hip hop dance shared significant terrain with the U.S. original, but wasn't a copy. The Lyonnais Compagnie Käfig, performing in the U.S. for the first time, replayed in reverse the arrival of American ballet companies in France, "ballet's original home turf." But Samuels adds that "the troupe's arrival will also be making a kind of multicultural statement—that no one place owns hip-hop anymore." Qualifying Käfig as a troupe that "melds French, North African and Spanish—specifically Andalusian—elements" she describes their practice as "cross-pollination" and sees their New York performance of "Recital" in a program shared with Bronx-based Full Circle

Souljahz as a "convergence of hip-hop's branches and roots." The recognition of a historical syncretism in dance, the discourse of métissage, and multiculturalism, all suggest the extent to which Käfig's cross-fertilization is a successful (rather than failed) multi-cultural development of and response to the U.S. form. While "the French troupe's dancing is more stylized and fully choreographed; the American's is rougher around the edges [...] Both remain true to the essence of hip-hop, expressing a belief in the power of community and the human spirit. Moreover, Käfig's six dancers all have Algerian roots, making their experience as immigrants and minorities in France not unlike that of the Latino, Caribbean, and African-American populations who originated hip-hop in the United States."[5] Rather than seeing a significant difference in two national signifying systems and their cultural products, this reviewer finds convergence and mutual inspiration.

The *Washington Post* review of Käfig's performance of "Recital" that same week in Lisner Auditorium by Lisa Traiger emphasizes the "elaborate production values of French dance theater" and other details that differentiate it from the U.S. form. The dancers' style isn't baggy jeans and big shirts, but features "trim sportswear" and "camaraderie not regularly seen in competitive hip-hop circles. [...] The men enjoy unison work and play off one another in a brotherly fashion with little animosity. Instead of stony glares and gangsta poses, they smile broadly while spinning, popping, sliding and flipping." Traiger mentions a seventh dancer, "Franck Louise, " whose score channels "Middle Eastern and classical music" and who plays a ghostly hooded conductor onstage.[6]

While prized for virtuosity in the U.S., hip hop in this French version does something more: beyond the grace and strength of precise moves, Traiger describes Käfig's "tongue-in-cheek tweak to the poses of American hip-hop practitioners." Their elaboration of the form is not only not a copy, but already a *commentary on* a less sophisticated, more rigid *gansta* battle mentality. Käfig, in this review, has "created a piece that unifies the pluralism of popular culture with the high art of the concert stage." And ultimately, Traiger qualifies it as "plain fun." Somehow as if ahead of their U.S. counterparts and predecessors, this company of "French Algerian descent" can move on and elaborate the popular form into art. These two reviewers understand, in a first exposure to French urban dance, how it develops from the US original, and what it does differently.

How this French form developed, how it recast an original form to raise questions about and respond to its own national context, is the subject of this book. While the difference of French hip hop is the most striking factor that I attempt to explain, it follows that readers will want to compare my case study to other outcomes in other places, to the hip hop that has developed globally in multidirectional relations rather than simply the one-way relation to the United States. In "Global Hip Hop and the African Diaspora," Halifu Osumare has emphasized, in Cuba and Brazil, the similar construction of hip hop as a positive community force rather than a counterculture commercialized around concepts of machismo and bling. She underscores the origins of this positivism in the movement itself.[7] While its styles may recall the look of US rappers, French hip hop has, for much of its history, avoided commercialization and focused on community and personal development, an "aesthetic," and a bohemian urban lifestyle of peaceful multiculturalism and coexistence. Tim'm T. West considers how homophobic tensions have dominated in US hip hop;[8] in the multicultural paradigm in France, such tensions have been largely absent, in spite of the relatively late arrival of women's and gay rights' activism and public discourse. In France, some of the community and pedagogical sides of hip hop dance come close to what in Britain is called "community dance" and have been instituted as a social program, often in economically depressed neighborhoods.[9] Many scholars writing now on global hip hop music and dance conclude that the youth practicing it are cultural agents or theorists who are synthesizing local and global cultures and acting as cultural agents or even entrepreneurs.[10] Many agree that it is the global or synthetic dimension of hip hop (rather than a national or local focus) that gives its practitioners political power in individual contexts, even when that power is recuperated or manipulated by the state.[11] Significantly, some hip hop that has been politicized declares itself uninterested in politics,[12] and in some contexts, such as in China, hip hop has been used to allow youth some cultural freedom that appears to substitute for other political freedoms.[13] All of this research focuses on hip hop's multiethnic and multiracial world and emphasizes diasporas, "interracial" interactions, and local contributions.[14]

Whereas in the economic capitals of the world, dance performances on big concert stages are often seen as "the icing on the cake," a wonderful product of economic surfeit, dancing in the developing world is often associated with notions of "authenticity" of cultures not only less developed economically but in colonial history often deemed "primitive." French hip hop addresses this strange divide, as a concert form reflecting the importance of dance performance in bourgeois European culture, but also speaking simultaneously of the US-style global capitalism of some forms of popular entertainment and also of their working-class origin, that resonates in the pre-history of those forms and echoes in their global spread. Indeed, French hip hop is constituted by a range of forms—concert dance as well as the battles considered "authentic" with their gymnastic bravado and sports-style following. French hip hop, indebted to US inner-city culture, funded by France and Europe, danced by citizens with immigrant backgrounds, simultaneously strikes all three chords: the European *politique culturelle*, the articulation of minority identities in the Anglo-Saxon model, and the projection of "otherness" onto immigrant and post-colonial subjects.

The "French" part of my title is meant to be provocative. First, while the journalists I have just cited point out the visible *national* style of French hip hop, which it is my goal to describe and analyze here, within France itself the idea of a "French" identity—an idea with a long history—has recently been contested as a critique of immigrant and in particular Muslim populations. Interviewed in May 2011 on French television, former immigration minister Eric Besson, who headed the debate on French national identity in 2009–2010, declared the debate closed and yet responded angrily to critique of the debate as a "stigmatization" of Muslim citizens or residents of France.[15] These recent debates about French identity will be discussed in chapters 2 and 3.

Focusing on a "national" culture is also problematic because, as is well known, cultural theorists have abandoned the notion of national cultures, considering them rather as "deterritorialized" in order to explore global cultural influences in what Arjun Appadurai refers to as "genealogies of the present." Appadurai proposes the idea of "ethnoscapes" to replace former geographically located concepts of villages, communities, or localities. In *Modernity at Large*, he writes that "genealogies reveal the cultural spaces within which new forms can become indigenized" while "histories of these forms may lead outward to transnational sources and structures."[16] In this sense, while I sketch the history of the arrival of hip hop in France, I focus on the genealogy of its local development there and then its international "mission" as an emissary of "French culture." In this, I am also following other researchers' approaches to local hip hop phenomena: Alison Fensterstock, credited with inventing the term "sissy bounce" for a New Orleans variant of rap music, argues, "rather than try to place it within the current spectrum of American hip hop, it makes much more sense to understand it as an outgrowth of New Orleans music culture itself."[17] Considering French hip hop dance within French cultural and performance traditions, I too am looking "deep" here rather than "wide," but without losing sight of the fact that many of hip hop's French citizens have immigrant family histories or personal backgrounds.

Appadurai also uses dance (in this case, cabaret performance in Mira Nair's film *India Cabaret*) as an example of how "imagined lives are negotiated" and of what he calls the "self-fabrication" of dancers' identity—in this case through performance. In this example, Appadurai emphasizes "how ethnography in a deterritorialized world might handle the problems of character and actor, for it shows how self-fabrication actually proceeds in a world of types and typification." For Appadurai, the example of these Indian dancers, migrating to the South for work, shows "the tension between global and local that drives cultural reproduction today."[18] While I believe that performance always constitutes a special case of the fabrication of identity or its negotiation with an audience, the example of French hip hop both calls for such a deterritorialized ethnography and yet also suggests the power of the local—even national—example. Its dancers are simultaneously claiming a kinship with African American culture, with the global youth culture it has inspired also in places such as North and Sub-Saharan African, where these French dancers may still have family; yet they are also claiming citizenship and equality in France. Through these references to other local or global cultures, this demand for recognition and rights from the nation they feel they have been excluded from works through their particular version of the global gestures they adopt and adapt. "Frenchness," then, is not simply a label I impose on this hip hop generation, but a claim they are making in their movement. With French *hip hoppeurs* working out their problems via hip hop, it is less the American or global circulation of hip hop that is at stake for them and more the specificity of French histories of immigration and assimilation. At issue is the performance of a certain kind of inclusion in the cultural production of the republic rather than the exclusion from it that many hip hoppers have experienced. "Frenchness," then, is defined as belonging or associative rather than any intrinsic quality evoked by the debates on French "national identity" of 2009–2010, deemed by many to be racist and reactionary. But belonging in France has also signified—it is important not to forget this detail—a nation that chose to fund hip hop rather than the US-led war in Iraq before joining the war in Afghanistan. The use of the term *francophone* allows me to describe a "national" context in which a nation is not defined by its borders and instead considers the particular mix the nation's situation has produced.

New patterns of migration in France and Europe make it difficult to hold onto the "francophone" part of my thesis, and new dance languages evolving make it difficult to insist on any particular "hip hop." But in these new developments, the questions of language, dance language, and identity remain central. More recent immigration from non-Francophone countries, from Eastern Europe and from British former colonies in East Asia and South Asia, has added another layer to the complexity of immigrant identity in regard to the French state. In comparison to the francophone migrants from the Maghreb, for example, these new migrants (often coming to France via the UK or since the closing of the UK frontier) have arguably a more difficult time following the historical assimilation model and integrating into the French system. Yet they also represent a global Anglophone culture, that France aspires to in a different way. The growing presence of migrants from South Asia, Indian, Pakistani, Bangladeshi or Sri Lankan populations in Paris, some with visibility in businesses such as telecommunications and internet storefronts, has changed the mix of a historically francophone immigrant population. With this more recent wave of immigration, France is more closely linked to Britain, but also to global migrations (the US, the Middle East) than in its post-colonial migrant phase. It is beyond the scope of this book to consider the role that this new migration plays in French hip hop. The most visible dancer of Bangladeshi origin in Paris in 2012 is the contemporary British dancer/choreographer Akram Khan, currently *artiste associé* of the Théâtre de la Ville. While in Britain, Khan's work may be seen as representing minority populations in a concert dance form that also draws from kathak dance, in a recent issue of the French dance magazine *Danser* he is shown as a tourist in his parents' native country, as an artist representing European rather than indigenous forms.[19]

At the same time, the "Frenchness" of the hip hop I am describing here crosses borders, as does the hip hop dance form. The Théâtre de la Ville in 2012–13 is featuring urban dance choreography by Sébastien Ramirez and his partner Hyun-Jung Wang, who describe themselves in the program: "We are a couple, a Frenchman with Spanish and Catalan roots living in Germany, and a German-Korean woman born in Germany. In life, one accumulates identities." The program goes on to describe their dancing: "Sébastien Ramirez is an autodidact, coming out of the hip hop dance culture, running his own company in Perpignan. [. . .] Hyun-Jun Wang was born in Frankfort and lives in Berlin. After a ballet formation, she learned b-girling techniques, newstyle and house dance. [. . .] Together they are developing a stage language that one could call 'Urban Tanztheater' that deploys this dance vocabulary on the subject of 'cultural difference.'[20]

In *Ethics After Idealism*, Rey Chow defines two conceptions of culture prevalent in intellectual debates of the late 1980s, at the moment that hip hop arrived in France:

> One conception, derived from anthropology, refers generally to "lifeworlds" or "ways of life"; the other, more closely defined as the sum of refined achievements of "civilized" life, is usually associated with literary, artistic, and musical classics, which together make up what some call "high culture." The first of these conceptions of "culture" is a foundational one: it sees culture as inclusive of common beliefs, attitudes, and behaviors and as basic to every group of human beings.

The second conception, as pointed out frequently, is ideological and exclusionary, based as it is on the hegemony of particular class interests. At the same time, the two conceptions could also shift their emphases to generate cultural politics of a different kind. For instance, the potentially democratic idea that everyone possesses a "culture" could lead to the conservative culturalist view that every culture must be understood strictly and only in its own "specificity." Conversely, the notion that culture is "high culture," though elitist, may nonetheless allow for "achievements of refinement" to exist in every country, so that "culture" becomes viewed paradoxically with equality, as a cross-cultural, rather than local, phenomenon.[21]

This perspective in which cultural categories can become inverted speaks eloquently of the situation of French hip hop developing through the 1980s into the choreography of *la danse urbaine* without losing its working-class grounding in the following two decades. While I hope to point out the specificity of French hip hop's development, it is not in order to emphasize an elitist view that French hip hop is somehow "better." At the same time, this book emphasizes the socialist politics, the inclusive francophone poetics, and the anthropology of practice underpinning the French approach to funding dance classes, companies, and choreographies. In pointing out the French "achievements of refinement" in this context, I am critical of the now global market fueled by the US culture industry but, at the same time, want to question why the local French situation appears to grant not simply state "recuperation" of artists but also a kind of equality, an artistic opportunity, often unavailable to dancers in the United States. In so doing, I do include alternate voices, such as Bill T. Jones's, naming the weakness he finds in the French choreographic system. The goal is to show that French hip hop creates something new *in its context,* responding to a French critique that says that labeling dance or dancers as "multicultural" does not serve them well, and marks the abandonment of French republican (meaning revolutionary) universalism.[22]

This book attempts to define what I refer to as France's "republic of culture," (along the lines of what Mireille Roselle has defended as "tactical universalism" or "Republican multiculturalism")[23] then, in the most positive sense: funding hip hop to produce art, bringing the *banlieue* into the broader public sphere, a figural dance language, a body-based poetics that nuances the politics of bodily identity by moving beyond appearance, and an intellectual climate that understands dance as a practice of bodily knowledge, that accords dancers a *statut civil,* an intellectual and economic status as performers and teachers of a *technique.*

I will focus on French hip hop's exemplary transformation into *la danse urbaine* (urban dance), participating in a global performance culture both influenced by and influencing the domains of politics, new media, and debates about identity. But it must begin, as all the French narratives do, by focusing on the US and African-diasporic roots of the form, if only then to show how these roots are recast in "French" dancing. There is a growing corpus of work with an interdisciplinary impetus in dance and performance studies considering African dance forms as they are reprised and varied in US modern dance, new work on the history and actuality of African American performance forms, and broad reconsiderations of visibility and corporeality in dance as a political (not only politicized) form of expression. Research on African dance and the African diaspora, on black dance in the United States, has considered both specificity of the forms and their global reach and syncretism. Writing in 2002, in the introduction to his edited volume, *Dancing Many Drums, Excavations in African American Dance*, Thomas de Frantz links the analysis of the forms to complexities of theories of race and notes that "studies that acknowledged the slippery nature of 'race' in dance began to appear in the 1990s with the publication of work by Anne Cooper Albright, Sally Banes, Ramsay Burt, and Susan Manning," but that "few African American dance artists have received full biographical exploration" and that "the development of journalistic criticism that can engage the complexities of 'black dance' and acknowledge its political dimensions has been slow to emerge."[24] An explosion of work on global hip hop dance has accelerated this process, but such research rarely focuses on this genre of concert dance.[25]

Hip hop is also identified globally as black dance, with African roots, and for many it represents what dance scholar Brenda Dixon Gottschild calls an "Africanist aesthetic."[26] But its French dancers are both closer to Africa (most coming from families with immigration history, many from Africa, a majority of North African origin) and further from hip hop's African American or Latino origins. Caribbean French citizens relocating to the Hexagon from the Antilles are perhaps closer to the music culture that inspired early DJing and dance parties in New York's Jamaican, Latin, and Caribbean neighborhoods, but they have their own particular beats and song traditions. French hip hop's complexity echoes that invoked by De Frantz: it is also subject to a different discourse about race in the French Republic in which *black*, *African* (solidarity across North African and Sub-Saharan African immigrant communities in the suburbs), and the term *race* itself carry a particular resonance, to be discussed at length in chapter 3. In the French context, the African American influence circulates alongside the more immediate presence of the cultures of African immigrants, questions about the assimilation of North and Sub-Saharan Africans and their descendants and now about minority representation that may take its cue from the United States but reflects a different national discourse. Indeed, as I will discuss in the next section, themes and images from black America are sometimes seen as substituting for the lack of such discussions, in the French *metropol*, about Africa and North Africa, serving to raise questions about colonialism and postcolonialism that have come more slowly into public discussion there. Thus, between what Nelson George called "Hip Hop America" and global hip hop, something—I argue here—has happened in France that is a recognizable part of this global cultural traffic and yet quite different. After a decade of exploring the terrain in France, I cannot help thinking that when I say "hip hop" in French, it means something different than the same word spoken in English. It is precisely my point here to study the national specifics of a transnational form, arguing for France as a particular case and emphasizing French (and Parisian) particularities. In this book, I do so by focusing on the microclimate for hip hop dance in Paris; on the *observation participante* of dance classes, round tables, rehearsals, debates, and performances; and through participation in research funded by the Ministry of Culture, carried out in French, and focused on the local rather than the global. Indeed, France's unique support of hip hop, and the history of its *politique culturelle* and cultural protectionism (*exception culturelle*), requires that we see this case as a "national" example that recasts in significant ways the global flow of performance forms.

Within France, urban dance is said to represent minorities in France and, by extension, the world of immigration and thus of global forms. From a perspective outside of France—one represented by Bill T. Jones and discussed in chapter 2—it is a strikingly *French* form that represents first its French development and then a multicultural diversity inspired by African American culture, as well as informed by source cultures of its dancers and world dance performance traditions. Finally, it has been used by the state and also strategically by state cultural programs, becoming global, as it were, in reverse—through state-funded and organized touring. With this layered complexity of development, this history of state recuperation, the professionalism and civic status of the form, it can be hard to remember its countercultural origins and the social critique at its heart.

POLITICS, POETICS, AND TECHNIQUES

This book offers three rubrics for analyzing hip hop dance in France. First, I argue, it is a political as well as politicized form. Chapter 1 emphasizes the nature of the intervention hip hop performs in the social sphere of the republic. It is a political art not just because dance, as symbolic action, is always potentially political, which I will argue here through the work of both philosophers and dance theorists, nor because hip hop has been extraordinarily politicized around the globe. In France, in fact, it should be identified as a *socialist* dance, at least in terms of a "party affiliation" or the name of the government(s) first finding it important enough to support. This "use" of hip hop dance for a socialist party platform would seem to locate it somewhere other than the mainstream of US and global capital; indeed, for many years, as one cultural agent describes in chapter 2, French urban dance developed in state art contexts rather than in the commercial market. Those readers unfamiliar with French cultural politics may find this formulation naïve, but the cultural program that French urban dance was part of, as *le hip hop*, was, I believe, admirable.

In this case, the political component of French hip hop is enacted by the social profile of its dancers, representing a *francophone* or postcolonial perspective on the issues of difference, integration, and universalism. Danced by working-class suburbanites, hip hop provides a forum for the "excluded" part of society who come, via dance, to figure the universal—that is, to link their exclusion first to the history of African Americans but also to humanity in general. Their choreographies can be read as commentary on these questions of citizenship in France; beyond their narrative content, the dances also represent the mobility of dancing subjects in the republic: some of these dancers move out of the suburbs and onto national or international stages; some move beyond fixed images of their communities. As French sociologist Isabelle Kauffmann has argued, dancing hip hop has offered *banlieusards* an alternative to assimilation and their "assignment" to the suburbs.

But in France, the "way out" for hip hop dancers has not been purely through commercial success. Rather, it might be success in being programmed at national dance institutions—centers and stages—or in getting regional state funding for choreographic development. "Getting out" or escaping through dance has also meant using dance's transformative power to say something *different* about dancers in the suburbs. Urban dance is often praised for relating the situation of its own dancers—true to "socialist realist" form—but has also nuanced their situation, represented the complexity of cultural difference and bodily appearance. In chapter 1, I argue that what has made this suburban form political is not its politicization (its political recuperation), but what Etienne Balibar refers to as a political, collective potential: as politics, and as a movement poetics.

The second term I adopt to analyze French urban dance is poetics: hip hop there is closely linked to the national language of French, bringing diverse (and especially recent immigrant) populations together. Chapter 2 relates how hip hop came to "speak French"; how the US form was transformed in France, through cultural agents and the state, as well as its dancers; and how it used the African American experience at the roots of the form to "speak" of the cultural difference and political situation of its dancers, finding themselves in the 1980s without a "voice" and, in the 1990s, seeking a vocabulary to express the differences that led to unequal opportunity. This hip hop dance is 'francophone' in that it is linked to an international (and, in some ways, colonial) *francophonie,* the shared culture of language that unites the Hexagon with former colonies. In its French version, hip hop has in fact come to be called—by cultural administrators—a "francophone" dance, articulating the "minority" and "immigrant" background, the often "postcolonial" situation, of many of its dancers or of their families. Yet as a dance form in France, it builds on the historic civic role of dance in public culture and on a wealth of dance texts appreciating and theorizing bodies in movement. As a movement poetics, it signifies through reference to something else, shifting the terms of the debates about the role of bodies in cultural practices and cultural identity. In this way, my work differs from those who focus on hip hop's "power moves" and defines the French model differently.[27]

This book charts what hip hop dance contributes to *idées reçues* about immigration and *francophonie,* most recently manifest in the question of "French identity." Urban dance, I argue, nuances debates about "Frenchness" in the field of French cultural studies, and its performance brings a new perspective to the question of citizenship posed in the French context by Balibar *because* it "speaks a different language"—other than English—and because it speaks "differently"—extraverbally.

Chapters 1 and 2 also consider the history of this cultural transfer from the United States to a different social organization in France. While previously I saw only how much better off French youth were even in their suburban housing projects than our US inner-city youth and what greater opportunities they had, for example, in this artistic development of hip hop, I now understand—in part because of the 2005 riots—that in spite of these differences, French youth have also been abandoned by their government and social structures, and that hip hop was one way for them to speak of this otherwise inadmissible reality: first, to articulate the difference that universalism ignores, the differences that have made youths in the suburbs less "equal"; and second, to declare that the French projects had failed in their own way as miserably as the US projects, and that French youths of all ethnic origins, by espousing hip hop, declared solidarity with the specific struggle of African Americans of their generation and of an earlier generation. Finally, to choose this dance, to make it "speak French" and to make it an art respected and valorized in France, gave an outlet for the rage—the frustration of the reality of inequality that found no place in the discourse of universalism and no language in which to speak of it.

These dances refocus a culture thinking universals onto the image of bodies not fixed but themselves circulating meaning—bodies that, along with their gestures, signify difference, whether it is defined as ethnic, cultural, or racial, and stage this difference, collapsing onto performing bodies the problems raised recently, for example, in the Musee du Quai Branly's exhibition of cultural diversity. Performed by dancers seen as representing diversity, who are often also the choreographers of their movements, the question of multiculturalism raised by the museum comes alive in this dance. It emphasizes the lack of representation—artistic and political—among France's minority populations, vastly underrepresented in the French National Assembly. It also points the way to new understandings of bodily identity and data gathering about such identity in a "wired" republic, shifting the terms of universalism from one that excluded through suppression of differences to one that can only be accessed through recognition and representation of differences. It is not the bodies dancing themselves—or not only—that make this shift possible, but rather what these bodies do: the poetics rather than the muscle power of their representation.

The third term I introduce here to explore French hip hop is *technique*. If the politics are socialist (dancing "of the people" supported by the state) and the poetics are French/francophone ("saying something different" or "saying differently"), the *techniques* studied here are those bodily techniques emphasized in French anthropology and theory of practice of the past four decades but, at the same time, working in parallel with a high-tech modernization, live and body based in an age of information. Although dance performance is often linked to notions of cultural authenticity, to pretechnological cultures, *le hip hop* has both used the dominant technology of its time and counteracted the "sluggishness" that theorists argue is brought on by it, integrating the technological and the live, the ancient and the hypermodern capacities of dance. Finally, then, far from socialist realism, this dance offers an embodiment that is a political representation ("we are a visible minority," "take account of us") at the same time that it is a figural projection ("we are something other than we appear") and an intellectually valorized body of knowledge rather than a somatic simplification of identity. Hip hop has emphasized bodily difference and exclusion—the physical side of citizenship—to represent something broader. Dance techniques are learned and developed in a context that signals not simply submission to a cherished institution (concert dance tradition in France) but also the practice of some individual agency, embodied engagement, or personal expression. This example engages theories of bodily agency, performativity, and social resistance or change playing out in choreography and on the dance stage as well as in the studio and the street.

It is, ultimately, in a setting that valorizes dance not only as a *poetic* and *civic* art but also as an *intellectual* practice, a mise-en-scene of ideas, and as *technique*, a knowledge practice, that this dance form could assume the importance that it has. Chapter 6 concludes the section on technology and techniques with a reading of some key French texts on the theory of practice, explaining the intellectual background understanding bodily practice *as* thinking and opening the way for the cultural politics focused on hip hop. Shaping the intellectual environment for redefinitions of culture and cultural practices over more than three decades, these texts also help to link dance to new technologies through the concept of technique as a form of bodily knowledge. This book continues my earlier attempts to integrate dance performance into the cultural and intellectual production of its time, to give dance its place in the history of ideas and in the history of bodies shaped and conceived by the dominant technologies of their time and also responding to them. I want to understand how a dancer such as Storm (a German dancer from Berlin who often performs and teaches in France) can be described by French hip hoppers as a *bon technicien* (with the best dance technique), using the same word, *technicien*, that one would use for an engineer, and find useful, for this, Andre Leroi-Gourhan's idea that even in prehistory, dancing isn't primitive or a-technical but a manifestation of *motricité figurative*.

Chapter 6 puts hip hop and its pedagogy into the context of this French theory of practice, considering how a climate created by French intellectuals focusing on practice and understanding bodies as sites of cultural production and knowledge allowed hip hop to be taken seriously by ministers of culture and a left-wing elite. Reading the work of Leroi-Gourhan, Bourdieu, and de Certeau anticipating and accompanying a shift to an idea of culture as practice, using dance as a subject, an example, or a metaphor, provides here a context for the appreciation of the countercultural form and an explanation of its "recuperation" by state agencies for social purposes, and in particular the institutionalization of its transmission or pedagogy. Chapter 6 also documents how hip hop dance technique is learned, complementing these theories of practice, and the concept of mimesis is discussed in the transmission of hip hop moves. The use of the mirror in the dance studio allows a double reflection on the aestheticization of the form in class training and the constitution of a community in performance, significant for the Malian-Parisian teen described earlier, who comes to hip hop class without her family's consent.

Many of these same texts contribute to the argument of Carrie Noland's recent book—also discussed in chapter 6—*Agency and Embodiment: Performing Gesture/Producing Culture*, which argues for the active role of bodies in shaping culture, in particular in performances that do not simply reproduce cultural norms, because of the way in which gestures both "embody culture" and "submit it to transformative variation." In this book, I argue that it is not only a cultural or anthropological understanding of gestural meaning but also a choreographic figuration, a meaning through reference or metaphor that is fundamentally poetic, that allows dancing bodies to be understood as more than they appear to be. When Goye Tangal, whose nickname is Tip Top, slides backward across the stage in Compagnie Choream's *Epsilon*, what he is doing may recall or refer to African dance; when he travels to Africa for the first time with Choream, he is representing France in some former French colonies, including the country his family emigrated from. But while these hip hop choreographies encode elements of many different kinds of dancing, they also allow their dancers not simply to "stand for" or represent an ethnicity that they physically resemble, but to move beyond such resemblance to a realm of bodily expression that finally gets beyond bodies. The theoretical texts that attribute to bodies a certain knowledge, a *savoir-faire,* whether conscious or subconscious, inherited or adopted, voluntarist or mechanist, such as Bourdieu, de Certeau, and Leroi-Gourhan attach to certain gestures or practices, set the stage for a significant valorization of dancers as more than simple agents of cultural reproduction.

Chapter 3 considers *how* hip hop choreographies express this cultural difference in France. This dance has been "used" for integration under the banner of its universalism, serving as a visible reminder of difference even as it emphasizes the nonvisible complexity of cultural, ethnic, or religious identity. Two choreographies by autodidact dancer and choreographer Farid Berki stage thinking about colonial encounter and conquest, and about postcolonial exodus and emigration, about mobility and identity. Drawing from a range of moves, both from within the hip hop dance vocabulary and from outside of it—modern dance, capoiera, Latin popular dance— Berki's choreography is among those that expand the hip hop dance idiom into a choreographic language. One of the works considered here is also one of few to consider the *history* of colonial domination and slavery, set in a tropical landscape; and his work over two decades provides a continuity between that imagined history and the contemporary, global state of exiles, the subject of a more recent piece.

Chapter 4 presents the alternative to the fantasies of dance's cultural authenticity or resistance: exposing the historical links between dance and technologies, the elaboration of visual technologies in sync with dance, and wondering about the role that dance plays in regard to new media. Two full-length hip hop choreographies in the mold of the machine ballets of the 1920s, one by Franck II Louise and the other by Compagnie Choream, comment on the wonders and horrors of technology and the hybridism of human and machine. French hip hop choreographies discussed in this book respond to a range of discourses about dance, from the "primitivism" projected onto it as a physical form to a means to represent a futuristic, hybrid body; from traditional to hypermodern dance; from sport to art; and from popular to classical and concert dance.

In my previous work on dance, I have explored the historical side of choreography's interaction with institutionalized thinking about bodies. Two earlier books have analyzed dance performances in their production contexts to show that they were not simply miming or collaborating with institutional structures—presenting performance as a pathology or as productivity—but rather commenting on and even leading ideas about what and how bodies mean. Here I am exploring our own contemporary history, again "recuperating" dance as more central to political thought and social theory than is usually thought, and giving it a central place—if not a leading edge—in opening discussions about bodily identity and difference in a context from which such discussions (although prevalent elsewhere) had been largely absent. In this, I have ultimately focused less on "the body" or bodies dancing—questions of the flesh, questions of pleasure—often raised in work theorizing the body. Instead, I have focused on the performing bodies not as an end in themselves but as vehicles of meaning, vehiculating meaning irreducible to an essentialized body or bodily identity.[28]

I have shown, in my historical cases, how performing bodies exposed the cracks in the institutions that supposedly regulated them, how they revealed the nonclosure or noncompletion of institutional codes or interpretations of bodies. Thus, while arguing that the romantic ballet was far more than the idealized prostitution it was reduced to in the public imagination, I showed that that prostitution was itself a function of the institution and of the imagination, arguing not for ballet's purity or innocence but for the institution's collusion with the very practices its ideals seemed to ignore. I showed as well that dance did more than mime or sell an institutional productivity associated with scientific management, commenting critically on such productivity even while giving it a choreographic face. The idea has been to show the radical invention of certain movements by focusing closely on the historical context of production, emphasizing both the uniqueness of the historical moment and the dance inventions it produced and performance's power to create its time and eventually recreate it.

While very much a product of high-tech France, hip hop choreographies such as *Drop It!* (2000), *Epsilon* (2001), and *Zou* (2008) refer to the attractions of new media while also reminding audiences of its toxic effects. This simultaneously high-tech and low-tech form reminds us that dance has often figured technological modernity in performance history, and also that high-tech often works to "naturalize" technology—in other words, to make it look natural. Concert dance has often staged the human machine, the mechanics or thermodynamics of movement, and many themes of the "machine ballets" of the 1920s are visible in French hip hop. But it has also paralleled and critiqued new conceptions of technology, including telepresence in a globalized world, "virtual" subjects, hybrid bodies, social webs, and mobility and instantaneity. *Zou*, by the Compagnie Los Anges, offers what I will call a socialist-utopian view of technology that marks the historic situation of hip hop over the last two decades and dreams of a sustainable national future. While digital performance is not the subject of this book, *Zou* reminds us that hip hop in France did rise in sync with it and did take advantage of largely state-generated technologies, a vision of France as a hypermodern, highly functioning, high-tech space. While ostensibly a low-tech form danced by those without access to "information," hip hop has registered and responded to the benefits and pitfalls of modernization.[29] Discussed in chapter 5, Yiphun Chiem's solo *Apsara* pairs break dance with Cambodian traditional dance to describe the layering of identity in the migrant experience and suggests the impact of both live performance and recording technologies in the global communities transmitting dances.

I argue here that France has made urban dance, *le hip hop*, possible. But what, in turn, does this dance make possible in France? A discussion of bodies previously ignored or marginalized; a revaluation of bodily citizenship (there where one is); a reconsideration of the new positioning of bodies in a culture facilitating mobility, anonymity, and telepresence. Hip hop was strategically developed within and naturally grew out of such an environment: it comments on those conditions of its production, and it is danced with passion by new generations of French with other cultures and languages in their background, drawing new audiences. While the days of hip hop funding may be over and dancers nearing forty describe themselves as "over the hill," these forms of institutionalization of hip hop *à la française*, as different as they may be, have not dried up its potential for social engagement or to produce young dancers and new choreographies and bring to the theater a public who might never otherwise attend. French hip hop's live roots, its discourse of authenticity and solidarity of the suburbs, have strangely not disappeared in the highly produced, high-tech theater form it has become. While its potential for "selling out" to US-style consumer-driven forms increases—for example, hip hop choreographer Bianca Li (although never one associated with old-school "authenticity") judging the television show *Dancing Show*—a "French" model of arts funding is still also viable, with one of the regional choreographic centers, the Centre Chorégraphique National de la Rochelle now directed by hip hop dancer/choreographer, Kader Attou, founder of the group Accrorap.

Dancing—whether on stage, in one's room, or in the lobby of a station or a public building—is a way of responding to one's situation and in particular to current conceptions of bodiliness (bodily customs and behaviors). In France, dancing hip hop is a *parti pris*, a self-positioning in the world and in the public sphere. It is more than steps; it is more than muscle, the pain of physical discipline, or the pleasure of aesthetic self-expression. It is, like all dance forms, a form of both individual and community development; it is a commentary on the current state of life in bodies. For many of the dancers in hip hop dance class with me, it was a way out, and a way in.

Arriving at dance class by bus or metro at night, all of us were getting out of our apartments, out of our bodies, by getting into the moves and, ultimately, getting into what is called *le mouv*—the movement. We all wore sneakers and came into class with our sneakers on—street shoes in a dance studio, an exception. We might economically reproduce a movement sequence to the beat, or even master and enjoy it, or chip away at more difficult moves that would take many more days of practice. We would push ourselves to do what our teachers were doing and recognize our limitations even while seeing them realize a dream of movement with ease before our eyes.

Earlier in this introduction, I mentioned that in the dance studio there was very little that was new to a dancer trained in the full spectrum of modern dance, from ballet to jazz to tap, improvisational and social dance forms. But this statement needs qualification. Hip hop's basic steps may be familiar—humans have two legs, and only so many combinations are possible! But the energy, the attack and *élan,* of the so-called up-rock or standing form distinguishes it and brings it close to those forms, especially of African dance, in which the feet barely appear to touch the ground. There is an emphasis on the "up" rather than the "down" part of the leg gesture. The spring in the step—the "hop"—is associated with male dance forms worldwide: rather than emphasizing the ground or the downbeat, hip hop springs up from the ground with a certain enthusiasm and yet maintains a relaxed upper body. This is not the same "upward training of the body" identified by Georges Vigarello [30] or associated with the ballet's *danseur noble*, but it does require some of the same skills. Its performance requires not simply natural ability, but the discipline of every dance form, and for me it was hard to get right. Something of this energy, the hovering over the ground, the cool on top of the hot footwork that marks other modern forms such as tap, lingers even in the transformation of the form into urban dance.

This book describes the dancers and teachers, choreographers and performers, students and "stars" of French hip hop dance, and recounts their practices and performances as well as my situation as outsider and insider in their movement. Even in class, there is a kind of rage in the form: some of the moves are outrageous. We are taught to move frenetically, not just to the beat. We learn to crawl on the floor and skim over it backwards. We all try to spin on our heads. But these moves are all at the service of a performance that is disciplined, skill that is acquired, and dancing that is not only for oneself but also for others. It is not jazzercise and it is not gym; it is a dance class with a recognizable format.

More than the hip hop battles or *soirées* (parties) that punctuate *le mouv*, this book focuses on the dance studio and the stage, far from the US inner-city neighborhoods that are constantly generating new forms, new steps, and new confrontations but also far from the now glamorous global hip hop music industry. In France, the dance studio has become a place of invention where the hip hop vocabulary was elaborated from its recognizable idioms—popping, locking, "up-rock" standing dance forms, smurf and skating, as well as break dancing, "down-rock" on all fours, or balancing on the arms or the head. With state or local funding, arts grants, community grants, and choreographic development, it is this dance taking the stage at dance and urban culture festivals, this particular choreographic language, this "French" hip hop, that I experienced and that I try to relate here. How did these moves—stomping, shaking, freezing and unfreezing, crawling, twisting, spinning upside down—come to speak "French," and how did they come to animate a social movement—artistic and political—in France? Hip hop moves are globally seen as American, and it would be easy to argue that it was performing a kind of "Americanness" that helped hip hoppers get out of their "assigned" place, or that it was an American conception of community that helped them "in" to a more visibly constituted minority community, or that hip hop represented a tradition of American dance forms innovating from popular forms. The source cultures of French hip hoppers' families, data about their ethnic background or *dominante culturelle*, are not the subject of this book, nor are all the minority communities in France discussed. Exploring the French exception, I am considering *le hip hop* not as part of a culture industry, but as a product of their republic of culture—a context in which dance nuances bodily identity politics with a bodily poetics and in which it is considered a *technique* of the body, a knowledge practice qualifying dancers for a *statut civil*. In this context, in this book I ask: what sort of "French" hip hop is being made by these dancers even as they emphasize their difference, identifying with an African American form or a global form, making a claim for Frenchness even while contesting its borders? And how has that "Frenchness" made them move?

PART ONE

Politics and Poetics

CHAPTER 1

Hip Hop Citizens

Politics, Culture, and Performance

MITTERAND *HIP HOPPEUR*

French histories of *le hip hop* usually begin with the arrival of African American dancers—"the pioneers"—in Paris in the early 1980s.[1] There followed the diffusion of a movement, music, and graffiti culture from US inner cities via TV and video, and with both popular and institutional support. The famous photograph of French President François Mitterand posing with first-generation *hip hoppeurs*, sporting a backward baseball cap on his noble brow like a laurel wreath, became an icon for his administration's enthusiastic promotion of youth culture. Embraced by the so-called *gauche caviar* (the elite "caviar Left") after Mitterand's election in 1981 and led by his culture minister Jack Lang, French hip hop lent itself to a *politique culturelle* that supported the teaching of this dance in the *maisons des jeunes et de la culture* and in gyms and public meeting rooms of housing projects in big and small towns, and that would eventually fund dance companies and hip hop choreographies. With an entirely positive tone of inclusion masking the social realities of unequal opportunity, hip hop developed as a *banlieue* form in France with dance companies surrounded by debates about social welfare and antiracism. By the late 1990s, French hip hop had developed a choreographic language; self-trained dancers were regularly coming into contact with modern dance choreographers and dance vocabulary and expressing ideas other than the state of things in the suburbs.

In France, no one contests that hip hop is an American form, and yet it is impossible to overestimate the role played by the French state and by the Ministry of Culture and regional cultural actors in this development. By 2000, hip hop dancers, after an initial stable engagement, could attain the status of *intermittant du spectacle* and receive unemployment benefits when not working in the theater. Choreographers received public funding as commissions for festivals or evening-long pieces for hip hop companies. Hip hoppers began to be hired to appear with groups like the Cirque du Soleil, to appear in the Olympics and other festivals and parades, to dance on television, and even to dance with the corps de ballet in opera productions, for example, in the 2001 production of *La Chauve-Souris* at the Paris Opéra de la Bastille. *Danse* is only the first of the impressive list of forms of "urban culture" (*Danse Théâtre Musique Expos Multimédia Vidéos Débats Ateliers Librairie*) included on the poster for the annual la Villette festival in Paris, the *Rencontres des Cultures Urbaines*. It is at such festivals that several US hip hop dancer/choreographers, including Philadelphia's Rennie Harris, whose choreography is discussed later in this book, first found support from French funding structures.

The French adoption of American hip hop takes on an added dimension when considered in the context of the *exception culturelle* protections applied to cinema. Although France moved eventually, in the early 1990s, to put quotas on the projection of blockbuster Hollywood films, the importation and development of hip hop dance follows a different model, in some ways closer to the pattern set by modern dance, eventually institutionalized as *la danse contemporaine* alongside classical ballet. Thus, rather than a form of cultural imperialism, this importation might be viewed as an often-repeated pattern of French absorption of avant-garde or foreign forms into its cultural institutions. French funding for modern dance has also been exceptional and has drawn American dancers and choreographers over the past three decades. It could be argued that in some fields, US artists and performers have historically found themselves more appreciated in France.

No image distinguishes French hip hop from its US source better than that of President Mitterand, *hip hoppeur*: in direct contrast to the disparaging of rap and hip hop musicians during the Reagan and Bush administrations overlapping his own two terms from 1981 to 1995, Mitterand's public embrace of the *génération hip hop* suggests not so much its politics as its politicization. Ministries of culture and culture budgets have paid for a hip hop or "urban dance" inflected with a European tone and for the most part avoiding commercialism—or rather, being promoted as "high culture" with a socialist rhetoric and spirit of "popular culture."

This view of French *hip hop* as a successful, socialist-utopian form has only recently, with the election of a Socialist president in France on May 6,

2012, become a dominant discourse again in France. Social ideals were crushed by financial crises, political fractures, and, only a few years after Mitterand's election brought an end to twenty-three years of domination by the center Right, the loss of a coalition-left parliamentary majority and the return of the Right via a new "cohabitation" government headed by Prime Minister Jacques Chirac. Worse, of course, from the left perspective was the rise of the extreme right Front National Party headed by Jean-Marie Le Pen, winning more than thirty seats in parliament in the legislative elections of 1986, and the eventual sidelining of the *Parti Socialiste* entirely from the second round of the presidential elections in 2002, when voters chose Chirac over Le Pen. In 2012, with many of the same factors and parties in place, the idealism represented by major arts funding and a hip hop Ministry of Culture in France appears once again to be mining this historical moment for inspiration. François Hollande's speech to the crowd at the Place de la Bastille in Paris on the evening of the election spoke of a diverse France unified rather than fractured by *communautarisme*, echoing sociologist Edgar Morin's recent formulation of "la France une et multiculturelle."[2]

The role of dance and especially "urban dance" in this cultural politics, launched first by Mitterand but visible in the European Union highlighting cultural production, continues to distinguish the French model from the American. It was made clear in a touring lecture by the (French) European Minister of Culture Renaud Donnedieu de Vabres in the United States in 2008. Not a socialist himself, Donnedieu de Vabres described the importance of culture to the "project" of Europe ("We must get Europe back on track through culture!") and emphasized that the "theme of cultural diversity is a truly European message. This fraternity, this respect, this equalitarian dignity of cultures, religions, languages, artistic and intellectual expression is a European message of prime importance."[3] The speech ended with a rousing series of *vivas* building in crescendo to "Vive la diversité culturelle" ("Long live cultural diversity!"). Listing back to back the "achievements of the intellect in all fields: from science to poetry, from the visual to the corporeal art of dance, from cutting edge technology to the rarest, most fragile of crafts," Donnedieu de Vabres emphasized culture's power to bring to discussion issues of "identity, pride, open-mindedness, roots, creation, tradition, modernity, values…words which seem to be banished from our vocabulary when it comes to talking about Europe!" Culture's work is no less than helping Europeans find a "frame of reference, meaning, repossession of their own history" as well as "freedom and democratic power" and bringing Europeans together "to halt the spiral of fear" and "to reconcile our diversity."

Here "dance" means of course the publicly funded contemporary dance centers, thriving across France (the regional nationally administered choreographic centers), and the ballet or opera dance companies brought to life over the past decades by contemporary choreographers such as Mark Morris at La Monnaie, in Brussels. But it also means, significantly, hip hop or urban dance: "embracing urban cultures" means admiring hip hop for its promotion of cultural diversity. From the perspective set out by Donnedieu de Vabres, hip hop's dancers, regardless of their ethnic or cultural background, are the diverse "others" of Europe. That dance seen on one side of the Atlantic as counterculture from the start could be, in Europe, part of the "political, economic, and spiritual perspective" on Europe's future, an agent for the reconciliation of differences, makes clear that hip hop, a popular form across Europe today, is more than a matter of cultural transfer. Perhaps most striking in this "embrace of urban cultures" is the political project now more than two decades old; it remains to be seen whether, following the "recuperation" Donnedieu's discourse vows to continue, hip hoppers elsewhere have themselves been influenced by the French version.[4]

How did this dance, described in the 1990s by its French dancers as a dance of "rage," become the dance of European union? How was this form, countercultural at the roots, recuperated for a redefinition of French national culture in sync with a European "project"? What potential did French ministers see in hip hop, and why did they emphasize hip hop's "otherness" (rather than its global centrality) to serve their ends? How did hip hoppers in return "recuperate" their spaces and themselves? For any reader following my argument from the introduction through these pages, it might be tempting to dismiss French hip hop as "recuperated" counterculture, as a socialist veneer glossing over a capitalist global form, or as miming rather than addressing problems of violence, inequality, and minority invisibility in France. But in this chapter I argue that French hip hop dance has done something more, both in spite of and because of the national program for it, its strategic importation, and its eventual exportation as "French" culture. It is in response to debates in French studies—the notion of a "French" cultural identity, the history of a French "cultural exception" worth protecting, and the opening up of that cultural identity to other, "multicultural" influences—that I am drawn to ask what difference dance performance makes when considered in these debates. But it is through work in political and performance theory that I will shape that response.

In his review of Mitterand's *politique culturelle*—the *Grands Projets* and the cultural programs initiated during his presidency—Panivang Norindr emphasizes that Mitterand's focus on a national cultural identity was a utopian, Renanesque vision. Urging *oubli* and assimilation, Mitterand's program repeated the colonial error of attempting to erase ethnic identity and difference. Norindr concludes:

> Until a more pluralistic notion of Frenchness and "nationhood" is elaborated in France—that is to say, one that would recognize the untenability of a return to an essentialist notion of culture and nation and account for the transcultural nature of cultural exchanges and dialogues—the *français par acquisition* or unassimilated minorities will continue to be considered aliens and will be unable to find a legitimate place in this "nation-space," a complex discursive formation capable of preventing new cultural expressions that constitute *la nouvelle francité, la plus grande France*, from rising in the new French urban landscape.

In this book, I suggest that—not without difficulty—they danced their way in.

HIP HOP IDENTITY POLITICS

The French embrace and development of hip hop dance is contradictory at best. The socialist *politique culturelle* understood early on the potential popularity of this form and, in establishing it in nationwide youth centers and programs based in town halls, effectively channeled its rebellious power, or so it seemed until the 2005 uprisings in the suburbs. Those who found the uprisings unsurprising, or limited in scope—a perspective shown in the widely circulated parody of a French weather report, showing flames popping up all over the map of the Hexagon—would certainly argue that hip hop's radical potential had long been defused by its state "recuperation." Rather than counterculture, hip hop has served a public function in France and has benefited from arts funding at the national, regional, and local levels; yet hip hoppers who don't believe they've been "co-opted" or "recuperated" by politics argue that they themselves are "recuperating" their communities. What interests me here is that both energies are present in the *mouv'* as in the moves themselves, and that artists and practitioners may be funded but are not ultimately controlled by the state, just as they may be angry but are not expressing only anger in their dance. While hip hop in France was manipulated to cover over the reality of consumer-driven culture, both in its public performances and individual practices, it has seemed to labor for something else.

If I am arguing here that the focus of French hip hop turns out less to be the United States, the global dominance of American culture or consumerism, than postcolonial realities in the Hexagon, it is also because, as Pap Ndiaye has argued, African American culture has been studied in France and substituted for the largely unstudied and undertheorized presence of minorities, arising from the immigration of the last thirty years.[5] It should also be noted that "immigrant," a label often used to describe French citizens who are minorities and their art, does not have the same resonance in the United States, broadly described as an immigrant nation, as it does in a France that has often focused more on an essentialized heritage rather than its own migrant history. In the debate between French- and US-based researchers over multiculturalism, the term itself is contested. French *multiculturalisme* is inspired by the United States, the so-called Anglo-Saxon or communitarian model, but its subject has become France itself. Yet in representing this "new" multiculturalism in France, in the development of a choreographic language, hip hop dance has turned from staging the situation of its own dancers to speaking figuratively—poetically—about the world stage. The description of multicultural France through the metaphor of *francophonie*— usually applied in France only to the areas of the world in which French is spoken—will serve me here to describe the "Frenchness" of this dance that is also a movement poetics, using "French" or the French cultural program and choreographic institutions to elaborate a broader language of identity, community, and citizenship.

An exploration of French urban dance brings to debates about identity and difference the materiality of dancing bodies but also the metaphorical potential of gesture and movement. It stages *hip hoppeurs'* identification with black America but restates their case as visible minorities—African and North African, Asian, and Caribbean—in terms of immigration and the French context, and as "French" cultural patrimony, as art. It registers changes in bodily behavior brought by social and political change, by the cultural influences on a new generation, but also by new technologies. It posits a corporeal identity against an assimilationist universalism acknowledged as a failure, unequal opportunity, and against a background of new mobility and anonymity made possible by new media and telecommunications. It raises the question of appearing and belonging, citizenship and rights, as Etienne Balibar defines it, not in a postnational context, but rather *there where one is.*

Across the three topics of the state's cultural politics, the protectionism offered to French cultural products, and the introduction of a theory of multiculturalism into the national-cultural profile, this chapter will explore this French particularity at issue—both the vague concept of "Frenchness" that has animated debates in the academic field of French Cultural Studies and the specific debates in France around cultural politics and its contribution to "French" identity. I ask here what hip hop has to do with it. In every case I study, in this and the following chapters, I am asking: what does it mean to signify with one's body? What does dance's particular bodily and nonverbal expressivity bring to discussions of art's role in the reconsiderations of a cultural identity? How was this particular expressivity mobilized by a cultural (national) political program, and how does it exceed programmatic limits? What does it mean to define identity through appearance, through corporeality, or to define citizenship linked to place and presence in a climate in France in which an idealized republican universalism ignoring particulars of ethnicity, religion, and cultural practices is shifting to one drawing on those differences? In which now there is an acknowledgment that bodies "mean" or that judgments are made *as if* bodies mean something, through their appearance as well as their expression?

In recent performance theory, performance has the political force of action. I will argue here that French hip hop has a civic component and opens a discussion of ethnic and social differences that have long existed but rarely been discussed in a positive way. Hip hop's danced "discourse" suggests a political representation of difference that calls attention to it but also moves beyond it, "enacting" (to borrow a term from recent performance theory) a new way of thinking about difference that both respects and resolves it. I will call this representation "figuration" in the national debate about identity, a call for minority representation but also an emphasis on the poetics of this political representation, a creative redefinition of belonging as a citizen to a universalist republic. This discourse emphasizes the particularities of material being (life in bodies), bodies as bearers of universal as well as particular meanings.

It is not correct to say that in France there has been no public conversation about race. But the vocabulary and ideology in this conversation are very different from in the United States and must be explained in depth to readers unfamiliar with French politics: in a culture in which the word *race* still produces a *frisson* created by its negative connotation, racism is an everyday occurrence. In France, a discourse about "race" has followed three different paths, explored in detail in chapter 3: The concept of race has been linked first to the entirely negative history of the treatment of French Jews during the Nazi occupation; all attempts to label individuals by race, to use racial criteria to identify or link people, has been seen as a negative operation foreshadowed by the deportation of Jews under the Vichy government's collaboration with the policies of the Third Reich. Discourse about race has also been identified in France with colonial policies of ethnic identification and subjugation, also now broadly condemned. Rather than a banner of pride or identity politics, racial identification has been seen as a state operation with dire consequences.

Combatting this stigma, the Association SOS-Racisme, founded in 1984 and presided over by a familiar political figure, Harlem Désir, from 1984 to 1992, adopted another line of discourse. In the second half of the 1980s, the motto "Touche pas à mon pote" and the graphic design of a hand held up as if to pacify or ward off danger became a common site in Paris. My French roommate suddenly appeared with a pin on her lapel, and I wondered what it meant. First, the address of the motto was in informal rather than formal language (using the "tu" form for the command and the slang form for "friend"). Translated roughly as "hands off my buddy" (or "don't touch my pal"), the warning seemed to me to invoke a white majority rather than raise consciousness about minority identity per se. But its visible and active fight against racism has animated much of the hip hop movement in France. The association adopted a positive language about "valeurs de sympathie" and is now concerned with the human rights violations of the "exclusions" of residents of foreign origin from French terrain.[6] Its former president, Harlem Désir, has served as a European deputy since 1999 and in 2012 was chosen to head the French Socialist Party.

The SOS-Racisme website identifies the "ethno-différentialisme" of certain right-wing groups as the enemy. Defending the new Socialist President François Hollande as a "unifier," or *rassembleur*, Harlem Désir describes the Left now in power as "diverse." Rather than seeing "diversity" as the introduction of difference into the political landscape, this thinking now proposes the unity of a preexisting diversity (rather than the unity of a monolithic French identity). To the partisans of the French Right (the Front National), Harlem Désir said in a televised interview that this is not the time for "hatred" but for "coming together." Rather than seeing socialism or "the Left" as exclusionary, he is proposing it, according to the party platform, as the site of unification or *rassemblement*.[7] This has been part of *le hip hop*'s program all along: unity across diversity. In the French political landscape, it is also possible to see the influence of Barack Obama's inspiring rhetoric of American unity in diversity.

While dance responds to the stereotypes linking appearance to meaning or to character, French hip hop dancers arguably manifest a self-presentation informed by hip hop's African American and Latino American styles and ask to be "figured in" or counted. Yet *la danse urbaine* goes beyond this call for political representation based on self-representation to include a metaphoric element, precisely because these hip hoppers may be African but not American, or Caribbean but also French. The risk of representation of difference, or *particularisme* in French, has been to sacrifice equality; but once equality is shown to be nonexistent, such identity politics becomes a way to redefine and claim the universal rights that have been denied to an excluded group. Yet stereotypes are also projected onto dance and dancers: a misunderstanding that bodies are what they do, that in dance they are telling some form of bodily truth rather than manifesting both a figural system and a technique (discipline, work).

French hip hop dance, then, isn't only about "becoming visible" or "asking to be counted"; it is also about "enacting" something, with political potential. This chapter considers French hip hop as a cultural product that takes a political form, but one working through expressive poetic structures as well as techniques and new technologies. I will argue in this book that French hip hop allows a new conception of minority identity and its representation in both political and artistic forms, and participates in a redefinition of citizenship in the context of postcolonial and global migrations and in the context of the mobility brought by new telecommunications technologies and new media.

The idea that hip hop is a "political" dance form—that dance itself can express a political view—is not new; hip hop falls in line with other "performances" of human rights, with community activism, and with minority visibility.[8] But in this case, I will argue that French hip hop solidifies a new discourse about minorities and *egalité de chances* (equal opportunity) not simply through embodiment or the mobilization of bodies, but through the poetic figures that choreography permits: allowing bodies to refer to something else, to become other than they are. Through reference to African American culture, French hip hop calls attention to the exclusion and inequality faced by minorities; through the poetic self-transformation permitted by dance, it shifts the conversation to one about art rather than self. Representing their own exclusion allows these dancers access to a greater universal humanity; in the French context, they might be described in terms used by Jacques Rancière, as those without rights whose struggle comes to represent the demand for universal rights: the rights of those without rights ("une part des sans-parts.")[9] Yet—with a few significant exceptions of some "underground" dancers subject to extradition[10]—*hip hoppeurs* are for the most part French citizens who are staging or performing their exclusion as *sans-parts*.

In outlining this political potential for hip hop—as it were, from "below" and in the face of its politicization from "above"—I am inspired by Etienne Balibar's political philosophy and in particular his commentary on the 2005 riots in the French suburbs. For many philosophers, dance is symbolic action; in this case, it could be argued that French hip hop was a strategic investment by public structures in dance's potential to channel suburban collective energy. It might be seen as an alternative expression of the violence that surfaced in 2005. But it is, to use Balibar's terms, not so much any political content as a political potential (or "becoming political") that brings together hip hop dance and the 2005 manifestations of violence. While urban dance was and is part of public culture in France, and such culture is central to French self-definition, it has also allowed the development of young artists, choreographers, and dancers beyond what the state may have planned for them. In what follows, I sketch the history of the *politique culturelle* in the elaboration of a French cultural identity and its openings and closings onto the world market (in the so-called cultural exception and in a turn toward "multiculturalism"). In the face of the universalism linked to French culture, *le hip hop* has carved out a space for particularity, with political potential.

THE *POLITIQUE CULTURELLE*

Understanding the politique *culturelle* mobilized around French hip hop means considering the significance of culture to the French nation and the key role of a conception of universalism in social and cultural domains. From the *exception culturelle*, set up to protect French cultural products in global markets, to the *multi-culturel* debated and located in French hip hop, this *politique culturelle* has manifested a double conception of French art as universalist and as unique.

Roger Celestin and Eliane DalMolin, in their *France from 1851 to the Present: Universalism in Crisis,* describe France's uniqueness through its adherence to universalism. They locate, in a changing world, "not the disappearance of France itself, but the disappearance of what we would like to call the *compatibility* between France and the world in which it exists, the disappearance of a basic congruence between its universalist principles and ideology, and those that obtain in the world today." While this formulation might appear to exculpate the French in a global power shift in which it no longer leads, it locates the problems inherent in French exceptionalism and "the essential place held by republican universalism in its definition."[11]

This concept of universalism—to be discussed in the next chapter as it operates in hip hop debates—is also foremost in definitions of culture in France. Even while "borrowing" culture from other sources, France defines its own cultural *bouillon* as uniquely French. The logic is consistent with the rhetoric and practice of universalism, which has now come under challenge. A kind of absolutism has governed culture in France, even as it is known for absorbing and adapting other forms.

There are, of course, different conceptions of French culture, and its importance to national self-definition has put it at the center of political debates. Many of these debates have taken place in English, in UK or US academic contexts, reflecting on French particularities. France only became a nation culturally in the late nineteenth century, Eugen Weber pointed out, when rural masses had to be integrated into a dominant culture (as they had been integrated into an administration), akin to the processes of colonization.[12] In recent work, Richard Derderian gives Jean-Philippe Mathy's critique of Weber's concept of a "steamroller" promotion of Jacobin values and cites Michel Wievorka's argument that what we are witnessing in France today is not the survival of an older national identity but a nostalgic retreat from an unsettling present.[13] There has since been a shift, Derderian emphasizes, from a "universalist all-embracing notion of culture."[14] Brian Rigby points out that while Pierre Bourdieu argues that few in France would be willing to call culture into question, many labels have been attached to it: linking it to universalist humanism (from "la Grande culture" and "la culture générale" to "la culture désintéressée" and "la culture désincarnée").[15] Culture is linked to the nation: "la culture légitime" and "la culture officielle" or "savante" or "universitaire." Culture is linked to dominant social groups: "le pouvoir culturel" and "la culture dominante." The idea of "francité" is linked to a belief in the "essential superiority of French culture."[16] In a more critical vein foundational for the *Situationiste* attack on the *société du spectacle*, for Henri Lefebvre, culture is a state ideology and is promoted as a consumer product; leisure society is nothing more than a facet of this oppressive mass culture: "Leisure is no longer 'la fête' or the reward for hard work, nor is it yet free activity done for its own sake. It is a universal spectacle: television, cinema, tourism."[17]

While it is easy to gloss the historic embrace of US popular culture in France, from jazz to hip hop, it is also important to understand the range of critical perspectives that underpinned the development of French protections on their cultural products. Richard Pells has described the resistances that characterized both bourgeois concern for popular culture influenced by radical US social movements and avant-garde disdain for US consumer culture. Far from simply embracing US culture after World War II, Pells argues, European families—even those with fathers surviving the war—worried about the increasing influence of rock and roll, and eventually hippy counterculture, destroying traditional European cultures.[18] In *Not Like Us: How Europeans Have Loved, Hated, and Transformed American Culture since World War II*, Pells lists a series of influential figures, both marginalized and idolized: Elvis, James Dean, Beat Poets, Black Jazz, Native Americans, hippies, urban poor in the 1980s, and basketball stars. He links these influences to the gradual adoption of English, noting that by the 1990s, 70% of European youths (18 to 24 years old) studied or spoke English, a figure that had almost doubled twice over the two preceding generations.[19] While considering, in particular, the affection that children of immigrants displayed for US basketball stars, adopting their apparel, Pells emphasizes that these US products reflect not insurgency but affluence. Citing the subtitle of Godard's film *Masculin, Feminin,* Pells describes this French generation as "the children of Marx and Coca-Cola," critical of capitalism even as they embrace its products, with the implication that, at a certain moment in French history, Coca-Cola was a radical product, its consumption an implicit critique of French cultural (gastronomic) traditions. At a crucial point, the anti-Americanism of the '60s youth engaged in Vietnam war protests and anticapitalist politics turned to a pro-Americanism linked to mass culture. While it would be easy to link this to a generational and demographic shift in the '80s and '90s, the hip hop generation was in fact anticipated by the generation of *soixante-huitards* (activists from the May 1968 movement).

Published nearly twenty years ago, *Popular Culture in Modern France: A Study of Cultural Discourse* by Brian Rigby focuses on popular culture, mass culture, and the state and culture since the Popular Front and World War II. French intellectual treatment of popular culture, he finds, turned in the case of the United States from disgust and distaste to admiration and theorization. Writing in the early '90s, Rigby notes that few of the texts he focuses on are translated into English; he hopes to accomplish the work of familiarizing Anglophone readers with the arguably unique situation of "culture" in France and its debates.[20] At this time there was agreement among intellectuals writing on the question that France follows developments across the Atlantic with a certain time lag. The French debate in the 1960s, about mass culture, "elite culture," and "high culture," Philippe Beneton argues, evolved at a time when it was already losing some of its vitality in the United States.[21] Since that time, an entire field of French cultural studies, headquartered at universities in both Britain and the United States, has brought these questions forward.

Hip hop is also part of the historical pattern of cultural transfer from the United States to France, in line with the French popular dancing (often inspired by African American culture) that preceded it: from the Charleston brought over by the Revue Nègre and popularized by Josephine Baker, to the *apaches* (whose dancing is mimicked in one of the sequences in *An American in Paris*), to *le rock*, a couples' swing dance that has little to do with rock music, but is close to swing, danced now by at least two generations of French students from bourgeois families. If the French are "missing the point" of this music or dance, does it really matter? Music and dance have always been globalizing cultural phenomena reflecting local performance conditions. But in these antecedents, US black culture came to influence French or European white culture, whereas in the case of hip hop, it first mobilized minorities.

Le hip hop has benefited from the centrality of the arts in French life and French politics and the significance of French concert dance as a national "product" and even export. Beyond French culture budgets, one reason for this is of course the historic place of dance in French culture, its "invention" of ballet in its court and concert forms and linking of dance to the nation and the national cultural profile. But it is also a broader appreciation of what is called "physical culture" and (as I will argue in chapter 6) of what is often referred to in theory as "practice." In French, the word culture is attached even to sports, under a broad rubric of *culture physique* that includes all forms of physical training, discipline in competition, and artistic performance. One could argue that physical education was long valued in the US academy, but in France this linking of culture to bodies in motion prepares the ground for intellectual readings of dance performance that allow it a place as a political or civic activity. Concurrently with the arrival and first moves of hip hop in France, in 1983, physical education became a field in which students could receive the *agrégation,* and in 1984 it was "placed amongst the first group of subjects for marking the Baccalaureat."[22] Hip hop dance was well positioned in France to benefit from new attention to the popular arts, the popularity of sport and its status in education, and a push toward high-tech modernization.

French culture budgets during the two terms of Mitterand's presidency developed in tandem with a push toward modernization that included rather than excluded new art forms. It was precisely *against* the mechanization and industrialization typical of the late twentieth century, Malcolm Cook notes, that the French state came to play an educative role in supporting a cultural politics championed by Mitterand and by his culture minister Jack Lang. Lang's report *La Politique culturelle 1981–1991* published by the Ministère de la Culture, de la Communication et des *Grands Travaux,* in 1991 emphasizes the doubling of the budget from 0.5% to 1% of the state budget.[23] But this program for popular arts such as comic strips, street theater, the *nouveau cirque* as well as hip hop, was developed in parallel with new technologies, telecommunications and new media.

This *politique culturelle* itself became a subject of study, with the publication of articles, research, and, in 2000, the 650-page *Dictionnaire des Politiques Culturelles de la France depuis 1959* under the direction of Emmanuel de Waresquiel and including entries by many researchers from the Centre National de Recherche Scientifique (CNRS). Ultimately, during this period, culture was specifically seen as a "right" following the UN 1948 Universal Declaration of Human Rights, and from the French perspective, Cook writes, "culture in its broadest sense is related to political freedom."[24]

The interesting development, for the purposes of this book, is the shift from an intellectual critique of US culture linked to mass culture to an appreciation of all things American not only in popular culture but also among a certain French elite. Pierre Bourdieu describes a process by which forms formerly "on the way to cultural legitimation" such as cinema and jazz have become part of the long-accepted cultural heritage.[25] Along with this process, a shift of taste and politics by French intellectuals "converted" to mass culture, the generation of Maoist protestors of 1968, have turned toward the new individualism and made a "religion out of what comes from America."[26] As Rigby points out, there was no resistance to mass culture in the generation following the *soixante-huitards*; they considered Anglo-Saxon rock or pop music to be part of their own living culture. Hip hop charts a shift over to the full embrace of American culture, in a context in which US culture was the mode and the norm; in which "people are keen to be part of U.S. consumer society";[27] in which the consumer product is both more broadly available and no longer looked down upon by the elite, and by extension the state; and in which there was a history of the translation of US forms into French. But the "global" hip hop marketed around the world took a different form in French urban dance.

FROM THE *POLITIQUE CULTURELLE* TO THE *EXCEPTION CULTURELLE*

The period in which French hip hop flowered and in which France moved to defend certain of its cultural products against free markets saw the development of a "cultural exception" protecting cinema. In her coedited volume on French cultural studies, Jill Forbes argued in 1995 that neither America nor Japan appeared to pose a threat to French cinema: "arguably the most confident and lively cultural form of the late 1980s and early 1990s, typically celebrating cultural and ethnic diversity and the erosion of gender distinctions."[28] A film such as Olivier Assayas's 1996 *Irma Vep*, reflecting on cinema's French centennial in its story of an attempted remake of Feuillade's Les *Vampires*, refers to the threats posed by Hong Kong and US blockbuster cinema to France's art film tradition but also stands as an example of that protected tradition.

Moving somewhere between the so-called beur or *banlieue* cinema[29] with its low production values and populist, popular feel and the MTV aesthetic adopted in films such as Mathieu Kassovitz's *La Haine* in 1995, hip hop began in France with a link to television rather than cinema and in live performance has often been seen in counterpoint to the cinema. While I have suggested that hip hop was never as counterculture in France as it was perceived as being in public culture in the United States during the conservative Bush governments, it was in the '80s and '90s more closely associated with a *banlieue* aesthetic, low production values, and low-tech rather than high-tech culture. Forbes comments: "there is an obvious mismatch between a cultural policy which attempts to generate a form of national unity with its emphasis on the French 'heritage' and the often counter-cultural practices of artists throughout the post-1981 period."[30] Referring to contemporary debates about French culture, Forbes shows that the United States was not insignificant in them, with Marc Fumaroli arguing in favor of a market economy versus state intervention in cultural practices, and Alain Finkelkraut attacking multiculturalism and pleading for reinforcement of the French "identity" through culture in *La Defaite de la Pensée*, which was attractive, Forbes argued, to a contemporary movement for a statist, centralizing impetus in calling for a return to Third Republic values.[31]

Forbes further points out the economic politics behind the French turn to protect its audio-visual cultural products, the basis of the "cultural exception." American television was embraced, she says, because the Giscardian protectionism in the electronics industry was not complemented by support for program making: "the 1974 reforms and privatizations of the 1980s actually hastened and expanded imports of foreign material, much of it from the USA, which was the principal source of programs that were cheap enough for the new stations to afford."[32] French stations imported inexpensive American series in the 1970s and 1980s to make up for a shortfall in French production. Yet the result, Forbes argues, was that at least in its early years of production, "French television accompanied the 'désenclavement' (opening up) of the country which was accomplished by improved physical communications," and new stations brought new material: M6 was intended as a youth music station with French-produced video clips. "The domestic experience of the 1980s undoubtedly lies behind the French government's unswerving promotion of European film production and inspired its successful demand that audio-visual products should not be included in the GATT free trade agreements concluded in 1993." This is the so-called exception culturelle.[33]

Forbes also traces the influence of US media and media culture on French intellectual life and cultural debates. After the well-known initial critique by the *Tel Quel* group, they, "like so many French writers before them … [,] were seduced by the exoticism of America and the possibilities for cultural transcendence which it appeared to offer, and in the Tel Quel issue, *Etats-Unis* 1977, the United States was presented as "une autre solution à l'impasse occidentale" (an alternative solution to the Western impasse) because of "la multiplicité de groupes sociaux, ethniques, culturels, sexuels, des discours' (because of its variety of social, ethnic, cultural, and sexual groups and discourses.")[34] Forbes cites *"look"* filmmaker Jean-Jacques Beineix identifying any reference to America as positive, because "it is part of our cultural heritage."[35] This embrace of America and American popular culture turned on its head what is sometimes referred to as the leftist critique of the United States by the remnants of the European historic avant-garde, or the critique of the culture industry by Adorno and Horkheimer. In other words, US multiculturalism became a beacon and a model, and the adoption of US culture was—in some quarters—cast no longer as domination by a mass cultural model, but by a multicultural one.

LE MULTICULTUREL: PERFORMANCE

Alongside this protectionism, then, "multicultural" was the label given to the art opening toward outside (non-French) influences, or more precisely, representing a certain diversity within France. While keeping the creation and protection of French culture on the horizon, I want to turn now away from the general cinema market and audience and focus on the specific differences of urban dance as live performance and on its minority performers.

In *North Africans in Contemporary France: Becoming Visible*, published in 2004, Richard Derderian argues that the concept of "recognition" was key in using culture to comment on political realities. What was unique about the period 1981–1995, he argues, is the way in which the children of immigrants, no longer content to remain within the confines of their communities, began to "mobilize both culturally and politically into the public sphere" and advanced their collective and individual efforts "to convey the experiences of ethnic minorities to French television and museum audiences." During the Mitterand years, "French cultural institutions became supportive of projects to make the past and present experiences of ethnic minorities visible to the French public."[36] But beyond becoming "visible," there was a struggle for "recognition" that, Derderian argues, "cannot grow out of the elimination of differences" and that involved "breaking silences."[37] Derderian cites as an example the collapse of militant theater and the neighborhood-based associational movement "eclipsed by powerful professional organizations such as SOS-Racisme and France Plus" and remarks that their demise was based on the failed attempt to make the transition to professional theater.[38] While hip hop dance could be located, in France, within this history of a call for "recognition," it can also be understood as a figural form, moving beyond self-representation to a motivated and more complex range of representation. While Derderian argues that some neighborhood efforts to professionalize local theater groups failed in the face of the better-funded associations, hip hop has managed to keep this grassroots "association" profile while professionalizing.

Some scholars in French studies have emphasized the "breakthroughs" made by French "immigrants" in the worlds of music and cinema as opposed to a tightly controlled publishing industry. Alec Hargreaves suggests that performance has been a realm in which this cultural work of announcing difference and questioning integration happens first because publishing is too structured: in the case of artists of African origin, their "most forceful impact has been in non-text-based cultural forms, especially film and music, where commercial considerations and generational transitions have outweighed the conservatism of more literary-based cultural milieux."[39] Writing in 2003, Hargreaves does point out that "[s]ince the 1980s more than 100 narratives have been published by second generation Maghrebis."[40] Yet he emphasizes:

> The cultural forms in which African minorities have broken most effectively through these kinds of barriers are film and music. Where academic institutions are dominated by an older generation of gatekeepers steeped in traditional literary culture, the film and music industries are driven more by market demand from younger audiences who find audio-visual cultural forms more appealing than text-based art.[41]

For Hargreaves the shift in generations also signals an opening up of nationalism and a bond across majority and ethnic minority youth:

> In contrast with the generations who still dominate academic institutions, who were raised in a world where national boundaries and identities seemed of self-evident importance, young people in contemporary France are far more likely to see themselves within a global cultural dynamic in which the United States plays a leading role....Rap was originally developed as a form a counter-culture by African-Americans who were tired of being excluded from the American dream. It was taken up initially in France by minorities in similarly marginalized positions. But, alongside the subversive aspects of rap, its American origins give it a glamorous dimension in the eyes of young people outside the United States. In this way, a shared (but not necessarily identically constructed) interest in American cultural references has been helping to bring together majority and minority ethnic youths within the French cultural sphere.[42]

Significantly, this inclusiveness of the "black-blanc-beur" generation is produced through the cultural adoption of African American hip hop. Yet it also leads a movement in minority rights, a visibility that has been linked to essentialism and the Anglo-Saxon tradition of community lobbies and identity politics. While in the hip hop world in French dance, a certain kind of success can be seen as "selling out" to a more commercial "inauthentic" form, Hargreaves points out that some negotiating has to take place to get minority art out into the broader public; he sees the challenge confronting minorities to "widen their cultural resonance together with the boundaries of French culture itself."[43] I argue in this book that against the background of their exclusion in France, hip hoppers are working to present themselves as citizens of a republic of culture.[44]

Other researchers have suggested that hip hop and other popular forms provide a challenge not only to French universalism but also to what has now become institutionalized French studies itself. Winnifred Woodhull remarks that, along with fiction from francophone writers not living in France or part of the immigrant history, documents from popular culture such as hip hop necessitate an end to "business as usual" in US French programs.[45] In responding to these debates highlighted in French studies, I want to consider the contribution that can be made by a consideration of performance: to suggest why dance is important in France, the part it plays in these debates, and the fresh perspectives its study brings to what has been essentially a political-social debate. While performance culture is often acknowledged as significant, it, especially dance, has not received equal attention within these debates on integration or assimilation into the French system: the problem of a universalist program coming to terms with a society without equal opportunity, unrest in the suburbs, and the civic positioning of youth vis à vis the republic and the globe available via the Internet. As a form highlighting bodies and navigating both popular culture and the national stages, embodied citizenship and the mobility brought by new media, urban dance serves as a crucible for these questions, especially given the heightened role that new technologies have played both in the arts and in the nation. The performance of urban dance can be understood as a way to find a "voice," expressing belonging to the republic while expressing difference "within," asking for representation and representing oneself, and, in this way, enacting a performative citizenship.

THE PERFORMANCE OF CITIZENSHIP: BECOMING POLITICAL

In his "Uprisings in the *Banlieues*," Etienne Balibar emphasizes the infrapolitical or apolitical tenor of the 2005 riots. The very choice of the word uprisings to describe the movement responded to the lack of a French vocabulary or the charged alternatives: "hardly anyone in France spoke of a 'soulèvement' with respect to the events of November 2005, at least publicly: bordering on *insurrection*, the term strongly connotes a revolutionary tradition.... The French press oscillated between the idea of a *révolte* (rebellion) and an *émeute* (riot)."[46] The youth involved were described as *rebelles*, *casseurs*, and *dealers* assigned to the register of delinquency. For Balibar, the undecided question was one of the political or criminal logic of the actions, usually polarized: Were the activists bandits from the "frontier" border area of the *banlieue?* Was the violence spontaneous? Was it not provoked and amplified by government policy and discourse? "[W]e have to ask if it did not in fact seek to touch off an episode of 'criminal' violence to boost its own legitimacy and law-and-order propaganda." Balibar argues that this government repression assumes as a pretext some illegal activity on the part of youths and even brings it on. The reference here is to then-Interior Minister Nicolas Sarkozy's much-publicized remark about the *racaille* or "scum" of the suburbs that needed a "power-wash" purging.[47]

Balibar emphasizes that the violence, in part self-destructive, shows how what is "theirs," the object of destruction, "is in large part a 'thing' from which the young rioters are contradictorily *excluded* as 'non-citizens,' to which they only have limited, illegitimate access, but of which they are *themselves a part*." The violence thus manifests their exclusion in a despair fused with nihilism and depersonalization, referred to as an "*internal exclusion*" or, via Agamben, "the *permanent state of exception*" in which the law is said "to suspend its own effectiveness."[48]

Balibar's well-known concerns with the operations of difference, otherness, and exclusion lead to a reconsideration of the term immigration so often used in the "official" discourse about hip hop dancers as *issus de l'immigration*. For Balibar, "immigration" is a label that sticks across generations and that "has become the 'name of race'": for Balibar, religious discrimination is the new racial discrimination. The *banlieusards* face a double discrimination of class and race, a double bind in which "*each stigma prevents them from freeing themselves from the other*, crushing their individual and collective futures." This double exclusion produces a void of belonging for those citizens who feel they are excluded.[49]

In these uprisings, Balibar also considers the role of technology and the response to the technological infrastructure in which the *banlieusards* are inserted. The spectacular character of the violence, the destruction of consumer items and symbolic places, he writes, "marks the advent of a new age in which the means of mass communication acquire the role of *passive organizers* of social movements."⁵⁰

> This "virtual violence"...*transforms* real, endemic social violence, to which it responds, *into spectacle*, thereby at once making it *visible* in its intensity and *invisible* in its everydayness. It expresses a desperate will to affirm not so much a "cause" or a "project" as an *existence* that is constantly forgotten or denied by the surrounding society, using means proper to the experience of reality in contemporary society (there is no recognized existence other than that which can be represented; reproduced by the media).
>
> [These means...] return against those who use them by imposing a certain identity on them. In this sense reference to the "practico-inert" and "stolen praxis" in Sartre is as useful as reference to Debord's "society of the spectacle" or Baudrillard's "hyper-reality."⁵¹

Reading these lines of Balibar, we must rethink French hip hop dance practice in its relation to the suburbs and citizenship, public space and public arts, and multiculturalism and the media. Is urban dance a detouring and deterring of violence into symbolic action, a spectacle in its own way? For Balibar, the rioters' actions were *infrapolitical*:

> [T]his formula can mean two things: either that the riot *does not* (and will not) *reach* the level of collective political action, be it because that is not its aim or because, as such, it "has no aims" aside from a cry of rage; or that a riot is *still far* from political action, separated from it by several steps that have yet to be taken, and that it does not in itself contain all the conditions (consciousness, ideology, organization, tactics and strategy, etc.)....A movement's continuity and its becoming political depend on its capacity to transform the sense conferred to illegalism by the dominant system and to resist repression (or to turn its effects back on those who practice it).⁵²

Yet hip hop in France has political potential both because of and in spite of its recuperation by the state: it manifests what Balibar calls "becoming political." Indeed, Balibar will argue that politics can also occur through its opposite—*antipolitics*—when citizenship is emptied of its content, when a country such as France exhausts its ability to represent and "speak for" its popular classes and its excluded, for example, the young unemployed "immigrants" of the *banlieue*. Balibar reminds us that

> [political representation] does not only have this passive face, conferred "from above" (oligarchically, technocratically, hegemonically); it also incorporates

pressure "from below" that transgresses earlier prohibitions and imposes other types of representatives (not necessarily parliamentary—to the contrary...) or forces the existing representatives to convey (but also to try to appropriate) the speech and claims of those "outside the law" in an open dialectic... (that which exceeds representation, creating a void.)[53]

In conclusion, Balibar will argue for this *becoming political* of the revolt— its political potential (even for insurrection) in spite of double exclusions operating against those "*pushed or left outside* representation, and their manipulation by an image-hungry media and state seeking fantasmatic actors to replace real actors and to represent the 'foreign body' in the imaginary."[54] If I adopt this conclusion for the situation of French hip hop, it is in large part because of its "associational" base, its continued social service and its working for solidarity even as it develops as concert dance. For Balibar, this political potential hinges on the possibility or impossibility of a *collectivization*:

> [H]ow could association and communication emerge from exclusion and its doubling, "secession" or provocation? What constitutes an insurrectional movement—be it the American civil rights movement and black power in the 1960s and 70s...—is at once its radicalness and its "transversality" its ability to express or echo other revolts in its own code. The radicality of the revolt of the *banlieues* is indissociable from its power of refusal. Here the absence of objectives... is not a failing.[55]

In this example, Balibar argues, the echoes include stopping the *reduction of politics to the police*, the "internal" mobilizations of social workers and secular and religious resident associations, and the recognition of differences within those judged as different, the people *d'en bas*—including gender.[56]

My conclusions about hip hop in France in this book are drawn from such written and theoretical texts, in addition to observations of the teaching and staging of choreographies, analysis of the choreographies themselves, and exposure to the world of "associations" as well as "official" structures— festivals, debates, programs, etc.—surrounding hip hop. These associations exist on websites as well as in community centers, and their potential to organize "collectives" is one that depends on technologies as much as it does on bodies. Hip hop serves as an example of a professionalized art form that continues to be based on associational structures. A typical example arrives in my e-mail as I am finishing these introductory pages. One of the many hip hop mailings I receive, this one about the Hip Hop Danse/Tanz festival organized each year by Moov' N Aktion includes a link to a new group called "Hip Hop Citizens." Organizing their own two-week festival, "Paris hip hop," they emphasize their civic profile:

> Hip Hop Citizens will continue to bring its expertise and savoir-faire to the organization of Hip Hop events that involve local youth. An Association for the promotion of urban cultures and mediation for youths, Hip Hop Citizens has been working for several years to help youth get access to citizenship via culture. While "Paris Hip Hop: Two weeks of Hip Hop" remains the focal point of our activity, we are also developing along new axes aimed at improved outreach to youth proposing projects coming from hip hop culture. Facing a lack of both institutional and private funding, it is important for us to remain mobilized, to guarantee that the voice of an entire part of French youth and such a prolific artistic movement, is heard. It's also about bringing alive the hip hop culture *à la française* in the rest of the world through exchange and development of international projects.[57]

While focusing on France's problems, including cuts in the number of social workers and tutors, youth advocates called *educateurs*, this association nevertheless emphasizes the significance of hip hop to disenfranchised youth in France and France's contribution to global hip hop. The metaphor remains vocal—participatory and choral rather than communitarian. The closing phrase is, "With more of us, we will be stronger, and stronger we will be better heard/understood!" ("Plus nombreux, nous sommes plus forts...plus forts, nous sommes mieux entendus!")

In spite of—or perhaps because of—hip hop's global reach, and in spite of its European development (in EU cultural programs), French hip hop has become a site for the working-through of specifically national, as well as more broadly European, challenges. In the wake of the 2005 uprisings in the suburbs, Balibar has considered how current "postnational" definitions of citizenship do not match what is happening in France, where the question being raised is "nationality": the French presuppose nationality to be the precondition of citizenship: "it is French which in certain circumstances implicitly subjects the notion of citizenship to the possession or acquisition of nationality."[58] In the United States, Balibar points out that the question is, "where do you enjoy the rights of citizenship—which country of citizenship?" In "Historical Dilemmas of Democracy and Their Contemporary Relevance for Citizenship," Balibar recasts the question as one of "where" people have rights: "where" they are citizens. Arguing that democracy is a process, not a form of state, and thus constantly in process, and referring to a citizenship defined as "in the world" rather than a global citizenship "of the world," this text ultimately suggests that citizenship is less a question of image or "virtual subjects" and more a question of bodies.

Via French hip hop, one could argue for an embodied citizenship in France, based on the demand for rights there where one is (not in some other place where one might be a citizen) based on bodies and even bodily difference, as liberatory rather than regulatory. One can link the focus on embodied identity to the Négritude movement in France, a political valorization of bodies in the colonial situation that connected to the US civil rights movement, in the anticolonial and postcolonial theory to be discussed in chapter 3. The mouv' in France also takes its cue from Aimé Césaire, one of its founders; at the time of his death in 2008, his image dominated the great hall of la Villette where the Rencontres were taking place: "the strength to face tomorrow." (See Figure 1.1) Césaire exposed the false motivation of a colonial policy of assimilation: "The French had followed the politics of assimilation unrestrainedly.... [T]he idea was to turn [an African] into a Frenchman with black skin."[59] But today, both the necessity of considering race and the pitfalls of racial essentialism are being debated. Patrick Lozes, a founder of CRAN, a group collecting data on black communities in France, states: "The idea behind not categorizing

Figure 1.1
Homage to Aimé Césaire at the Grande Halle de la Villette, home of the annual Rencontres Urbaines hip hop festival, Parc de la Villette May 2008, Paris.
Photo Credit: Felicia McCarren.

people by race is obviously good; we want to believe in the republican ideal. But in reality we're blind in France, not colorblind but information blind, and just saying people are equal doesn't make them equal."[60] CRAN associate Victorine Mbengue describes their attempt, in France, to turn the discussion from one about "diversity" to one about "minorities." Assigning "diversity" to some people or groups functions as a handicap, she argues; in the United States and elsewhere, there is no such process. Rather, the necessary discussion is one about the rights of minorities who are underrepresented. While it has been said that data has never been collected on minority communities, she argues that such data collecting has always gone on silently in France: in criminal arrests, for example, or in housing discrimination, appearance and country of origin have always factored in.[61]

Multiculturalism is thus the label that has been applied to cover questions of identity and citizenship, immigration, and race—many with a colonial component.[62] But the recognition of postcolonial realities in France has come late and was heard at its loudest in the rejection of the February 23, 2005, parliamentary vote passing a measure requiring the teaching of positive aspects of colonial history ("les bienfaits du colonialisme"). Responding to the events in Clichy-sous-Bois of November 3, 2005, in *Le Parisien*, rapper and actor Stomy Bugsy claimed that his "hip hoptimism" was in fact the product of the ethnic mix of the suburbs.[63] He goes on to remark on the colonial history such neighborhoods seek to redress and repair: "Why doesn't France recognize its responsibility for the colonies? The day when we learn what really happened, we feel betrayed.... However, I am sure that the sons of immigrants are happy to be in France....We've eaten here, we've grown up here, we love this country. But we'd like it to be given back to us."[64] Responses such as this one, and Balibar's reading of the 2005 events, suggest that French youth in the suburbs are far from the virtual or transnational subjects who feel their roots are elsewhere or who are headed somewhere else.[65] They suggest an embodied citizenship, made possible in part by the technologies of communication and globalization, mobility that is redefining the rights of bodies where they are.

An invested bodily identity, focused on the question of difference, is significant in a climate in which technologies arguably make bodies less important, simulate or substitute for movement in the real world, and create a global, virtual community. But performances respond to the dominant technologies of their time, to conceptions of life in bodies and what might be called the current state of bodiliness. The new visibility and mobility brought by technologies make possible an embodied citizenship where people can insist on difference without losing their stake for equality and avoid a racism defined through ethnicity or redirected against immigration or religion: the very cultural diversity that is celebrated in the arts. This book, while presenting hip hop's embodied citizens, emphasizes their metaphoric and technological potential for self-transformation that does not stop at representation.

While one could argue that personal mobility, new movements and gestures, and new performances of a national character have been charted before in French studies, created in French cinema or enacted in French stadiums, we might argue, with Balibar, that now it is as if a standing conception of liberty, guaranteeing personal liberty even at the cost of that of others, is being replaced by a sense of personal liberty guaranteed by the personal liberty of one's neighbors: not a transcendent sense of liberty but a liberty based on equality, not an individual realization of liberty but a communal one. Such banal actions as smoking or dog walking, previously executed, for example, in urban areas such as Paris, in the full exercise of one's rights, are now limited and controlled in order to guarantee the rights of others: not to breathe smoke, for example, in a public building or restaurant, or not to encounter a dog-befouled sidewalk. While certain habits have been slow to change, surveillance and reprimand are now being performed by a younger generation and are effective with a younger generation: in the foyer of the Opera de la Bastille, a young man in uniform approaches a patron in order to tell her, gently, that smoking is forbidden in the foyer. In Mayor Bertrand Delanoë's Paris, the streets and squares are equipped with bags to aid dog walkers in clean-up. Along with this reconception of personal physical liberty as dependent upon the other's liberty and the community's as a whole, concrete rather than abstract, comes a new sense of freedom itself as a bodily condition: the right to be who one is (bodily difference, gender, race, differently abled), the right to difference, the turn from an abstract definition of belonging to the nation (via universalism) to a concrete definition.

In "Historical Dilemmas," Balibar returns to a concept of "equal liberty" or, written as one word, "equaliberty" in a 1994 work, redefining democracy as a process of ongoing democratization. Balibar traces the concept of "equal liberty" to Rawls,

> who bases his *Theory of Justice* on the notion of "equal liberty," only to explain that between the two concepts there should be established a "lexicographic order," meaning that liberty is a condition for equality and has absolute value, whereas equality is not an absolute condition of liberty and can therefore be relativized or limited if its implementation becomes a threat to individual and public liberties.[66]

This order or preference explains the practice of individual rights even to the reduction or exclusion of other people's rights and is reversed now in the curtailing of individual rights for the public good. It also explains the conflict between difference and equality in the French universalist context: pointing out difference without giving up a claim to equality. Balibar's discussion of "equaliberty" in the French or European context suggests a change in ethics and in the relation of the individual to the state, but a change in bodily condition significant for hip hop dance has also followed from the adoption of new technologies and their implementation by the state, as well as their recent failings twenty years after. It is precisely the rise of a newly technological state, technologies affecting bodies and bodiliness, *along with* the cultural politics described here that set the stage for the new bodies proposed by French hip hop.

PERFORMANCE THEORY

Balibar's definitions of citizenship and his analysis of the 2005 uprisings in France focus on performance (rather than "media") in political life and suggest the significance of performance theory to an understanding of debates about "Frenchness" itself. Anchored first by Austin's linguistic "performatives," the term performativity, write Eve Sedgwick and Andrew Parker, "has enabled a powerful appreciation of the ways that identities are constructed iteratively through complex citational processes."[67] Performance theorists have emphasized the broad reach of the concept not only for identity formation but also for cultural production and cultural memory; Joseph Roach defines "performance as the transformation of experience through the renewal of its cultural forms" that "keeps the dead among the living."[68] He emphasizes that for African American forms in particular, "the contributions of other cultures to Western forms tend to become disembodied as 'influences,' distancing them from their original contexts" especially apparent in the African antecedents in now-ubiquitous American popular culture.[69]

Performance theory has turned toward a consideration of political action, most visibly in Judith Butler's work on the embodied agency represented by performative speech acts.[70] The agency embodied in the performance that is called gender, "the gendered stylization of the body" that is "manufactured through a sustained set of acts," poses, for Butler, the question of "whether the materiality of the body is fully constructed."[71] Butler's model of gender as performative rather than as an internal "essence" leaves aside the question of whether the body's performances are "fully constructed," that is, the question of a bodily materiality (underneath, inside) that is not performed. While in this theory the question seems to be: do bodies mean (without language) in their attitudes, appearance, gestures, and other stylizations?, my work has been asking a somewhat different question: how do bodies mean by dancing (in other words, not simply by existing or appearing), and especially, how do dancing bodies mean in the face of print culture, a culture of public debate, even when their dances are nonnarrative? Rather than refusing or opposing language, I have argued, bodies dancing address in a different language contemporary debates about bodies, and their movement is a language with representational (rather than simply "presentational") potential. In the next chapter, I will argue for French hip hop that it is precisely through structures of representation or self-transformation (close to those of language and poetics) that choreography performs political meaning, even when it is nonnarrative. That is, it is not simply through having a body or calling attention to one's body that urban dancers create choreographic meaning, but rather how they use that body—in movement, in choreography—to mean.

Performance is also a major concept in thinking about new media and the practices it has created. New media theorist Henry Jenkins lists "performance" (defined as "the ability to adopt alternative identities for the purpose of improvisation and discovery") as one of the "needed skills in the New Media culture" and in particular what he calls the "participatory culture" of online authorship, communities, and creation.[72] Against the history of markets, protectionism, and national culture that has been traced in this chapter, hip hop is a resolutely live art, but one imbricated in the rise of new technologies and techniques implemented by the political-cultural programs outlined in this chapter.

Recent theories of performance attempt to come to terms with the material presentation of bodies performing along with the representational reach of performances of all kinds. French hip hop dance can be understood as a form of performance that enacts rather than simply refers to a historic, socioeconomic reality, along the lines proposed by performance theorist Chris Salter, who understands "performance as an entanglement among humans, instruments, algorithms, and machines on the stage, in the laboratories, and through the streets of cities"[73] and archives different combinations of technologies and performances, "performance as practice, method, and worldview" across new media, sciences, and social sciences. Rather than focusing on the mechanical or repeatable functions in performance (as some theater and performance theory has done), Salter concludes that performance "unfolds in an operative or immanent mode."[74] Performance in this definition "yields new knowing about the world through its sudden presence and equally sudden disappearance."

My study, too, focuses on the materiality of bodies, the local practices as well as universal gestures made possible by technologies, and the difference between "knowing that" or "knowing about" versus "knowing how" that Salter traces to the performance theory of Dwight Conquergood[75] but that I trace here to Bourdieu and de Certeau. For Salter, performance as "method/worldview suggests…that there is not a reality pregiven before one's experience but rather that the world is enacted or actively performed anew."[76] "Enaction" is borrowed from Francisco Varela, as action "bringing forth of a world" not through representation but through "constrained imagination" or a historical process of "active living."[77] While Salter goes far in uncoupling the usual polarizations between live and nonlive performance—"screen vs. scene, the materiality of media and real time, dynamic and interactive processes that mix human and technical presences"[78]—in this description he clearly repeats a major debate in performance studies. He argues that Varela's theory of enaction, considering the embodied and dynamic interactions between the neural-cognitive system of an organism and its environment, resonates with the cultural theory of performance and implies "a world in which subject and objects have not yet come into being and, even if materialized, are always in a constant state of flux and transformation that is unstable and difficult to repeat."[79] Focusing his argument through the work of Karen Barad, he cites her description of how "the move towards performative alternatives to representationalism shifts the focus from questions of correspondence between descriptions and reality…to matters of practices/doing/actions."[80] Salter concludes, "Like Butler's use of the word, which proposes an active practice, a doing that constructs gender, 'performative' implies that the world emerges over time, continually transformed through our history of interactions with it."

The socialist and utopian ambitions of French hip hop are largely in sync with Salter's conclusions about the "performative transformation of the everyday through increasingly sophisticated and hidden pervasive technologies." But in his book, he asks, rather late, what are the repercussions of machines (now like humans) performing? In my work, I have argued that it was part of an orchestrated industrial policy both reflected in and inspired by dance. Here, what Donna Haraway called the "frighteningly human" aspect of machines is not an afterthought, but the first step that urban dance moves both to represent and to counter.[81] The idea of performance as both an embodiment and a representation seems to me to parallel precisely a French minority politics that both insists on and moves beyond difference and a francophone poetics that "speaks" about difference, but in a figural language. By dancing, these youths are doing something about their suburbs; by choosing dance, they are saying something about the debates about them, about their identity and their place in the nation. Yet it is precisely in a culture of *"anytime, anyplace"* that this embodiment works as social critique, as identity elaboration, and as a technique in itself. Embodiment is only the first step, the most obvious visible layer, of this form: the "enacting" of their situation, or its representation and transformation through figural dance language, is highly manipulated and highly mediated. Following this political analysis of French hip hop, this book focuses on the poetics of its dance language and the techniques as well as technologies that it engages. An example of the crossing of cultural politics, multiculturalism, and staging what can be described as a socialist-utopian view of technology can be found in the recent hip hop choreography *Zou*, which will conclude this chapter in showing the French specificity of hip hop dance especially in the face of national politics and the cultural face of new technologies.

ZOU

This book's first choreographic example, the 2008 choreography *Zou* performed by Compagnie Los Anges, weds a utopian vision of technology to a hip hop concept of citizenship. Its choreographer, Stéphanie Nataf, describes this collaboration with a videographer as a reflection on "the line" of relation between oneself and others that mass communication has troubled rather than facilitated. Through the lines of train tracks, then of a Vitruvian geometry, and then the curving lines of wind turbines, the piece is meant to inspire respect for others and nature through the planning of an ideal *cité* whose virtual architecture permits this respect and relation. While the tone of the piece is decidedly "anytime, anyplace"—seeing technology as a web that binds but also ultimately frees us—it is concretely grounded in the social program of urban dance: the exploration of identity, recuperation of family roots, or cultural influence of ethnic dance in Stéphanie's choreography. *Zou*'s opening focus on train tracks and trains does recuperate some family history: the choreographer noted that her maternal grandmother was a *cheminot* and her grandfather, denounced as a *saboteur* in his early twenties during the German occupation of World War II, was killed by German forces with a group of young resisters in his village. While the train is presented as a vehicle of a dizzying modernity in the opening sections, it also permits the voyage out, as the dancers open up the lines and head toward the *ville utopique*. *Zou* stages and plays with the idea of individual mastery of space but gives way to the idea of group effort; technologies used responsibly trump the chaos of modern urban life. The vision of technology presented in the piece is, one might argue, in

the mode of utopian socialism. In this way it seems to represent a generation of socialist modernization that deeply shaped French hip hop.

For *Zou*, Stéphanie Nataf established a new company, holding an audition at the NPE du Spectacle, to which eighty dancers came, all of them
hip hoppers. This particular company of dancers, *Los Anges*, was formed by
Stéphanie for this piece and is made up of both formally trained dancers
and autodidacts who began dancing later in life.

The choreographic process for *Zou* represents a change from the choreographer's earlier work with Compagnie Choream, whose dancers had for the
most part been trained by Stéphanie and José Bertogal, Choreoam's cofounders, in their Montreuil classes. Stéphanie refers to them as the "children of the
Centre de Loisirs" where she and José began teaching and founded their initial collaboration, the group Macadam. While some dancers who started later
came later to Choream, all were from this area and they formed a close-knit
group, often collaborating in the choreographic process.

Zou represents a different way of working, with Stéphanie as sole choreographer (and sometimes dancer) rather than simple collaborator. At the
same time, with *Zou*, Stéphanie wanted to work with a group and with a
video artist, and while innovating she declares, in an interview, that some
of the projected scenes or sequences simply didn't work. Some of the dancers, she says, weren't able to do what she wanted them to, or sequences
meant to be synchronized with video projections proved to be too compli-
cated to achieve. While professional dance companies whose dancers are
paid often encounter such difficulties in the development and refinement
of their performances, this particular experience and the finished choreography seem to reinforce the working atmosphere and mentality of the hip
hop dance world. Even with a commission, even with professional dancers,
the focus seems to have been as much on the process as on the product.

In order to arrive at six dancers, the choreographer ended up having
to dance herself in the piece. Dancers are often deployed in threes, with a
frontal presentation to the audience of synchronized steps on stage—an
element familiar from show dancing, tap revues, and ballet but often abandoned in modern dance composition. This ensemble performance of the
unison dancing, often to music with a heavy beat, is a familiar figure in hip
hop choreography. While Choream dancers moved easily in sync, the dancers constituting this new company, Los Anges, found it more difficult: some
of the dancers who excelled in solo work were not as strong in group sections. But the choreographer and the choreography insist on these figures
seemingly as part of a hip hop "mentality."

Zou itself is a reflection on modern urban life and finishes with the idea
of a utopian city, the "city of our dreams" as the choreographer calls it, a "real

architectural planning project" that the dance can only gesture toward, but that she wanted to do "for real" with the dancers, presumably in concert with urban planners. Choreographed in collaboration with a video artist, Gregory Coston, and described as a work of "Danse/Vidéo/Hip Hop," its opening scene stages the chaos of urban life and the crushing pace of its technologies. (See Figure 1.2) The speed of contemporary life is evoked in a series of images projected onto the backdrop and at times onto the bodies in front of it: the time code of cities around the globe, metro interiors and metro maps, the word SECURITY, and lines that are linked to a unidirectional sense of time, movement, and transport that are converging. This scene was apparently meant to last only a minute but came, the choreographer says, to take its place as a scene in itself. The social commentary is evident and the hip hopper spinning on his head amidst these skewed lines suggests that hip hop has always represented this urban crush, the world upside down.

Music by Aarvo Part opens the second section in which the skewed lines turn to red and a "day" scenario—to be followed by "night"—recalls the mechanical era, heavy labor, and the blazing sun; replaced by white light and a deep blue background, the following section pays homage to the role electricity has played in creating a new environment for bodies. Evoked in solo by a dancer doing extremely fine movements of popping and locking,

Figure 1.2
Zou, choreography by Stéphanie Nataf, Compagnie Los Anges (2008): the Metro.
Photo Credit: H2O Photographe.

Abdou (who began dancing inspired by Choream) moves in and out of the light, sometimes in silhouette, as a Laurie Anderson text plays, suggesting the fragility of the new body shaped by electricity and the fine shocks as opposed to the brutal blows of the mechanical age. With mounting intensity, the next scene opens with fragments of daily encounters rendered with a stroboscopic effect, suddenly illuminating action in one part of the stage and just as quickly fading out, then again flashing on action between a couple in another part of the stage and fading out, giving tremendous evocative power to the brief movements glimpsed in the light. These individual, fragmented scenes seem to take us far from the programmatic hip hop unison dancing of earlier sections. The lighting recalls the special effects of rock concerts (representative of the lighting designer's background) or, for example, of David Parson's well-known six-minute solo *Caught* where he is caught in the air—in more than one hundred leaps—through a stroboscopic series of illuminations. It closes the opening moves of this piece in which the dancing bodies seem to be at the mercy of the technologies deployed around and through them and leads to a section in which dancers appear to play with, if not control, various technologies, or to live in greater harmony with them.

The first indication the piece gives of this new relation to technology is a dancer's tracing of lines through space. In a grid that now resembles a hand-drawn square (or diamond shape, *losange* in French—the company's icon), then cube, in a deep blue environment, the dancer comes to stand like the Vitruvian man, with arms and legs giving the cue to the lines that structure the universe around him. The image will be confirmed a few minutes later when the famous drawing by Da Vinci is projected for a few seconds only, in a suite of images. Onstage, the mastery of the lines and their geometry is shown to be an illusion: it is rather a hesitant manipulation proceeding step by step. When three lines of light seem to hang vertically from the top down to the stage, three dancers standing in the light seem able to gently direct them, as if each held a pendulum and shaped its arc. (See Figure 1.3) The choreography depends on illusion, the illusion of movement and the illusion of space created by movement. The three dancers appear to open the lines, to move from rigidly defined space into a free space. During the section where the lines are being traced into an environment, the sound score includes a tape of philosopher Gilles Deleuze speaking in a seminar, in French, about the relation between three individuals—A, B, and C. This segment is taken from a commercially available DVD of Deleuze and overall seems to serve as commentary on the "Vitruvian" reference while providing a narration that might be said also to follow the choreography, as the three dancers open the lines and enter into relation. (See Figure 1.4) Press materials for the piece declare that more communication doesn't mean

Figure 1.3
Zou, the line of relation.
Photo Credit: H2O Photographe.

Figure 1.4
Zou, Vitruvian space.
Photo Credit: H2O Photographe.

"communicating better" and that in a time and space that have become relative we have lost our relation "to the other." (See Figure 1.5) The focus of the piece is to draw "the line of relation from oneself to others" to find that relation ultimately in a "*cité idéale* whose virtual architecture allows us to find that path to the other." Ultimately these "life-lines" create a web that separates and binds, yet also reconnects and frees the dancers.

In the following scene, with hypnotic music and imagery building to the emotional peak of the piece, the lines of light descending from the top of the stage become visible as wind turbines with their long curved arms slowly rotating and casting their shadows across the bodies onstage. (See Figure 1.6) The score shifts to stylize the sweep and pitch of the wind-mills, but in a pleasingly dreamlike rather than disturbing sustained tone. The reference to alternate energies suggests that this scene complements the earlier mechanical and then electrical scenes, suggesting also an alter-nate human energy that parallels the technology. To generate the images and sound for this scene, the choreographer and videographer recorded turbines, just as they had recorded the passage of a train (sound and image) projected in the red section at the beginning of the piece.

The piece's final scene follows a missing scene described by the chore-ographer as the departure to the *ville utopique*, the *ville de nos rêves*. The

Figure 1.5
Unison dancing by the cast of *Zou:* Alexandra Réa, Céline Lefèvre, Magali Duclos, Feroz Sahoulamide, Abdou N'gom, Jean-Charles Zambo.
Photo Credit: H2O Photographe.

Figure 1.6
The landscape for alternative energies: *Zou*'s wind turbines.
Photo Credit: Mathieu Trinquart

last environment created by projections suggests a lawn strewn with red poppies, a space in which the dancers will frolic. (See Figure 1.7) Here virtuality comes to be associated with leisure or play; the virtual space of this garden suggests that technology can be a space of freedom, of vacation. The relationship to technology is entirely different from the chaos and oppression of the choreography's opening scenes; while it is only sketched out in the piece, the choreographer argues, when the video and the dancing are in sync, it is convincing. At the Avignon festival performance, it was well received. Audience members responding to a survey at the Avignon festival ranked the piece second after Sankai Juko, the choreographer notes.

While her earlier collaborative choreography *Epsilon*, to be discussed in chapter 4, suggests the creation of the world, here the subject is more precisely the creation *of a certain world*, a project of urbanism that combines hip hop values of the group, solidarity, and balance, even in an upside-down world, with a utopian reorientation of space and social relation. From the shock of too much technology through the illusion of the mastery of space via geometry to the conscious group effort toward alternative technologies, the choreography tells a story, not perhaps in a clear chronology but in a clear choreographic development of themes and movement expressing these themes. Combining modernist abstraction and the illusion of modern dance movement with the more concrete concerns and movements of hip

Figure 1.7
Frolicking in a space created by new technology: *Zou*'s *ville utopique*.
Photo Credit: H2O Photographe.

hop, the piece seems to argue for a place for hip hop dance within concert dance and new media performance. While the piece's final environment calls to mind the stage strewn with artificial flowers in Pina Bausch's well-known choreography *Nelken*, the dancing here has its heart elsewhere than in the Wuppertal tradition of modern dance theater. The piece's unison hip hop dancing, to heavy-beat techno or hip hop–style music, takes it out of that mold and gives those passages a very different tone. But in this way, and in this context, it is also a social commentary on its time, as Bausch's choreography was. *Zou*'s effect is to make us think of an entirely new generation of machines, quieter perhaps or less visible, but as dominant on our future landscape as the giant wind turbines, along with the new energies they create and the bodies they will shape. *Zou* itself represents a new generation of dance responding to those technologies and expressing them.

To view this choreography a few years after its creation, on tour in 2010, is also to understand the piece's project as a continuation of a socialist dream of effective and responsible technologies. With a generation of older machines now failing, and without continuous attention or technical support, many of the technologies put in place twenty or more years ago are obsolete or malfunctioning. In a way, one might argue that France has now returned to the state preceding the push to high tech introduced during Mitterand's two terms as president.

While in the United States alternative energy is associated with a discourse about innovation and new business, research, and development in the private sector, in France alternate energies have long been led by an argument about the importance of nuclear energy. The same countryside dotted by wind turbines, crisscrossed by train rails and, of course, by tractors, has also welcomed nuclear power plants. In France, the discourse about nuclear power has been linked to creativity and innovation: in a series of ads sponsored by the state owned energy company a decade ago, artists and creators using power find they can continue through blackouts and power outages, playing their rock music or thrilling audiences with innovative performances. The motto "It's not electric, it's nuclear" was developed to "sell" the idea of nuclear power as innovative and productive of innovation even in the cultural realm. Such an approach to sources and management of the power grid suggests a utopian idea in which art plays an important part.

The point is not that France is a high-tech country but that, like other countries, it follows a rhythm of investment and development over a generation and then, with political programs flagging and budgets falling, passes into a phase where things don't work for a generation whose expectation is that they will. Staging the failure of old technologies and the utopia of new ones, *Zou* seems to reside firmly in the space cleared by a socialist culture and technology policy, linking it to hip hop even as it moves toward innovating new forms. A reconsideration of nuclear and push for growth of alternative energy industries was a part of the Socialist platform for 2012. The next project for Los Anges, another video/choreographic collaboration, *Pixelle* mixes many of the same themes with a response to each performance environment through improvisation. Far from replacing live dance events, the choreographer wants to use recording and projection to enhance the live event, to see what is possible in the interplay between the well-planned, previously filmed and the experience of the present moment that dance performance brings.

CONCLUSION

What does urban dance bring to the discussion of French cultural identity and politics? This dance, in this context, enacts a reconception of the body as agent and actor, transforming the idea of corporeal identity. If this book can argue for an embodied identity and citizenship in French urban dance, making minorities visible even as their lack of representation becomes acknowledged, it is through the vehicle of metaphor that bodies are permitted to do more than simply "present" themselves. It is the goal of this book to show that embodiment, rather than a dead end in a republic aiming for universalism, becomes a figure within the mobility brought by new technologies and the social mobility it promises for all. Choreographic embodiment, in urban dance, lets bodies tell other stories, or tell stories differently, moving beyond appearance and experience to the realm and practice of figuration. At the same time, new media make possible new bodiliness and mobility, modulated by but not enslaved to new technologies.

When Rancière describes the "absolute right of those without rights," a concept also debated by Balibar and a terminology I invoked in reference to *hip hoppeurs* earlier, he is referring to those whose "absolute right...can only be exercised by another party" in a sort of transfer he calls "humanitarian" interference.[82] This is not the case for hip hop citizens: they enact their own integration into the political system, ironically by pointing out their nonintegration. The politics of *Zou* are not only identitary. Here, *le hip hop* has moved on, while rooted in banlieue experience and grounded in dance forms recognizably African, American, and European, to a performance staging technology, community and civic participation. Dancing here doesn't simply represent a general Frenchness but poses the questions of citizenship, environmental consciousness, and the creation of new environments.

What does hip hop dance propose in the French political-cultural field? Perhaps, through its transformational poetics and techniques, something akin to what Balibar writes as one word, *equaliberty*: being counted and being equal; being counted in rather than out (as "different," "multicultural," or "other" = *issus de*); accessing a certain freedom of identity by being counted as "French" (*there where one is*) rather than "immigrant"—an idea of a freedom to come from that taking account of, beyond being accounted for, and instead giving one's own account.

CHAPTER 2

Hip Hop "Speaks" French

Droit de citer

The American dancer/choreographer Bill T. Jones sees French hip hop as a little too perfect and a little too "national":

> Whenever I see works in France, they are usually very well made, but they are superconscious of style. Not just break dancing, but the best example of break dancing.... [I]n another word, it is never going to be gauche. And I wonder sometimes if [French choreographers], need a more challenging crucible, like the United States, that wouldn't just tolerate [them] as ... artist[s].[1]

For Bill T. Jones, French dance reflects state funding rather than the crucible in which US dance forms burn into existence; he does not see cultural funding as advantageous for choreographers, and instead gives a positive spin to the difficult conditions most dancers and choreographers encounter in the United States. In describing the French particularity of this dance form, Jones emphasizes not only its national profile, the "best example" that can be produced by big culture budgets, but also its choreographic language, a dance "style" that is recognizably "French." In France, hip hop dancers may bring their own minority cultures or local aesthetic to the form as much as they adopt a global American form, or they may layer it with any of the world movement forms visible in French cities: *capoiera*, yoga, Bharata Natyam, African dance of all kinds. In the last chapter, I argued that what has made it "French" was public funding, a *politique culturelle* and civic positioning of dance in public culture. But it also becomes French in its dialogue with French universalism: the specific context of minority dancers choosing hip hop within the national discourse that has ignored diversity while privileging the universal.

It is tempting to compare the French embrace of *le hip hop* to its historic embrace of *le jazz hot*. But there are significant historical differences: the French promotion of African American jazz musicians offered opportunities not available to them in the United States in the 1920s, and it was precisely through access to French means of production that musicians and dance performers attained commercial success, as I argued for the case of Josephine Baker in *Dancing Machines*. In the case of *la danse hip hop*, a US commercial model was countered by the French state's *politique culturelle*, which did bring funding opportunities to US choreographers, such as Rennie Harris, but not following the model of the music or show business market. Yet in both examples, it could be argued, dancing that resonates with free expression, with youth culture, became a mainstream form—reflecting its "recuperation" not just by cultural forces but by the French state itself.[2]

In the case of hip hop, one might argue that the form is a commentary on the "melting pot" of US culture that French dancers can only gesture toward. But French arts funding, a national and civic profile for dance, has made of *le hip hop* something recognizably French. In focusing on what makes French hip hop different, I am of course going against the grain of studies of global culture and its circulation. I seem to be emphasizing the exception rather than the general rule. And in doing so, I am asking: is modernity really global or does it still have a national character and a particular national history in some places? Indeed, by asking this question I am arguing, via Balibar, that hip hop dance is a form with political resonance in France, one that is not simply gesturing toward global culture or the US model but making an intervention within the specific political context in France.

This chapter explores hip hop's translation and its elaboration of a unique French profile: how *le hip hop* became *la danse urbaine*. It traces the development of a choreographic language that is "French"—funded by state and local governments, featured in festivals, and sent out on international tours to represent France. In hip hop's transmutation into a French form, I argue in this chapter, it learned to "speak" French: not only as French rap music did, but also in a metaphorical way. It offered a language of expression for minorities becoming visible and seeking a way to discuss difference within the terms of the republic.

The "Frenchness" I refer to here—when not defined racially by the conservative Right—is usually defined by language, often through the concept of *la francophonie*, the world of French speakers. But this term also describes the linguistic identity of more than 200 million people in the world, only 60 million or so of whom are "French." By extension, in the United States and the United Kingdom, the relatively new field of "francophone studies" focuses on the history, actuality, integration, and exclusion of French speakers in immigrant communities in the Metropol, as well as the reach of French colonialism and its impact on postcolonial nations that continue to be francophone. In this largely Anglophone field, *francophone* is a marker for diversity within France and describes minorities representing former French colonies with varying histories and degrees of assimilation, as well as postindependence populations in the former colonies. *Francophone*, then, in English, refers to the diversity rather than the unity of French-speaking peoples, and as a field of inquiry focuses rather on the failures of an ideal of universalism and its uneven policies of integration of such diverse peoples into the French nation during the colonial and postcolonial periods. Whereas the term *francophonie,* for example, in the institution called the Agence Universitaire de la Francophonie, spreads a positive vision of French culture through the teaching of the French language, *francophone* in English tends to focus on resistances and differences and has tended to critique the ironies and inequalities in the colonial and postcolonial history of *la francophonie*.

The French concept of language as a unifying, national (and even international) force depends on a universalist view that ignores ethnic, religious, and cultural differences. Considering the significance of bodies, appearance, and behavior in registering such differences among diverse French populations, it is interesting to see how the term *francophone* has come to serve, in English, to identify minority communities in the French Republic. Given the French emphasis on *francophonie* as a unifying factor all over the globe, it is striking to see the use of a similar, parallel rhetoric for hip hop dance, a nonlinguistic or nonverbal form. The title of this chapter plays on the familiar idiom *droit de cité* or residents' rights, emphasizing its resonance in *citer* or the right to refer to or "quote" a formulation, to "cite." I am using the linguistic metaphor here because "francophone" has been a key concept in the redefinition of what it is to be "French" and also because the discourses specific to French hip hop (happening in the French language, all over the world) pose a challenge to theories of global English dominance, suggesting the continuation of colonial patterns within globalized culture. French hip hop "cites" the US "founders" or pioneers of the genre; but rather than simply inhabiting a global "Americanized" space, it carves out a particular French francophone space. Finally, the French poetics surrounding dance historically and the civic positioning of dancers in the French cultural realm put dance in a different position, one that hip hop (as urban dance) was able to take advantage of.

Why should I insist, in looking at dance, on its resemblance to language and its proximity to poetics? Doesn't dance provide us with a model that is based on the presence and plenitude of the body and gesture, rather than a language of lack or a sign of absence that has been the focus of language theory since Saussure? Dance appears to be, if anything, a motivated language whose signifying gestures or shapes resemble what they suggest or communicate. In particular, hip hop is often seen as a dance of "power moves," discussed in the introduction, signaling the empowerment of its dancers through embodiment, a bodily language that cuts across conventions, to speak its "bodily" truth. Yet dance, like language, also represents "something else": something other than what is simply visible, something beyond the bodies dancing it. It is precisely in the gap between what the body is doing and what it is suggesting, the moves and their ultimate meanings, that we find what Dominique Rabaté has called the "force figurale"—the figural power—that I will argue here makes dance, like literature, a vehicle of ideas.[3] The power of French hip hop dance is its power of metaphor or of figuration. In this gap between the figure and expression, where one often speaks of loss or lack, Rabaté sees the opening that energizes the upending of forms. Dance's challenge to the established norms of seeing bodies or to their place in the hierarchy moves through this gap: the metaphorical and metonymic potential of dance to say something "else" or to "say otherwise." Its "force figurale"—the power of its figures—comes through its very insufficiency, the cracks in its surface, the gaps it shows between our bodies and our speech. In this way, theories of figuration nuance my account of embodied performance.

Theorists of political and social change emphasizing embodied agency often exclude or separate language from this bodily existence. Butler's theory of the performative, discussed in the last chapter, describes a bodily remainder, not fully "constructed," or an underlying bodily truth (e.g., in gesture) that may belie speech or intention. Taken up by many performance theorists, performativity can be useful for describing the political agency and social engagement of subjects. But Butler (e.g., in *Excitable Speech*) and others begin from the linguistic performative and link language's effects back to the body, via their bodily effects. Butler writes, commenting on Shoshana Felman's reading of Austin: "the speech act is a bodily act...the speech act is at once bodily and linguistic."[4] Butler's theory, in Molly Rothenberg's re-reading, "reinstates intentionality at the level of the body," referring to the "truth of bodily gestures," and thus misreads the role of foreclosure in the formation of the subject.[5] For Rothenberg, speech acts exceed the intention of the speaker, not, as Butler claims, because of the body's ability to express unconscious motivation or resist interpellation, but because other people interpret them according to their own lights.[6] While Butler sees bodily agency as a way to remediate loss, opening the possibility for bodily expression unmarked by loss or lack and free from interpellation, Rothenberg defends a psychoanalytic perspective constructing not an essentialized bodily truth, but the open grid of interpretation of all forms of expression. Such a perspective opens out rather than closes off the signifying potential for bodies dancing.

If an insistence on minority discourse in hip hop suggests an essentialized concept of race, to be discussed at length in the next chapter, gender essentialism in France has had an equally conflictual history. If women were granted the right to vote only in 1945, recent laws requiring *parité* or equal representation by women and men in public institutions have outstripped gains made by political feminism in the United States: the government named in May 2012 is constituted of seventeen female and seventeen male ministers. The female hip hoppers whose dances I am describing here do represent an exception in the world of hip hop but not in concert dance in France, which has funded many female choreographers and named them directors of the regional modern dance and choreography centers. In *Essentially Speaking: Feminism, Nature and Difference*, Diana Fuss ponders essentialism's theoretical or political usefulness in French feminists' texts. For example, Fuss sees Luce Irigaray using essentialism not to imprison women in their bodies, but to consider whether the body stands in literal or figurative relation to language; she concludes that in Irigaray's conception of a *parler femme*, the body stands in metonymic relation to language.[7] This will come close to the language I argue hip hoppers are "speaking" in their wordless choreographies: they are speaking "from" their bodies, with their bodily movements, and ultimately about their bodily existence. But beyond calling attention to bodily or visible difference, they are using choreographic language to "say otherwise"—developing a figural language in which the body doesn't simply "do" what it "says" or reinforce how it "appears." While a certain body politics is at the core of French hip hop, as it is in so-called US identity politics, here the French essentialism is ultimately at the service of what is called French *universalisme*—or unity and equality—coming to terms with difference.

Rather than moving from speech to the body, my work begins from performing bodies and moves "outward" in looking at embodied expression beyond a bodily essentialism. Language is a given here, and this bodily performance of dance exists within and along with a culture of speech and text. But choreography is no more reducible to the bodies animating it than language itself is to the bodies using it. It supplements public debate by adding a choreographic language to the discourses (political, philosophical, social) being deployed and can evoke perspectives outside of the French debates. Yet choreography manifests the same desires and limits as language does: it imagines options for bodies (through gesture, movement) rather than reducing them to an underlying bodily truth. And it shows that bodies aren't the end point to which the debate about identity should be reduced, but rather the starting point for a rethinking of bodies' place in the republic. This is why I use the term *poetics* in describing dance: referring not simply to dance's poetic influence or inspiration, but seeing dance itself as a movement poetics. Drawing on the Greek resonance of *poesis* as creation, Luce Irigaray describes poetics as "a *poietic* language, a language which creates something new and does not communicate only something that already exists."[8] French urban dance allows its dancers to "cite" various forms and to make them their own.

This chapter will argue that the French concept of *la francophonie*—the areas where the French language is spoken throughout the world—as well as the US/UK-based research field called francophone studies can help us understand what makes French hip hop unique in the political and social work it accomplishes, as well as the choreographic language it has come to develop as urban dance. Debates about postcolonial immigration in France intersect with theories of globalization that include a *francophonie* in which many of the worlds' French speakers aren't French[9] and their simultaneous encounter with what is often called an "Anglophone" global culture, and in which performance culture plays a major part. Discussions about nations and nationalism have been influenced by literary studies and the history of literature's contribution to state building and national identity, as well as its deconstruction in more personal and theoretical explorations of language, authorship, and identity. But what does it mean to take dance as an example—both national and international—and think about nations unforming or reforming through it? Would this be the nation "without nationalism" and without racism as Julia Kristeva defined it, via Montesquieu's *esprit general*, in her open letter to Harlem Désir on February 24, 1990?[10] Here specifically I am referring to a national-focused form with international reach, responding to a colonial history and postcolonial immigration that trouble the definition of national identity.

This chapter will make a double argument for hip hop as a *francophonie*: first, deployed like the French language, and recognized as a lingua franca, across francophone populations; then in hop hop's translation into a French concert dance form, urban dance, through a movement vocabulary specific to the French scene—or what Bill T. Jones in the earlier citation calls "style." In a study of the hip hop choreography *Paname*, this chapter also explores how hip hop developed a choreographic language linked to French history and French popular culture, in a context in which French song expresses a transnational transgenerational *habitus* and in which choreography itself is respected as a poetics or "writing." The French (or francophone) development of hip hop into *la danse urbaine* in France, as in Belgium, is in sync with the fading of American rap music as the musical accompaniment to French hip hop and the constitution of a round of discourses supporting and developing urban dance for the stage.

With ministerial support, French hip hop developed—in dance—a "francophone" poetics. While dancing usually appends "-graph" as a suffix to describe its choreographic writing or drawing, here I am appending "-phone" as a suffix usually used for aural forms.[11] But "francophone" dance makes sense here for many reasons and significantly shapes the argument of this book. First, if the dance form began in American English, it very quickly moved from *anglais* to *franglais* in France—the inspired use of terms and slang from the United States by a young generation for whom English was not yet the official language of the European Union or the second language at school and for whom, in some cases, French was also not their first language, or not the language spoken at home. But this *franglais* was itself part of a French slang broadly calling up words from both Arabic and English, sometimes also from other European languages, and creating its own poetics of back-slang. Calling this dance "francophone," then, refers to these populations also called "francophone" who constitute the multiculturalism usually identified as resulting from immigration, in particular from former French colonies. Hip hop's dancers constitute this "francophone" multiculturalism (that is to say, representing ethnic, cultural, or religious diversity) usually identified with the working-class suburbs of the big cities—rather than a global monoculture. If I choose to use this term, however, it is also because in the past decade, the hip hop movement has openly advertised its *francophonie* and used the concept as a metaphor for travel and exchange with former French territories, arguably as an alternative to the more contested term of immigration: in the theme of a "voyage en francophonie" for a biennial dance festival in 2000–2001, and in the press materials of a hip hop company reclaiming their "francophone" roots by taking inspiration from the French songs of their parents' and grandparents' generation. These examples suggest, ultimately, the specificity of the French model inspired by but moving away from an American original.

Without underestimating the global charisma of American rap music, the *politique culturelle* outlined in the last chapter made it possible for French hip hop to develop its own language. Hip hop has often served to represent globalized US culture, and the music industry has led the charge in selling that culture. Although dance and music are often cited as "universal" forms because of their transcendence of language differences, and rap is marketed as a global music, dance's nonverbal status allows it to bypass a certain American "content" while remaining at the center of discussions of the social and artistic development of an entire generation. Discussing the commercialism of rap and its relation to French urban dance, Philippe Mourrat, whose title is *Chef de projet à l'Etablissement public de la Villette, Directeur des Rencontres des cultures urbaines*, said in an interview: "La danse a été protégée de ça" ("Dance has been protected from that").[12]

Critics writing in the United States such as bell hooks, Robert Stam, and Ella Shohat have pointed out that hip hop music, in spite of its origins in US urban, ghettoized counterculture, was diffused by US multinationals and became a signal element of global culture: "A highly Africanized diasporic music, hip hop has become the international lingua franca.... The same U.S. based and multinational corporations that disseminate inane blockbusters and canned sitcoms also spread Afro-diasporic music around the globe."[13] In their 2001 response to Pierre Bourdieu and Loic Wacquant's critique of US academic multiculturalism, Stam and Shohat use hip hop to characterize a great divide between Anglo-American and French intellectuals. Cultural studies has made important inroads in the United States and the United Kingdom in the exploration of such popular forms: "But in France there seems to be a gap between the highly miscegenated streets of Paris and Marseille and the theorization of culture by intellectuals, who seem invested in conventional hierarchies, at least in the realm of high culture and theory."[14] For Stam and Shohat, writing more than a decade ago, this was a gap within France that the case of hip hop music exemplified. They emphasize what they type as a "French" misunderstanding of a left intellectual undertaking in what they argue should not be typed as "Anglo-Saxon" intellectual milieus and defend the integrity of an intellectual field (multiculturalism) against what they characterize as Bourdieu's and Wacquant's dismissive summary of a "marketing gimmick promoted by Routledge."[15] Stam and Shohat argued that important work was already being done, for example, on French hip hop and *banlieue* culture in the United States and United Kingdom, sometimes by French-speaking scholars. Whereas hip hop is usually studied as a global phenomenon, for Stam and Shohat it is a site revealing differences between traditions—in this case "French" and non-French analyses, and "theory" and the streets. In fact, the difference to be found in French hip hop dance is in how it negotiates this divide, not only in its manifestations in theory but also in its artistic practice. In the domain of hip hop dance, cultural differences have distinguished its practice on two sides of the Atlantic. One wonders, for example, what is "African" for Stam and Shohat in a globally diffused music that has only in the past two decades included artists recorded in Africa; is the "African" they identify in African American the same as the "Africa" represented by immigration into France, especially since decolonization? At the same time, the African part of black US culture is often forgotten or disconnected from Africa.[16]

In the translation of hip hop to France, a certain draining of content takes place—akin to what Bourdieu and Wacquant called "dehistoricization."[17] They have complained that US cultural studies theorists impose a black/white binarism in their study of other cultures, an impoverished analytic approach that is a vestige of the historic particularity of American segregation. Yet, although a certain ignorance of US black experience,[18] and its language of expression, facilitates this French development of hip hop into something else, it is not entirely the "neutralization" that Bourdieu and Wacquant claim emerges from the circulation of ideas when academics theorize culture. Rather, it is the French artists themselves who pin their cause to black culture in the United States. Generalizing about French hip hop music culture, Steve Cannon notes the "specific character of their appropriation" of rap,[19] not the black nationalist or separatist, but a pluriethnic variety that rises from the French suburbs. In the wake of decolonization and immigration, the denizens of hip hop in France have stronger or more immediate links to Africa than their US counterparts but also access to an America that is in many ways, for them, more mythic: the use of the word *black* in contemporary parlance,[20] rather than *noir*, signals an alliance with America rather than the region referred to as *l'Afrique noire*. Yet as the tripartite title of one of the first French urban dance companies Black Blanc Beur indicates, the term functions not as the black/white binarism imposed in the segregated US model, but in sync with postcolonial France. Inventing new labels for French of African birth or descent (the *verlan* or "back-slang" coinage of *beur* for *arabe*), inventing new references and identifications, and performing back-slang on back-slang (in the next generation, *beur* has become *re-beuh*), the French appropriation of hip hop is nuanced by postcolonial history and goes beyond a unidirectional cultural transfer.

In more recent music, this debate has accelerated exponentially in France. On the question of "recuperation" or media manipulation of rap, Olivier Bourderionnet has written about French rapper Abd Al Malik's "conciliatory discourse" both in his songs and in his autobiography, *Qu'Allah benisse la France* ("May Allah Bless France").[21] In this work, Abd Al Malik—born Régis Fayette-Mikano, of Congolese origin, raised in Strasbourg, and a convert to Islam—identifies himself as "pro-Republic, pro-democracy, secular, black, Muslim, and Alsatian" ("*pur républicain, démocrate, laïque, noir, musulman et alsacien*"), a series of adjectives difficult to square in the French imagination. Bourderionnet emphasizes the media's inability to come to terms with such a discourse even as it attempts to promote it. Abd Al Malik is appreciated by a Parisian and music industry elite—but is significant not only because he references thinkers such as Deleuze in his lyrics, nor because his discourse differs so significantly from the destructive *banlieue* ethics, according to Bourderionnet, but because he is himself manipulating the concept of the universal that has more often oppressed and erased the *banlieue* experience. Invited to the Fes Sacred Music festival in 2010, Abd El Malik at first sounded out of place in comparison to the traditional, spiritual music featured there. But his lyrics and message, delivered also in commentary between songs, distinguished his songs from *banlieue* genres critical of France and linked his music to the Islamic spiritualism (especially that of the "magnificent kingdom of Morocco") that he embraces.

The particular situation of hip hop in France allowed what was described as "authentic" or "old-school" African American roots to develop with global dance forms. In the city of Paris, hosting touring dance companies from all over the world, with a passionate dance public, hip hop became a site like many other performance sites in which cultural forms were layered over one another: watching *smurf*, for example, in Paris, one thinks of the cartoon characters (now prevalent in video games) called the *schtroumpfs* (translated as Smurfs). In the French context, it would be hard to say if French hip hoppers learned to moonwalk from Michael Jackson (who learned it from street dancer Poppin' Pete, in some accounts, or from choreographer Paula Abdul, in others) or from French mime Marcel Marceau (who credited himself for having spread it in the United States). In the United States, however, the form is not seen as multicultural because it is street art; Wacquant does not see multiculturalism in the US form because in forms like this, and in dance in particular, it has been erased. The establishment of the Hip Hop Archive in the W.E.B. DuBois Institute at Harvard University, as well as recent scholarship on hip hop in the United States, emphasizes multicultural or multiethnic and positive elements of the movement that have been highlighted in France but often ignored in the public debates in the United States, and also missed by French scholars' and artists' thinking about the American situation. A different kind of incomplete understanding can be seen in the Hip Hop Archive's online entry for "France," which details the rise of French rap music against the background of Third Republic freedoms but as of 2011 did not mention dance.

EVERYTHING BUT . . . THE WORDS

When I first began my research, in 2000–2001, joining a group that Paris-based, American-born researcher Roberta Shapiro had organized, it was impossible for me not to wonder whether French hip hop, in spite of its reverence for the US pioneers and its roots in the concrete turf of the zones with priority for urbanization (ZUP), had completely "missed the point" of a dance developed in US inner cities. The language difference, the apparent ignorance of "the words," the reinterpretation of a counterculture for "positive" or "social" ends, and the funding of a choreographic project using a different soundtrack all marked French hip hop as different.

Charting the trajectory of hip hop music in France, André Prévos has described a three-step process of "borrowing" and then "adoption" and "adaptation"—the progressive transformation of an American popular form into a more clearly French one.[22] Recent debates in US scholarship on rap have focused on the question of the words and the beat. Although I assumed that the French differed from US fans of American rap in not knowing any of the words to their favorite songs, Mark Antony Neal has argued that lyrics remain largely unimportant compared to rhythm and voicing that links rap to other forms of black American popular music.[23] In *All About the Beat: Why Hip Hop Can't Save Black America*, John McWhorter argues against the idea that "rap is nothing but vulgar noise" but critiques rap as ineffective politics, "stasis as progress, gesture as action." When considering rap music he admires, he concludes: "even rap like this [Tupac Shakur's] is not as effective as 'politics' as we are often told."[24]

But in French translation, the words *necessarily* become less important, and the language difference does pose a problem. In spite of the admiration for American rap music and its presence in urban dance classes, in France the content of US rappers' songs and their critical messages are ignored or read as inspiration, the spirit rather than the letter of "gangsta" law. French parents take their young children to learn funky moves in hip hop dance classes where the recorded musical accompaniment can feature explicit lyrics in English, of which they seem to be blissfully ignorant.[25]

Although in the world of French hip hop the concern with authenticity includes using American words as a touchstone, they are only one of many codes in the movement. While the words may inspire countercultural thinking or identification even in their global commercialization, in French hip hop dance they seem to be insignificant. Far more significant are the French codes surrounding hip hop's working-class context; nearly as omnipresent as French *verlan* are the official acronyms for the ZUP from which hip hoppers come and the agencies supporting immigrant families, such as the FAS (*fonds d'action sociale pour les travailleurs immigrés et leurs familles*)—the third of the three partners (the other two are the Ministry of Culture and the Parc de la Villette) that until 2009 sponsored the biggest annual hip hop dance festival.

In fact, an entire poetics—beyond *verlan*—is generated around French hip hop. In one conversation, dancers remarked on the difficulty of using French institutional vocabularies (drawn from classical, contemporary, or jazz dance) for teaching hip hop, which the establishment of a diploma would necessitate. American words remain crucial in the teaching of French hip hop, but they are often not the same words as those used on the other side of the Atlantic.[26] Certain dance steps, for example, have a different name in French: the "electric boogie" was referred to as *le smurf*. The range of texts available on hip hop, including children's how-to manuals, contain lexicons and define these names and steps using both American and French slang.[27] But they often provide definitions giving words a different resonance than in the United States.

In France, the rhetoric promulgated by the funding and programming structures—as well as the dancers and companies—is one of inclusion in spite of the widespread acknowledgment, at least since 2005, of the exclusion of *banlieusards* from equal opportunity. In Steve Cannon's phrase, this puts French hip hoppers "well in advance of the forces of the official left"; their movement "has the potential to raise the colors of the 'flag of unity' way beyond its initial audience in the *banlieues*."[28] Adopted, in Cannon's view, from Africa Bambaata's model of "positivity,"[29] this discourse counters the use of the term of *exclusion* to describe the French equivalent of "underclass."[30] In France, this "positivity" so permeates the *mouv'* that terms like *posse* take on a communitarian, even familial tone, losing their connotation of outlaw justice or breakaway, sectarian individualism. In the first full-length book by an academic on the movement in France, ethnolinguist Claudine Moïse writes:

> In the beginning, in the hip hop movement, there is the posse: a kind of extended
> family to which each member feels attached, through their home territory, and

also by affinities. An allusion to a North-American mythology about the solidarity of a sort of troop of justice-seeking cowboys, the posse is a term without marked connotation, harmoniously resonating with the possibility of freedom, and letting everyone find his own place. . . . [31]

In opposition to the commercial culture of rap music,[32] hip hop dance created an atmosphere closer in spirit to the French movement of May 1968 than to the American 1980s. This positive tone, whether inspired by US hip hop's origins or ignoring much of its later content, animates the debates and roundtables, organized by the funding structures and also by collectives and associations that thrive around the hip hop movement. While "posse" now has a positive resonance in the United States (for example, via the Posse Foundation), this appears to be the active recuperation of the term from its sectarian and divisive gang-related history.

This positive tone seems to belie the social critique and rebelliousness and the frenzy at the root of the US form. In its different forms, hip hop performs a mockery of industrial productivity, a critique of the crippling of the worker in the machine age. At the same time, the parodic, pumped-up swagger of house or break dance is impossible not to see as a self-empowerment that is both carnival and critique. Brought to the concert dance stage by dancer/choreographer Rennie Harris's Puremovement Company, a Philadelphia-based company that began with self-trained dancers, it speaks eloquently of inner-city African American and Hispanic American experience. Rennie Harris's 1992 solo *Endangered Species* is accompanied by a tape of testimonials of abuse and violence within the family and in the neighborhood, and when I see it in live performance, it makes the psychoanalyst sitting next to me weep.

In the United States, Rennie Harris's Puremovement is exceptional: a company that had been composed of street dancers performing on concert stages and now recruiting dancers with diplomas; in France, such companies are the rule. By the '90s, French hip hop was developing into *la danse urbaine*, a form of concert dance. In a 2001 article in *Le Monde*[33] by Rosita Boisseau and Dominique Frétard, celebrating the tenth annual Suresnes festival, the French breed of hip hop is traced to US influences such as the Urban Bush Women and Doug Elkins, yet some of the US modern dance companies able to integrate hip hop into their repertories— including Elkins and Rennie Harris's Puremovement—have found crucial funding from French structures.[34] French dancers remain surprised that the great dancers they revere as the "pioneers" have never been recognized or funded—and work, for example, as pizza deliverers.[35] The French artists and social workers inspired by US hip hop both ally themselves with the marginalized and are themselves the agents who mainstream this popular culture, as they deftly use (and allow themselves to be used by) French institutions.

During much of hip hop's nearly three decades of development in France, institutional funding worked hand in hand with the notion of authenticity. In addition to supporting US companies, French institutional money could "buy" authenticity, in the form of subventions to dance companies—such as Käfig—bringing US hip hopper "Clown" to perform with them as they did for *Dix Versions* in 2001 or to film productions privileging the form's African American precursors. Choreographer Christine Coudun, cofounder of Black Blanc Beur, writing in 1996, set out a working opposition between "authentic" hip hop and the choreographic process, arguing that improvisation is the best working method for the elaboration of choreography and defining as good sense the "harmony between an authentic style of hip hop (preserved in the group over ten years) and artistic sensibility."[36] In this case, rhetoric about "authenticity" seems to complement rather than describe choreographic projects, and a decade later, companies such as Choream with dancers rooted in hip hop practice and style did not worry about it: Stéphanie Nataf stated in a 2002 interview that she and José Bertogal, codirector of Choream, no longer cared whether the label hip hop was attached to their work.[37] The tendency toward eclecticism in hip hop choreographies, imported through contact with dancers from other traditions or even cultural tourism, as in Accrorap's 2000 and 2001 collaborations with Brazilian or Indian dancers, does not efface the hip hop "content" in their choreography. For hip hop to continue to exist in institutional structures, it is being absorbed by contemporary dance institutions (the regional centers, CCN-sponsoring events), venues, and publics, even if it is moving more slowly toward the halls reserved for the best modern dance companies.[38]

In its choreographic elaborations, Rennie Harris's hip hop remains close to its street and community origins and speaks very particularly, and profoundly, of African American experience. French hip hoppers, referring to US black culture, are already one step removed, and thus represent something other than themselves. The importation of moves from classical ethnic and other dance traditions and the merging of hip hop with jazz and modern dance forms have added other layers of signification to French hip hop. At the same time, seeing choreography such as Rennie Harris's as simply reproducing the situation of its own dancers flattens its potential for representation and denies to its dancers the power to represent something else in their art, to speak figuratively rather than literally. This, too, was for many years the situation with hip hop in France, with its roots in the urban housing projects; as an art form *issu de l'immigration*, like its dancers, it has been surrounded by the discourse of support for *les travailleurs immigres et leurs familles* and structures such as the Fonds d'action sociale. Has the transformation of hip hop into an art, urban dance, eased integration tensions or exposed its failures?

REPRESENTING ONESELF REPRESENTING SOMETHING ELSE

In spite of this idealism about the United States in French hip hop, and in spite of its resolutely positive rhetoric, *hip hoptimisme*, it has also staged its performers' exclusion. French hip hoppers subscribe to black US culture to articulate their own differences. Using the African American form to speak of difficulties in France and identifying with the African American cause, the French version of hip hop nevertheless works major changes into the form. While passing through the United States, the Anglophone world of hip hop, the form comes around to speak of its particular context: postcolonial immigration, multicultural ethnic and religious diversity, an embedded tradition of dance as a respected art form, even a "national" art. French hip hop is inspired by African American culture and continues to valorize it, but it draws its strengths now from multiethnic urban France and reflects not only the source cultures of its dancers identified as *issus de l'immigration* but also the presence of "high art" concert dance and classical ethnic dance forms highly visible in cities like Paris and Lyon.

In his work on culture and universality, *Branchements,* Jean-Loup Amselle writes:

> [R]ather than protesting against American domination and declaring a state of cultural exception along with quotas, it would be better to show the ways in which contemporary French culture, its "signified," can only be expressed through a global planetary signifier, that of American culture. Speaking *franglais* is, perhaps, for the French, a way to articulate the truth of their culture, just as, for the group from Sarcelles called Bisso na Bisso, plugging into American rap is the best way to rediscover their Congolese roots. Contrary to the thinking of those obsessed with the purity of origins, mediation is the shortest path to "authenticity," the palimpsestuous relation being here simply the means to bring to light the identity of an underlying text. The practice of "sampling" expresses the originality of a culture that one would be at pains to call French, American, or African.[39]

Using the American form, then, allows the dancers to "articulate the truth of their culture," which is itself palimpsest, universal, in finding its specificity through relation to other global texts.

In other work, however, Amselle emphasizes that cultural mixing theorized by many anthropologists creates an intellectual problem in the French context. In *Vers un multiculturalisme,* Amselle argues that multiculturalism, or the emphasis on difference, is dangerous: that it tends to support the very cultural biases it hopes to destroy, that it is ultimately based on a notion of an "original" or authentic culture (for example, an essentialized African culture), and that it opens the window for a racism based on difference rather than basic universal humanity. Amselle's arguments are based on French contexts and rely upon philosophical understandings of French republicanism and universality; but the conclusion is that US-style affirmative action should be understood in fact as "affirmative exclusion."[40]

In Amselle's recent work, the idea of "banlieue identity" or of "multicultural" minorities is seen as reductive, serving both the Left and the Right, but not the banlieusards themselves. In *L'Ethnicisation de la France* he argues that "the identity of any individual is dynamic; it can't be classified through belonging to any particular group, precisely because he or she identifies successively or simultaneously with several of these groups."[41] Specifically, the *politique culturelle* concerning immigrants, in particular during Mitterrand's presidency, was *"liberale"* and "multicultural"—recognizing singular identities and thus in conflict with the French republican model; for Amselle this multiculturalism promoted by the Left also strangely served some on the Right by opposing the concepts of equity and equality, favoring a concept of equity through a politics of recognition.[42] The result has been, he argues, a "decline of the social" and the abandonment of universalism, following an American model of "the understanding of social phenomena in cultural terms." Multiculturalism, he writes, has "failed" in France, and in Europe, because it fragments the social body and opposes majority and minority identities, has created a boomerang effect against the appearance of ethnic, cultural and racial minorities in the public space, and a reinforcement of "white" identity that distinguishes it from the U.S. model.[43] Amselle states that no one (in France) is served by the kind of categorization typical of American identity politics: "We aren't helping those 'representing diversity' by locking them into their 'negritude' or 'Arabic-Muslim-ness". Turning social questions into cultural or ethnic ones is the best way to keep the *banlieue* youth under the yoke of power, the best method to keep them locked in their ghettos delimited both by geography and identity."[44]

The hip hop dance analysed in this book responds directly to this challenge: passing through another culture, an art of identity, to style oneself as other, but not the expected other. "Accumulating identities," as dancer/choreographers Sébastien Ramirez and Hyun-Jung Wang write about themselves (in the program described in the Introduction), and dancing a different universalism.

If in hip hop's first phase of choreographic development, the "urban" content of the dances was justified in a discourse about France's social problems, a similar "civil" discourse surrounds the next wave of choreographies that have moved far afield from the home turf. Why should dancers be bound to some kind of "authenticity" grounded in the *cités* any more than they were bound to an "authenticity" of US hip hop? Must hip hop dance bind its performers to representing themselves? This, of course, has been one of the problems with so-called *banlieue* films, often read as sociological documents of the metropolitan experience of second- or third-generation *issus de l'immigration*. Although many films of this genre tend toward realism in low production values, reading them as "realistic" would mean ignoring, for example, questions of representation raised by who speaks French to whom, and for what imagined audience, in a film such as Merzouk Allouache's 1996 *Salut, Cousin*.

In the well-known essay "The Work of Art in the Age of Mechanical Reproduction," Walter Benjamin–via Pirandello–ascribed this flattening of representation in which the actor plays only himself or herself to the mechanics of film (as opposed to theater, where an actor is able to create with theatrical distance, the illusion of playing someone else). In Abdellatif Kechiche's 2005 film *L'esquive*, the French high school teacher directing her *cité* students in a production of Marivaux attempts to shake her student Abdelkarim out of himself, to enter into his role: "sors de toi!" The order to act, to imagine himself other than he is, to declare in verse the very words that in real life he wants to say to the *lycéenne* playing alongside him finally forces the young man not out of himself but out of the room. In its wordless "French" form, hip hop dance can be seen to allow its dancers to *sortir* or "get beyond themselves" and to channel their anger in a broader expressive mode. In the words of hip hop dancer and choreographer Samir Hachichi: hip hop was the vehicle that allowed "us, as Maghrebians in France, to go beyond the place to which we are usually assigned" ("aller plus loin que là où on a l'habitude de nous mettre") (nous = les Mahgrebins).[45]

FROM *FRANGLAIS* TO A "FRANCOPHONE" DANCE

After its first steps in English, then, this form came to "speak French": first by speaking choreographically about the situation of its dancers and then, slowly, speaking figuratively about something else. Summarizing the "institutionalization" of break dancing as *la danse hip hop* in 2004, Roberta Shapiro emphasized that "breakdancing is undergoing not one, but multiple, interdependent processes of institutionalization. Consequently, hip hop ballet functions in polarity with another ideal typical form of practice—the hip hop battle."[46] Shapiro points out that the cultural entrepreneurs who tend to define break dancing in artistic and theatrical terms make up only one of three groups "whose actions are embedded in different worlds and who, in part, espouse different sets of values. Nevertheless, these people also participate in a common world structured by competing views as to how *la danse hip hop* should be defined and conducted."[47] The two other groups include those young dancers (identified as male and minorities) organizing battles as a "return to the 'real thing,' a reaction to what the participants view as an undue aestheticization of breakdancing and loss of control to non-hip hop agencies," and the group of social workers and educators who supported break dancing from the start. Shapiro emphasizes their important role in this institutional transition: "it was they who first took the activity seriously twenty years ago, designated it as dance (and not play), gained government support, and influenced policy," but they have also continued to encourage competitive hip hop battles. In these "two main ideal processes of institutionalization—promulgated by cultural entrepreneurs, on the one hand, and social workers and educators, on the other," my work complements that of Shapiro and our colleague and coresearcher Isabelle Kauffmann by focusing on the so-called hip hop ballet that both researchers date to 1992–1993 but that others identify as taking shape as a self-conscious choreographic language around 1999:[48] on the institutionalized form and its choreographic development, its teaching, and its performance. While embracing completely this institutional form, I do not wish to ignore its "popular" roots: its American references and its multicultural program. As both Shapiro and Kauffmann have shown in their work, "the two worlds are not that clearly divided"; battles continue to shape dancers' technique and ballets influence the development of steps in competition.[49] Both refer to Hugues Bazin's seminal work, *La Culture Hip Hop*, that traces, from a sociological perspective, the many facets of hip hop's visual and music culture in graffiti, in *soirées* ("parties"), and in a generalized youth culture, not explored in this book.[50] In response to these works, I should point out that my work barely touches on the main pillars of global hip hop culture, described by Halifu Osumare as "deejaying, rapping, breaking, and graf writing."[51] Yet it is not by accident that the hip hop dancer/choreographers whose work I focus on here—Franck II Louise, Farid Berki, Stéphanie Nataf and José Bertogal, and Yiphun Chiem—are well known as "self-trained" hip hoppers whose "authentic" credentials are not in question (even though some of them also went on to do formal dance training) and for whom the label "hip hop" never presented a problem.

Yet in its focus on dance, the French state gave a positive role to all of the arts surrounding hip hop. In a shift from teaching culture to embracing cultures (multiculturalism), the French state, it has been argued, continued to see the popular culture of hip hop as a national art, "fostering a national culture."[52] With funding and a significant national dance presence, hip hop dancers and choreographers worked miracles in the ZUP. Next, in creating this "national" dance form, *la danse urbaine*, hip hop's cultural agents strategically responded to contemporary critique of the "Americanization" of culture by emphasizing its Frenchness. Hip hop dance in France also crucially positioned itself as a pedagogy: in government programs for youth involving both art and sport, with a focus on dance in regional centers and national theaters, from local performances in the *salles polyvalentes* of the city hall to national festivals. In the United States, it is hard to imagine the local government as the place to look for a listing of hip hop dance classes offered in any community, but all over France, the town halls or *mairies* have offered or organized classes and disseminate information on this civic activity. This channeling of a form that has been seen as counterculture in the United States to serve ends that in France would be described as "social" (as in "social security" for the public) is key to hip hop's French history.

Because of its social positioning, French hip hop has been studied by sociologists as crossing class lines: as a "popular" (working-class) form that has broken through as an art form, recognized by journalists and having developed an aesthetic, and as a profession, even possibly worthy of a diploma. In separate studies, Roberta Shapiro has shown how journalists have in the past decade steadily applied the aesthetic and technical vocabulary for ballet to hip hop choreographies; and with Marie-Christine Bureau at the Centre d'Etudes de l'Emploi (CNRS), she studied the professionalization of young dancers and their "insertion" into the profession as *intermittants du spectacle*, who have the right to unemployment insurance when they are not working.[53]

From an American perspective, it was hard not to admire what the so-called left-wing elite or *gauche caviar* of Jack Lang–style socialism made possible in France. I agreed with sociologist Loic Wacquant on the lack of parallels between the US inner-city ghettos and the French *cités*, emphasizing the nonexistence of a French "underclass" and the cultural diversity of the *banlieue*, even if missing some of the multicultural elements merging into hip hop dance forms and music at their beginnings in the United States.[54] Before 2005, Wacquant argued that the conditions in US urban inner-city ghettos were vastly worse than in the French *cités*, where even the poorest suburbs house people of various cultural and ethnic backgrounds. Although the political situation of some hip hoppers who are *sans-papiers* is dire, and the question of disenfranchisement very relevant, especially clear since the uprisings of 2005, the rhetoric surrounding hip hop dance has been less oppositional or contestatory and more imbued with the positive spirit of the *mouv*: *black-blanc-beur* solidarity, self-expression, and the right to government funding. Hip hop, in this different form it takes in France, referencing but not simply copying US forms and merging with other dance forms from other traditions, has a certain *statut civil*: it has a civic political profile and gives its dancers a place in the community. The specific example of two festivals will show how that political cultural program worked to develop a specifically "francophone" dance.

HIP HOP DANCE FESTIVALS

What I am calling *francophone* hip hop can be more clearly defined in two rival annual festivals of hip hop dance in Paris, the Suresnes Cités Danse and the Rencontres des Cultures Urbaines at la Villette. These events resemble theater festivals rather than formal battles, but they do often include some informal dancing in hallways or lobbies. Both directors of these festivals have, for two decades, been bringing hip hop onto the concert dance stage. With very different strategies and rationales, both organizers are working toward elaborating a discourse about hip hop as a *francophonie*, referencing debates about universalism and particularism in France.

Olivier Meyer's Suresnes Cités Danse festival, for its first twelve years, hired well-known modern dance choreographers to set dances on hip hop dancers in choreographies presented in an art deco theater that is a gem of Paris's so-called *ceinture rouge* or red belt of communist (or formerly communist) communities. He presented the 2004 festival in a text in which classic metaphors of cultural *métissage* cede their place to universalism, the travel metaphor is here extended to other universes, and the subtext seems to position France as the metropolis that has long recognized the value of other cultures' products and ideas:

> Fermenting and brewing. Hip hop was the initial starter for the Suresnes Cités Danse festival. But far from trying to confine this performance of the urban body to a "catalogue" of socio-cultural products, I wanted to use it as a springboard to release its energy in a creative space open to other winds. The 2004 festival manifests this will to break out, in tracing a voyage into other countries,

other universes (Brazil, India, Cameroon or Italy)…as a way of recalling that the *cité* is today as it was yesterday, a space of brewing, mixing even within the confines of its heart, bearing witness to the fine diversity of cosmopolitanism. This is the shortcut that tempts Suresnes Cités Danse festival: from the territory of the individual to the universal.[55]

Mixing metaphors of the defined and yet cosmopolitan space of the city with cultural *métissage* and melting pot, the rhetoric about universalism deriving from the particular is an attempt to define an aesthetic human-ism that does not ignore the realities of racism and social class in France today.

The reference to "confining" hip hop to the "catalogue" of sociocultural products sounded at the time like a reference to the festival at la Villette, before its cancellation by administrative decision in 2009, included its direc-tor Philippe Mourrat. At stake in the rivalry between these two cultural agents is not simply a successful festival, programming the "best" hip hop companies, but the mission of inventing an art and its public. Each of these two programmers seems to try to outdo the other in terms of a "social com-mitment": Meyer insists on the high-art end of hip hop. La Villette, going in the opposite direction, has continually produced choreographies by young and unknown hip hoppers, some of whom are now successfully breaking through onto the big stages. Articulating a clear difference with the Suresnes festival, Philippe Mourrat emphasizes the creative energy that comes from these sites. Mourrat's could be described as a "bottom-up" approach against Olivier Meyer's "top-down." For the 2003 Rencontres, Mourrat emphasized the working-class sources and basis of this dance even while promoting it as civic culture; he locates it rising in cities across France and elsewhere, com-ing from urban youth, and as global or multicultural not only in its origins but also in its current practice. After 2000, he began to travel internationally to find hip hop companies in disadvantaged neighborhoods worldwide and bring them to the festival. Although references to the US pioneers have not disappeared from French urban dance, they have been largely superseded by a notion of global culture that looks beyond national differences.

A different view of hip hop's relation to *francophonie* emerges from the festival at la Villette. In one debate at the first Rencontres, in 1996, the link between hip hop and the cultural patrimony of *la langue francaise* was made explicit in this remark made by a participant: "Hip hop is like *francophonie*. The French language is so rich that, while developing it, there is no need to protect it. Hip hop is the same" ("Le hip hop, c'est comme la francophonie. Le français est assez riche pour qu'en le développant on n'ait pas besoin de le protéger. Le hip hop, c'est pareil").[56]

Published in the printed record of the *Rencontres* by the press of the Cité de la Musique, this remark solidifies a certain perspective that one could associate with the festival. Beyond the free-market tone of its promotion of French culture, I cannot help noticing that *ait*—the subjunctive—is included either by a well-spoken participant or by the editor translating the tape of the event into print. This is a world dominated by *verlan*, by slang and street poetics, a world in which I heard one hip hopper, a white French guy from the suburbs, thank the dancers at the end of an audition with an unimaginable error: "*merci d'avoir venu*" (meaning "thanks for coming" but using the wrong auxiliary verb). In this context, this little *ait* articulates something important: those fearless about protecting French, those who know how to use the subjunctive and yet do not feel the need to defend French against linguistic incursions, are also those who feel that hip hop can be the space of artistic development and of cross-class expression and, eventually, an international ambassador of French culture.

DANCE POETICS

In the debates on culture and multiculturalism in France, Max Silverman identifies dance with music and visual art as "arts of world interest" that are "not linguistically coded."[57] But, beyond the image, *la danse urbaine* has always been surrounded by language, inserted into dialogue and debate, and finally recognized, itself, as a form of *francophonie*. The hip hop world adopted a discourse of *francophonie* to emphasize its rightful place in joining the French *patrimoine*. Linking this dance to a language means emphasizing the cultural component of dance's form and practice, as well as understanding it as a complex system of representation; Daniel Maximin's list of cultural "francopolyphonies" includes dance with song, music, poetry, and other forms, as a cultural manifestation of common humanity, and raises dance to the status of language while attributing to it extralinguistic, poetic powers. It means localizing this global form in the cultural, national context of its institutions, actors, and agents in France in what Howard Becker calls "art worlds." It also means listening to the voices that accompany hip hop in France: roundtable debates, inter-views and workshops, and the institutional rhetoric, as well as the poetic back-slang—and not only rap music. It means reading dance as a form of writing, within a tradition of French poetics, and of understanding the dance as a hieroglyph or an ideogram following Mallarmé and Valéry. Finally, it means understanding how urban dance in France became linked to the cultural patrimony through this strategic cultural politics, the employment status of *intermittent du spectacle,* and a broadly respected notion of choreographic "authorship."

An example of hip hop's figurative language, described as a choreographic *écriture* and sent out on tour to Latin America, Central America, Panama, Peru, and Haiti, was the work of the company Choream, an alliance of dancers that has since re-formed under other company names. Championed by both festivals mentioned earlier, Choream was an example of mostly self-taught street dancers who succeeded in negotiating between the pedagogical and social commitment of the popular form and the invention of a new form, which they have imagined will eventually itself be seen as "classic." Company cofounders and choreographers Stéphanie Nataf and José Bertogal described, in 2002, moving beyond concern with hip hop "authenticity" or labels, yet they continued to be concerned with language, with developing their own choreographic language, and with identifying it as "French." The press materials for their 2003 choreography, *Paname,* spoke of it in terms of a *francophonie:*

> Can words or texts or lyrics be the motor for a choreographic piece? In this work we revisit the loveliest songs of the French repertory and dance to their marvelous lyrics. Our dancing follows these famous lyricists and their singers, the ones who rocked our parents and grandparents. Brel, Piaf, Brassens are here our sources of inspiration. *Paname* is the hip hop generation's homage to the previous one and to our roots that are solidly francophone. It's a bridge across the generations, an urban reappropriation of the classics of the French songbook.[58]

The use of the word *francophone* here signals a turn away from a notion of an old-school American "authenticity" by a company respected both for its artistry and for its roots. Instead, *Paname* celebrates the Paris of the parents or grandparents of its young dancers; an old nickname for Paris, *Paname* sets modern urban dancing to music by Edith Piaf, Jacques Brel, and George Brassens. (See Figure 2.1) Yet the dancing is resolutely late twentieth century/early twenty-first century, and the male dancers in particular retain the ambience of street dancers rather than the finesse of jazz or tap dancers interpreting these songs. (See Figure 2.2)

There can be no doubt that what is being spoken here is French, hip hop movements adapted into a generational commentary on La Belle France of an earlier generation. These dancers interpret this music and comment on it as much as dance to it. The young *danseuse* interpreting Brel's "ne me quitte pas" seems both to espouse the poet's plea and figure the rebel who is leaving him, suggesting both points of view in what becomes a reading of the song, an interpretation. Similarly, the male dancer dancing to

Figure 2.1
Paname: choreography by José Bertogal and Stéphanie Nataf (2003): homage to the earlier generation.
Photo Credit: H2O Photographe.

Brassens's song listing all the women he desires interprets it comically, in keeping with the singer's tongue-in-cheek tone: "when I think about Fernande, I desire her..." (the French is *je bande*—"I get an erection"), a phrase repeated for the many female names given in the song. (See Figure 2.3) Yet at the same time, in a gesture to be analyzed later, the dancer lies flat on his back on the floor, with his arm extended at a right angle toward the ceiling, mimicking the flagging erection during the lyric "when I think of Lulu, I do not desire her...." Rather than simply identifying the dancer with the singer, we see him interpreting the song and an entire era—a way of thinking about women, about sex—through his movements. His dancing is not simply a staging, but also a commentary on Brassens's famous lyrics.

Here hip hop is reclaiming francophone history and territory in order to talk about the shared culture of French music, whether it be in the colonies, in immigration, or in the Metropol. To break dance to Edith Piaf's

Figure 2.2
Paname: modern urban interpretation of *la chanson française.*
Photo Credit: H2O Photographe.

Figure 2.3
Paname: the cast dancing their different styles: Céline Lefèvre, Alexandra Réa, Melanie Sulmona, Laos, Thierry Lasserre, Jean-Michel Gast.
Photo Credit: H2O Photographe.

Figure 2.4
Paname: the breaker Laos interprets Edith Piaf, "incroyable mais vrai!"
Photo Credit: H2O Photographe.

or Georges Brassens's music is to show that hip hop speaks French and to translate these songs for a young audience, into their movement language. (See Figure 2.4) It is a way of saying, "we may look different, but we share this language and thus this cultural heritage of *francophonie*; we move beyond our bodies, our historical time, and our space. This cultural heritage belongs also to us; we reclaim it as we claim this city." At the same time that these young hip hoppers stylize an earlier period, they make the songs and the period their own; they are not simply representing themselves, nor "dressing up" as something other than they are, but rather representing their capacity for self-transformation through dance and music.

DANCING "ELSEWHERE"

After two decades of thinking of hip hop as a form about *metropolitain* urban experience, French hip hop entered an "international" phase. On the choreographic level, many hip hoppers have been including moves from other dance traditions (capoiera, belly dancing, Indian classical dance, Asian and African forms of traditional dance) that they have discovered on tour, in Paris, or in their own family backgrounds. Images of world exploration, of encounter with other cultures and other countries, has become the standard rhetoric descriptive of hip hop's integration of other dance forms or traditions into its movement vocabulary. A wide variety of texts surrounding the production of urban dance performances are indicative of this strategic attempt, on the part of programmers and *fonctionnaires*, choreographers, and managers, to cast hip hop not as a foreign form invading, but as a French form gone traveling.

For example, the program for the eleventh Biennale de Danse en Val-de-Marne devoted to hip hop included African and other dance forms. In a text by the Biennale's director, Michel Caserta, "Voyage en Francophonie...," included in the program, *les pays francophones* are something you travel to and work with, sharing common interests. Here *francophonie* is not a theme but a linguistic reality bringing together workers from different countries:

> Contrary to the preceding Biennale's themes, the 2001 festival calls upon a group of countries bound together by a common interest, the French language; that is, a space that we refer to as "francophone"...less as a theme than as the possibility to work with the countries of the Maghreb, black Africa, with Belgium, Switzerland, Quebec....It is more about shared interests than the elaboration of a theme common to all. This approach makes our exchanges, points of view, more dynamic. It is also an opening up to far away countries and the allure that they can create.
>
> A voyage beyond our shores, meeting up with great cultural and artistic riches.[59]

Although the subtext here is that it is people from these different places immigrating into France who bring it richness, it is expressed here as a discovery of other cultures facilitated by the *francophonie* of the inhabitants of the destination, and not recognized as already present within the Metropol. Mixing business metaphors with travel and pleasure, this formulation can be read as reversing the problems of unemployment and immigration in France, associated with hip hop, and identifying hip hop as the vehicle for movement and dynamic cultural exchange. In this same program, a text signed by the Président du Conseil Général du Val-de-Marne, Michel Germa, puts it in even more republican terms: hip hop allows solidarity between men, the euphoria of fraternity, liberty, and peace; and hip hop citizens are called upon to remain vigilant in seeking state funding:

> In choosing this Eleventh Biennale to bring dance from different francophone countries to the public, the festival once again focuses on encounter, dialogue and exchange with other cultures at the highest level.

It is the implementation of a project for solidarity among men, moving toward the satisfaction of their need to live in their bodies, to know others, to fully enjoy the benefits of fraternity, freedom, and peace.

In short, I cannot conclude without calling for vigilance and action on the part of all to obtain from the State the financial means that will make possible artistic creation that will find a broad public.[60]

These are incidental texts yet part of the mass of discourse produced within and around the hip hop movement that help to define this dance in social and political terms. Are the festival director and the Conseil Général of the Val-du-Marne insisting on the difference of those who are "not French" or on the presence of such difference within France, embodied by immigrants? Referring to a "voyage," the rhetoric shifts attention from the more contested term of immigration to reimagine relations with the former French colonies as other than a relation of domination and immigration—rather in terms of the business of culture and tourism. The call to arms at the end of the editorial, urging citizens to be vigilant in demanding arts funding, rings of the battle of artists hoping to encounter a larger public and answers the hysteria of the Far Right calling for the expulsion of immigrants from the French public sphere.

A program for sending hip hop dance companies, such as Choream, on tour—in particular, to francophone destinations—reflects this same strategy. Hip hop dancers become the goodwill ambassadors, ironically from the very suburbs to which people from these francophone countries have immigrated. What do the hip hoppers themselves say about such tours?

One of her goals with Choream's dancers from Montreuil, choreographer Stéphanie Nataf said in an interview, was to tour in "their countries" ("de les emmener dans leur pays"), which, she claims, "we succeeded in doing" ("nous avons réussi") in one case, on their tour in West Africa.[61] She describes in her youth wanting to be African herself, wearing her hair in dreadlocks and dreaming of travel to Africa; but she remarks of the black dancers in Choream "ils avaient honte"; they found themselves in a situation in France in which being African was stigmatized. On tour in Kinshasa, dancer Tip Top (Goye Tangal) met close members of his family for the first time and traveled to the ocean for the first time. It is clear in the choreographer's expression that she does not see herself as a beneficent patron, championing a cause, but rather as part of a group that set out on a voyage of discovery. For her, being the choreographer or leader of the group seems to have included a social responsibility to her fellow dancers, not simply to put them onstage or facilitate their self-expression, but rather to break out of the mold of the suburbs with them. Stéphanie emphasizes that her career in hip hop started in the environment of the youth center and that only later did she seek training in modern dance, jazz, and yoga. Hip hop, she argues, also gave to those coming up in the *banlieue* something to be proud of; learning to spin on his head (*la coupole*), for example, earned one small boy with glasses the respect of the entire neighborhood. Dance, she claims, saved her life, and her goal with Choream was to give others access to that dance. That she often identifies the ethnic group of the dancers in question ("black," "Jewish," etc.) suggests that this was an important part of their identity and played a contributing role in their self-conception and their social situation. For the choreographer, this discourse is part of a radical reclaiming of identity through dance in a context in which the creation of a discourse about minorities (generated by minorities) was a positive step forward.

It is significant, however, that the choreographer's goal was focused on the other dancers in her company rather than on herself. Her father's family emigrated from Tunisia when he was a teenager, but she was not encouraged to learn to speak Arabic at home. The focus away from Arabic suggests the very same *honte* or shame that the choreographer readily recognizes in the dancers with African roots who grew up dancing with her. Rather than embarking on a voyage of self-discovery to North Africa, the choreographer has faced the question of immigration and roots through the experience of the company's dancers of Sub-Saharan origins.

HOW "MOVES" MEAN DIFFERENTLY

The French version of hip hop speaks "French"—saying differently, and saying something different from its US model. Even within French hip hop choreographies, we can see the same gesture used to signify or suggest different things: the arm movement taught in a Choream class looks like *la danse orientale* and looks familiar to dancers of North African origin who see it having its source not in the United States at all. (See Figure 2.5) This same arm movement can be adapted to bodies using the floor and representing, abstractly, birds or serpents, waves of the sea or of time, in Compagnie Choream's 2001 piece *Epsilon*. (See Figure 2.7) And in *Paname*, it is used comically to represent that the "bandaison papa ne se commande pas" ("daddy's erection can't be ordered"): the body's failings or flailing, the sexual impasse, desire beyond control. (See Figure 2.6) This same movement signifies concretely and lets the body speak, but also speaks abstractly, moving beyond the body or allowing the body to move beyond its frame.

Figure 2.5
Demonstrated in Choream's dance class by Stéphanie Nataf, the arm movement as *la danse orientale*.
Photo Credit: Felicia McCarren.

As loquacious as it seems, as eloquent as it can be onstage, hip hop also expresses what philosopher Giorgio Agamben has called the "gag" of being-in-language,[62] choosing to move to music or song rather than to say,

Figure 2.6
In Choream's 2003 choreography, *Paname*, the arm movement punctuates the accompanying lyric by Georges Brassens about flagging desire.
Photo Credit: H2O Photographe.

Figure 2.7
The arm movement suggests flora or fauna in Choream's *Epsilon* (1999). Choreography by
José Bertogal and Stéphanie Nataf.
Photo Credit: Photothèque La Villette.

and pointing to the difficulty of saying even while expressing otherwise. In
their origins, hip hoppers' simple gags, headspins, and six-steps are both
their language of expression and a way of articulating the problems inherent in corporeal self-representation. If French hip hop has come to say
something different than US hip hop, if it speaks of "something else" to
its audience, it is also because it is understood as speaking differently. The
tormented gestures accompanying a text about abuse in Rennie Harris's
Endangered Species refer to the "gag" that censors discussion of social problems even in a culture of the talk-show confessional. The ludic gestures that
match Brassens's lyric of the *bandaison papa* ("daddy's erection") that cannot be willed in Choream's *Paname* are the "gag" that laughs at the attempt
to sound the mysteries of desire.

Yet in spite of the rhetoric, in spite of the funding, and in spite of choreographic development, what the French version preserves is exclusion—
made clearer since 2005. What the French examples make clear is, in fact, the
failure of language to speak of this exclusion; ironically, the very structures
that support it have labeled it an art of the suburbs—effectively requiring
it to stay there. In the United States hip hop has been seen as representing
a monoculture, the genius and rage of a particular socioeconomic group. In
this identification with black American culture, French hip hoppers under-
score the difficulties of speaking of difference in France, in French, a difference that, at least since the 2005 uprisings, we must understand as their

own ghettoization. But in identifying with the African American or Afro Caribbean origins of hip hop, French dancers—even while "speaking" about themselves—are doing so by referring to something else: they are saying otherwise, using their bodies to speak metaphorically or allegorically. In spite of having been ghettoized by the cultural agents promoting it, as an art of the *banlieue,* French hip hop recuperates dance traditions (some of them in the family background of the dancers) and comes to represent multiculturalism. Hip hop's *francophonie* suggests the degree to which it is French speaking— "globally" or "multiculturally" French—but it also suggests ways in which it has sought expression, in French, of "non-French" realities for those dancing it. Thus, at the same time that it comes to represent a unique situation in France, on French national stages, it speaks of "something else"—broader universals, the force of figuration, representations. This is the "French" hip hop that the state sends out on tour all over the world.

The example of French hip hop dance thus contradicts Bourdieu and Wacquant's critique of the globalization of imperial US culture, defying stereotypes even while recycling them. It has been supported by the centralized state and municipal funding agencies and studied by academics. It is both popular and a recognized art form, coming onto the biggest dance and theater stages in the country and touring to New York with the best-known modern dance companies. While prestigious theaters including the *scènes nationales* and avant-garde festival directors rival each other to program the best new hip hop, contemporary choreographers work with hip hoppers and, vice versa, youths keep coming up from the *cités*, dancing. There has been cultural transfer, transculturation, but there has also been strategic, French government–funded development and particular choreographic and cultural influences. Something has changed: the hip hop presented in 2008 at the "I Kiffe NY" festival in Manhattan, to be discussed in the next chapter, is *French*. As the very title of the festival shows, an "Arabic" component makes French different; while showcasing this difference in New York as exotic, it is a difference far from resolved at home.

When hip hopper Samir Hachichi, in Jean-Pierre Thorn's film *Faire Kiffer Les Anges*, describes after his brother's shooting death dancers wanting to "get past" the place they have been assigned, he means "getting out of" the suburbs but also out of a frame of corporeal signification of difference, using the body to speak "differently." It means going further than this universalism that has produced unequal opportunity, most often linked to racism against North Africans, further than the so-called culture of the suburbs or the *banlieue* "aesthetic." It means using this well-positioned dance to gain and give access to the universal of the body in particular and of bodies in general.

And this dance, in spite of its nostalgic charm, is also a dance addressing the problem of rage, "the rage to dance"; as the Choream choreographers noted, it refers to their francophone roots, to the generations that
preceded them in France—whatever their origins. With this dance, they
are signing up to the heritage of those French artists—from apaches to
beatniks, from black American jazz performers to the *sans papiers*—who
created French modernity. Dancing that on one side of the Atlantic speaks
of the forever-censored reality of disenfranchisement ends up, on the other
side, speaking of its dancers' self-enfranchisement as citizens of a republic of culture and as denizens of a global community of cultural exchange.
Shifting from a minority art to a kind of national art that internationally
speaks of Frenchness, and ultimately part of the *patrimoine culturel*, hip
hop has now outlived the cultural mission that promoted it. The program
of the Ministry of Culture that partly funded my collaborative research, the
"mission du patrimoine ethnologique," is defunct. It is interesting to note
its demise even as hip hop, representing France abroad, serves as a sign of
the success of the *politique culturelle* beginning with Mitterand's first term
described in chapter 1.

If US hip hop conquered a generation in France in the 1980s, and French
hip hop captured its home audience in the 1990s, it has since become the
not only national but also international phenomenon recognized by Bill T.
Jones at the beginning of this chapter. In the form of its French embassy,
hip hop has gone on tour: in 2004, Choream traveled for three months
of touring and choreographic collaboration in Africa, as representatives
not of a "global" hip hop, mediatized and diffused by television or music
videos, but of French particulars and universals. French companies appear
now almost every year in New York. Yet significantly, bringing this form to
"speak French," to speak of the French version of segregation in the suburbs
and unequal opportunity, in a gestural, figural language referring to US culture, makes a point about what is missing not in US culture, but rather in
French culture: a language in which to speak of difference and discontent, a
language in which to articulate rage and the very lack of a civic discourse in
which to address it. "Francophone" hip hop became a site opening discussions of difference, from a starting point of segregation, and elaborating a
poetics beyond assimilation: using the form to speak of cultural diversity
or constituting the body of minorities in the French Republic, referring to
ghettoization, to bring to discussion the history that universalism wishes
to forget.

CHAPTER 3

Hip Hop as Postcolonial Representation

Farid Berki's Invisible Armada *and* Exodust

INTEGRATION'S "ROCKY ROAD"

If French universalism staked a claim, in the past, to be blind to cultural, ethnic, or religious difference, it has not in practice guaranteed an equality of opportunity to everybody. The recent recognition of such *inégalité des chances,* or unequal opportunity, has now sparked the discussion of an inequality of persons based on difference. On the night of his election in May 2012, President François Hollande dedicated his five-year term to "justice" and "youth"—asking that his performance be measured in terms of what he accomplishes in these two areas. His identification of these two problem areas responds to concerns over the past few years: as a French student argued in 2010, about the attempt to open the *grandes écoles* to more minorities, "It's very dangerous for France to close its eyes and say, 'Equality. We have the best values in the world.' It's not enough. There has to also be equality of chances."[1] *The New York Times* article reporting this story is quick to point out that the idea of a "quota" doesn't work in France:

> There is a serious question about how to measure diversity in a country where every citizen is presumed equal and there are no official statistics based on race, religion or ethnicity. A goal cannot be called a "quota," which has an odor of the United States and affirmative action. Instead, there is the presumption here that poorer citizens will be more diverse, containing a much larger percentage of Muslims, blacks and second-generation immigrants.[2]

Yet quotas have been more and more often in the news: the imposition of quotas in 2011 for the opposite reason—to limit minority players from immigrant backgrounds on the French National Soccer Team, often held up as a visible sign of France's changing demographics—received both national and international criticism.

With the new terms of *minorities* and *diversity*, universalism and assimilation have not disappeared, but the debate focuses on the "integration" of those who are still considered different. The recent debate on national identity (2009–2010) in France, led by then-interior minister Eric Besson, was clearly orchestrated to bring to discussion such differences but became, according to its critics, an opportunity for the Far Right to use the debate about "identity" to legitimize racist complaints about immigrants.[3] What does dance performance contribute to French approaches to these questions today? What can a study of French hip hop add to these debates about identity, which have a different tone in French than they do in English? In France, these have been discussions about immigration and integration of "others" under a rubric of universalism, a legacy of the French revolution betrayed by colonial history, and the realization of the lack of an institutional discourse about cultural diversity that has been, in part, responsible for the resulting *inégalité des chances*.

In the United Kingdom and the United States, these have been discussions concerned with growing racism in France, racism that does not seem to be disappearing with the new articulation of cultural, ethnic, or religious diversity. While the French debates have been oriented around the questioning of universalism in the face of the apparent failure of integration, the "Anglo-Saxon" debates have been organized around the fundamental notions of communities and lobby groups, so-called identity politics.[4] French *multiculturalisme* is a relatively new concept, broadly thought to be influenced by American categories of thinking difference in order to constitute political representation. One might simplify by saying that on one side of the Atlantic the debate is cast as being about bodies, while on the other side it is cast as being about ideas. Significantly, as discussed in the previous chapter, French hip hop dance has specifically showcased urban "multiculturalism" and diversity, while the global form of rap music, for example, has more often been seen as part of a homogenized culture of imitation—a topic to be taken up at greater length in chapter 6. French hip hop has become a territory for working through questions about its immigrant populations, and more precisely the legacies of its colonial empire reflected in those largely francophone populations.

Yet even in France the "positive" multicultural spin given to hip hop can sometimes be seen as a thin veneer, an attempt to cover over rising racism and a legacy of inequality. In the fall 2008 festival "I Kiffe NY: French

Urban Cultures Festival" organized by the French Cultural Services in New York, urban dance was presented, along with films, music, lectures, and debates, as an art of the *banlieue* testifying to the struggle for integration. The Cultural Services' website for the event explained:

> The banlieues are France's equivalent of America's inner cities, except that, as their name indicates, they are located on the outskirts of France's major cities. Too often, these banlieues, with their public housing projects, evoke negative connotations, of hardship, gloom and menace. But such one-sided portrayals neglect their growing importance as a prime source of cultural dynamism and innovation. Certainly, much must still be done to better integrate the inhabitants of the banlieues into mainstream France, but on their rocky road to integration, they are producing some of the most exciting, dynamic and revolutionary works in France today.[5]

In this formula, no one doubts that integration is a good thing; it is the placeholder for "equality" and "equal opportunity." Yet, as this chapter will argue, hip hop may have been used by government bureaus to advertise the equal artistic opportunity of some dance artists and companies, but it also testifies to discrimination and to the difficulty of dialogue based on changing conceptions of race and rising racism in France.

Emphasizing the multiculturalism of French hip hop, the keyword in the description of the New York festival by the French Institute Alliance Française (FIAF) is "transcultural":

> FIAF is proud to co-present *I Kiffe NY*, a new festival produced by the Cultural Services of the French Embassy that focuses on the incredible vitality of French youth culture. Borrowed from Arabic, "kiffe" is French slang that means to love—or be absolutely crazy about—someone or something. The word, like so much of French urban culture, was born in the *banlieue* and has since swept the nation, much like hip hop, rap, parkour, forms of dance, etc. With so much inspiration drawn from American street attitudes, the ties to New York are strong to say the least. *I Kiffe NY* is a powerful testament to these latest forms of transcultural artistic expression.

According to this presentation, French dancers are effecting the cultural transfer of an American form, but they are also combining it with the "multiple traditions"—including "Arabic"—available to them in France:

> French youth and urban cultures have absorbed and disseminated the American urban tradition of hip hop through the Pockemon Crew, one of France's premier

and award-winning dance ensembles. Since 2006, the group has dominated hip hop dance's international scene. Comfortable with a variety of music—from cabaret style to traditional Arabic music—Pockemon Crew created *That's Life!?* as a visual event that juxtaposes the French urban experience with the multiple traditions that influenced the dancers.[6]

Yet the very "Arabic"—that is to say, North African—influences in the language and music surrounding the hip hop movement that are showcased in New York as multicultural and transcultural are still often seen at home in France as culturally problematic. And while "Arabic" might describe the music or even the dialect spoken in many hip hoppers' homes or serve as a classification for the *dominante culturelle* for the majority of such dancers, it hardly describes hip hop itself, nor its dancers—who might be North African, but also Berber or Jewish, or Muslim but of Asian or Sub-Saharan African origin. The complexity of origin, language, and culture that marks the Maghreb[7] is here reduced to "Arabic" and presented as "tradition," as "culture," and as "transculturation." The choreographic works by Farid Berki described later in this chapter identify a *colonial* antecedent and a *postcolonial* present to hip hop in France but have also moved beyond the politics of the *banlieue*. Berki's hip hop raises the question of whether "other" cultural forms become politically acceptable when aestheticized; the rerouting of their subversive potential by the state is now a familiar pattern in France. Berki's dances have focused on the legacies and realities of immigration but also mobilize a rich dance vocabulary that moves beyond notions of "authenticity" in hip hop culture to figural expression. In this way, it might be said, they are representing difference differently.

DEBATES ON RACE

In US academic contexts, the world of theater and performance arts has been an active site for addressing questions related to race and ethnicity, class, and gendered identities. The ATHE (Association for Theatre in Higher Education) organizes panels and focus groups such as the Black Theatre Association; Latina/o Focus Group (LFG); Lesbian, Gay, Bisexual, Transgender Focus Group (LGBT); Women and Theater Program; and others for its annual conference (ATHE 2011 conference: "Performance Remains, Global Presence: Memory, Legacy, and Imagined Futures").

While the organized focus or lobby groups of our social and political systems have not typified the French scene, they are influencing current debates in France. In the US academic context, we consider it worth pointing out the race, gender, and social situation of the dancers constituting a performance community—it adds a layer to the analysis of the performance images. In France, taking into account a performer's race has been seen as racist, just as—in the recent scandal over quotas imposed by the French national soccer team—taking account of young players' ethnic background or family origin has been described as an approach that is *raciale*, and any such "racial" thinking (taking race into account) has been deemed racist.

A recent report by French television, *De la Cité au Ciné*, considered how actors representing minority populations in France have drawn attention to their lack of representation in performance and in politics.[8] At the ceremony for the French César Awards, the equivalent of the US Academy Awards, West Indian actor Luc St. Eloy called a decade ago for more roles for minority actors who had in effect been excluded from cinema. In interviews with the journalist L. Hakim, performers of African, North African, and Asian origins described the limited roles available to them and the stereotypical or "exotic" nature of the characters they play. In dance, I suggested in the last chapter, performers can move beyond these stereotypes in choreographies that do not include language and that often permit the transformation of bodily appearance or its diffusion in movement.

The Centre National Cinématographique, a research and funding structure that supports French cinema, created a fund in 2007 to support diversity in cinema with scripts and roles permitting what the fund's founder Marc Chebsa called "justice" for minority actors. Chebsa emphasizes also that such diversity will allow French society to see itself represented—to represent itself—as it is, and as it will be in the future. In French cinema, there have been more such representations, positive or not, but bringing to debate questions of exclusion and inequality in France. Two films with hip hopper Stomy Bugsy (born Gilles Duarte, in Paris) suggest cross-over from the world of live performance into cinema and show the interest of films made in the Départements Outre-Mer (DOM) rather than simply showing diversity in the Metropol: Jean-Claude Flamand's 2005 *Nèg Marron* cast two Antillian rappers, Amiral T and Didier Daly, as young gang members alongside Stomy Bugsy, who moved beyond the hip hop world entirely when playing Communist journalist and *résistant* André Aliker in Guy Deslauriers's 2009 *Aliker*, written by Martinican novelist Patrick Chamoiseau. But a certain historical style has also informed moves, costumes, and music for some hip hop choreographies, such as the collective *Jeu de Jambes*.

Minority actors' demand for visibility, for more roles, has coincided with debates about difference in France and the rise of a discourse and a model borrowed from what is called the Anglo-Saxon model of *particularism*. The best-known film associated with the hip hop generation of the French suburbs is Matthieu Kassovitz's 1995 *La Haine* (*Hate*). In her work on the film, Ginette Vincendeau writes that *La Haine* focuses on the "common struggle of mixed-race groups against the police and bourgeois society," which has led Anglo-American critics to argue that "it sweeps racism under the carpet while *a contrario*, French writers derided the 'politically correct' black-blanc-beur trio."[9] The critique follows that the film is addressing issues of class, not race. Vincendeau emphasizes that "The French hip hop scene is also noticeably mixed."[10] There is an increasing hybridity of the populace and increasing presence of multiethnic individuals in a range of popular cultural products, but many of them remain national. *La Haine* broke through to a global audience but also signaled a breakthrough in showing the effects of the embrace of US popular culture in France.

Discussions of the concept of "race" in French studies, especially in recent works published in the United Kingdom and the United States, have focused on the way the historical construction of race has been at work in French political and social spheres, counteracting an Enlightenment and revolutionary discourse of universalism. While broadly supporting the growth of a French multiculturalism resembling in some ways the Anglo-Saxon model of communities, such studies have also tended toward critique without themselves being able to offer anything better. Another tendency is for such studies, supporting minority rights, to move toward a certain paternalism, seeing minorities as victims rather than seeking practical means of empowerment. It is easy to be surprised by a particular French institutional reference to the hip hop dancers as "others," but these terms, instituted by ethnography and anthropology, function within the discourses surrounding hip hop in France. It is worth noting—as my earlier work has done—that dancers have historically been located in the margins, representing a certain "alterity" even while posing the most piercing questions about a common humanity, human bodies and human rights, in their performances.

The performing arts and hip hop in general give a different face to a historically white France. Hip hop dancers represent in the majority "minority" populations: Maghrebian and African, they represent the "others" associated with immigration and the suburbs, even though they include French citizens from the French Antilles, Guadeloupe, and Martinique, who cannot be considered "immigrants." Along with other ethnic minorities or with working-class French issuing from inter-European immigration, these groups constitute the face of hip hop, a face historically underrepresented in government and in the National Assembly.

In *Deconstructing the Nation: Immigration, Racism and Citizenship in Modern France*, Max Silverman describes the ongoing conception of two distinct models of nation in contemporary France, the first based on the right of communities such as ethnic minorities (an Anglo-Saxon or Eastern European model) and the second the French model of individual adhesion.[11] In the debates surrounding the definition of "what is a nation," Stam and Shohat emphasize that the "French model does not recognize 'race' as a valid conceptual or institutional category" and in France, the assimilationist model reigns: "the very idea of multiple models is excluded."[12] Yet Silverman argues that the "universalism, assimilation and individualism" of the French model are not opposites of the "particularism, difference and collectivity" of the Anglo-Saxon. Analyzing the contradictions of the French model, Silverman investigates not the differences between "race" and "nation" or "racism" and "nationalism," but the "articulations between them in the development of the modern nation-state."[13]

In *Race in France: Interdisciplinary Perspectives on the Politics of Difference*, editors Herrick Chapman and Laura L. Frader also describe, in their introduction, the "polarizing debates that have sometimes characterized discussions over matters of race, the tendency to see the French republican model of assimilation and the American or Anglo-Saxon models of ethnic pluralism as oversimplified, dichotomous alternatives between which one much choose: color-blindness or race consciousness."[14] This volume, they say, attempts to move beyond "transatlantic or cross-Channel stereotyping" and to move "beyond the usual defense or condemnation of the French republican model." The editors emphasize that "what makes cultural racism in France potentially so pernicious a mutation of older, more biological notions of racism is that by insisting on the necessity of assimilation, it can bear so striking a resemblance to the avowedly anti-racist republican orthodoxy it rejects."[15] Overall, "the character of the anti-racist tradition in France has had a contradictory effect on scholarly writing about race and racism" because, unlike Anglo-Saxon audiences, "anti-racists regarded 'race' as an invention of the racist."[16] But the growth of immigration studies since the 1980s, the authors argue, has made it possible to look deeper into the actuality and experience that has contradicted the republican rhetoric of color-blindness and the practice of integration or assimilation.

Silverman's summary in *Facing Postmodernity*, chapter 2, "New Racisms," details the "dualism of sameness and difference" that underpins what he calls "modern 'logics' of racism." Silverman borrows the terminology of Pierre-Andre Taguieff to describe the two major discourses of racism, heterophobic/mixophilic and heterophilic/mixophobic: the first reducing the other to the same through universalism, the second reducing to an essentialized difference and exclusion. While taken from pre-1930s discourses, these terms need themselves to be historicized within the traditions of monogeny and polygeny significant to the French history of biology.[17] In his *Affirmative Exclusion*, mentioned in the last chapter, Jean-Loup Amselle historicizes the current state of multiculturalism in France through the theories of polygeny and monogeny and sees the depiction or description of difference as *métissage,* as a form of "soft racism." While the republican model is deficient because of its underlying polygenism, defined here as "a plural view of human populations"[18] that contributed to the theory and practice of universalism and assimilation, for Amselle, "the recognition of a multiplicity of ethnic groups in France thus offers ideal conditions for the rise of racism."[19]

> Through multiculturalism, what is being expressed is the right to difference, in the sense that this ascribed difference goes hand in hand with the recognition of the other as other, that is, as a problem. It is therefore clear that the theme of multiculturalism or of *métissage* is connected to globalization. At the human and anthropological level, globalization means nothing more than a return in force of polygenism.... While *métissage* as a concept seems to be the antidote to the problem of a purity of origin, it is nothing but a symmetrical and inverted form of it. Only a theory of common humanity can counter the underlying racialism of the theory of *métissage*.[20]

Amselle's concern about the "danger" of a certain kind of multicultural thinking signals the significant differences in the French debates on race, the history of a republic that has turned away from data gathering on ethnicity, and a tradition of thinking that talking about race is racist. Racism is indeed on the rise in France, as evidenced by the popularity of the right-wing Front National Party candidate Marine le Pen, who finished third in the first round of the French presidential elections in 2012; the Front National's party line deploys a concept of Frenchness that would exclude "others" born elsewhere, and even second- or third-generation French with ancestors from somewhere else. The anthropological discourse trying to take difference into account can be distorted toward a racist polygenism. Other researchers, whose work will now be discussed, argue precisely that to understand this use of the concept of *métissage*, one has to look not only at French republican values but also at the exceptions made in colonial history.

Counter to an insistence on the importance of universal theory lies the recent history of widespread acknowledgment of unequal opportunities both in colonial history and now for minorities in France and the call (echoed now by the government) for a "positive discrimination" in employ-ment and educational sectors that would take account of data on ethnic origin. Alec Hargreaves writes:

> [P]oliticians, together with the mass media, have been deeply involved in the ethnicization of French politics, which in turn is just part of a much wider dynamic in which ethnic differences have come to play a central role in many aspects of French society. In recent years, the gap between official discourse and the day-to-day praxis of social relations has become increasingly difficult to conceal and it has indeed narrowed. Politicians and researchers have become increasingly inclined to acknowledge that, like it or not, ethnicity is a significant factor in many aspects of French society. Moreover, after hanging precariously in the balance, attempts to document the salience of ethnicity through new forms of data gathering now appear to have overcome the main obstacles placed in their way.[21]

In fact, while minorities in France figure a visible difference that has led to discrimination and harassment based on visual identification, the reverse side of the coin is that, as many are citizens, they have a certain invisibility in ethnic data. The case of Antillean French citizens who are not technically "immigrants" into France is one example; another would be second- or third-generation immigrants who are French but still seen as "foreigners," for example, because of their culture or religion. Hargreaves emphasizes:

> As about a third of all immigrants and virtually all the descendants of immi-grants are French citizens, they are by the same token invisible in most official statistics. And as ethnic discrimination operates on the basis of color or culture rather than on the basis of formal citizenship, its effects are also statistically invisible. In refusing to collect data based on racial or ethnocultural categories, the Republic has allowed discrimination to remain beyond the reach of the stan-dards of evidence required for successful prosecutions."[22]

Thus while representing cultural difference, minorities in France have had little access to political representation, or self-representation: Hargreaves emphasizes the lack of any *député* (member) of North African origin or of Muslim heritage in the 577-seat National Assembly and the under-representation of minorities in the French media.

French hip hop documents and debates often refer to institutionalized segregation in the United States, but a broad understanding of the historic breadth and local practices of segregation seems to be missing in debates

I have heard. While the French hip hoppers' reference to US black culture may emphasize segregation as a way to describe their own situation, it is usually said that the situation in France has been different, as if the universalist rhetoric were unchallenged by historical practice and experience. But postcolonial theory, as well as recent work by historians, has shown that it is precisely in regard to its colonial history that the French situation has not been so different, as it was in colonial contexts that French universalism often was not obtained. In "Race and Sociological Reason in the Republic," Emmanuelle Saada reexamines the "French model" of national identity through the signification of race in the social sciences and administration of the Third Republic and argues that in spite of the French rhetoric or ideals of the republic ("the Revolutionary ideal of a civic community open to anyone sharing its political credo,"), colonial practice shows the use of race as a category, the confusion of racial and social thinking, and political concerns about race.[23] Saada's article emphasizes alternatives to usual understandings of race in the French Republic: first, it is usually held that France had a "civic" rather than "ethnic" model that made it exceptional, and that color-blind universalism and assimilation were the practices adopted in the Metropol following the revolution, but she argues that these were not always the practice in the colonies and that it was, rather, colonial practices (giving race a role in the construction of citizenship) that came in turn to influence metropolitan France that in this way was not an exception: "One must conclude either that the 'civic model' was not fully implemented outside metropolitan France, or that the practices and criteria surrounding citizenship *in metropolitan France* were something more than civic."[24] Second, she argues that the colonial history suggests the extended influence of "biology" or "raciological" thinking: science is still used to describe race and raciological thinking is used to describe social facts—racial and social logics are used together, simultaneously and complementarily— long after the Durkheimian sociological method (social facts explained only through other social facts) took over in the early twentieth century. Indeed, she concludes, Durkheimian sociology didn't debunk "scientific racism" very quickly or effectively.

While thinking about race in France is a highly charged arena of debate, for the reasons sketched earlier, the legacy of US segregation and the influence of the US civil rights struggle and the black power movement may also remain powerful in French hip hop because of the legacy of the leaders of *Négritude*, in particular, Aimé Césaire. The huge billboard at the entrance to la Villette, for the Rencontres festival in the summer of 2008, memorialized Aimé Césaire with his picture and poetry. A heightened awareness of colonial history and contemporary inequality, then, highlighted by Césaire, Fanon, and others, has paralleled a change in attitudes toward immigration in the past twenty years. Saada argues that a "traditional concept" of assimilation is being replaced by *métissage* and "métissage, hybridization, and creolization" are used interchangeably and become indistinct, "referring to all forms of identity across time and place, insofar as all have a fluid and porous character."[25]

In the United States, race is now being discussed in a broad variety of ways, as a social construct but also as a category that continues to be used by institutions such as the National Institutes of Health (NIH) and as a census category. While research has confirmed that "there is no genetic basis for race," biology continues to be "front and center" in new constructions of race.[26] DNA researchers agree that "Racism is not only socially divisive, but scientifically incorrect. We are all descendants of people who lived in Africa recently.... We are all Africans under the skin.... When you peer beneath the surface at the underlying level of genetic variation, we are all much more similar than we appear to be. There are no clear, sharp delineations."[27] Yet for medical anthropologist Duana Fullwily, because racial category and racial type continue to be used in biological and medical studies, for example, in medical genetics, race is not simply a social construct.[28] It is precisely this typing and categorization that is missing from the "official" discourse in contemporary France, even if it has been practiced, in particular, in colonial history. In leaving to one side the long history of debates about and definitions of race in the United States, I want to emphasize both the difference in French debates and how hip hop there, by the fact of its trans-Atlantic translation, refers to this history without, in some crucial ways, knowing it.

DANCING "OTHERNESS"

As a visual, performing art, danced by the very minorities at the heart of these debates, hip hop stages the very bodies that are in question. Yet to the potentially reductive discussion of minorities, it adds the complexity of cultural production that is also a movement poetics. While hip hop dancers are broadly thought to represent *themselves*, in a social-realist dance form linked to its political-social program, in fact dance allows dancers to present their bodies, in all their embodiments, as something other than themselves. While staging the question of visible difference, dance performance remains an art of the visual rather than the entirely visible; it poses a challenge to reductive categories.

Dancing hip hop, these "minority" bodies are not simply social signifiers in a realm of appearance but signifiers in a complex bodily poetics, producing cultural meaning through reference and suggestion, through abstraction in addition to their concrete physical presence. Dancing shows that we both are in our bodies and can get beyond them—it manifests both rooted notions of corporeal identity and, through the discipline of training, the ability to use the body to say something else, to say "differently." As discussed in the last chapter, dancing simultaneously gives us an identity and a location yet allows us to bypass or outstrip these; it goes beyond the registration of difference in physical appearance or cultural practice that establishes cultural diversity in France. Even while staging such difference, it allows the expression of a poetics of the human body that is, in its own way, universal: the being-in-the-body parallel to the being-in-language that is the human experience.

As we can see from the I Kiffe NY festival, hip hop dance has played into a perspective in which dancers are exoticized; but it also provides a forum to bring into question the reduction of cultural diversity to physical difference. While dance is often described as an altered state or a superhuman practice because of its physicality, it raises and stages the question of our common—bodily—humanity. At the same time, it challenges received knowledge about the visibility of difference and the underrepresentation of cultural, ethnic, and religious minorities in France: hip hopper Farid Berki, for example, on his website describes the "invisible heritage" that dance can explore, in particular in taking into account the different and yet overlapping vocabularies of different dance traditions. These movement vocabularies enrich his work, to be discussed later in this chapter. Berki's choreographic works cast hip hop in France as part of a colonial history and postcolonial present, but they have also moved beyond representing hip hoppers as France's internal "others."

It is not difficult to find cultural theorists arguing that dancers are "others" and that dance provides an example of an authentic culture in the face of a dominant global culture or colonization. In *Welcome to the Desert of the Real*, Slavoj Zizek condenses the two sides of the coin: "the other beats his wife and dances fantastic dances...."[29] Dancers, wherever they are from, are agents of "otherness": speaking "otherwise" with the body and representing an "elsewhere" that they make present in their performances. The "other" who, in Zizek's analysis, dances fantastic dances as incomprehensible to "us" Westerners as wife beating is simultaneously an agent of cultural "authenticity" and also "mediatized"—represented unidimensionally by the media and out of reach of the media: all the pictures in the world of him doing things unacceptable to the West won't change his behavior. The conflation of a "fantastic" dance culture with a violent domestic culture in Zizek's barbed formulation suggests that both are equally mysterious from the Western perspective. It is worth exploring in two examples how dancing by colonial or postcolonial "others" has been represented recently in francophone studies in the United States as precisely this kind of "inexplicable" that is constitutive of culture, or of a cultural "authenticity" in the face of colonial projects.

Dancing, in spite of what we call its "technique"—the specificity of its movement vocabulary, its professionalization, its transmission—has also been considered, and continues to be considered, "preindustrial." Even while wedded to Taylorist choreography of labor or the highly functioning machine or used as the image selling the iPod device, it often remains a repository of cultural specificity and ethnic and religious differences. My previous work has explored the particular symbolics of dance in a culture in which it has become problematic—a print and work culture in which its wordlessness and nonproductivity mark it as a vestige of something else. My interest until now has been in dancing in places where it was not an unproblematic "natural" expression. Here I want to explore how dancing gets assigned the task of representing the pretechnological state of culture, even as it is called upon to figure globalized, high-tech modernity.

In these contexts, body language plays a significant role: first, representing the profoundly local ("authentic" or untranslatable) essence of culture even while also seen as speaking a universal language. In her introduction to an edited collection of essays, *Remembering Africa*, Elizabeth Mudimbe-Boyi includes dance as one of the "texts" that are "untapped sources of representation" (of Africa): along with "colonial discourse, the *objets d'art* of museums, dance and drums, paintings, stuffed animals, literary productions, as well as personal recollections" are the "primary matter" of the volume.[30] In ethnographic dance scholarship, expressive forms such as dance have been seen as allowing colonized or suppressed peoples to "speak" through a nonverbal form, expressing "resistance" in Barbara Browning's example of Brazilian popular dance or supralinguistic cultural complexity in John Middleton's comment that in certain contexts, the Lugbara dance because "verbal statements alone could be too crude."[31] In Boyi's collection of essays, dance is even used to figure the mutual influences of transcultural contact in Mary Pratt's "mirror dance" of imitation, between colonizers and colonized, or travelers and "travellees."[32]

But because of its iconic status and the universality or accessibility that accompanies its enigmatic code, dance has carried the banner of a certain cultural authenticity, one that is often, perhaps too easily, adopted by cultural theorists. It is important to problematize this by reconsidering dance's historical engagement—for example, under French colonial rule—both with local cultures and global (metropolitan) technologies. It is important to consider the use of dance within francophone studies as both a cultural sublime and a highly trafficked form; in the case studies that make up the chapters of this book, I have considered examples of dance performing a technological modernity, even while representing a kind of alterity, expressed through rather than in spite of a certain Metropolitan context. These dances are "francophone" themselves, because they respond, precisely, to the issues raised in current research (especially in English, in Britain and in the United States) in the field of francophone and postcolonial studies.

While dance in France has represented the "high culture" of the national patrimony, it has also eloquently represented other cultures and within France has often been the face of colonial others, the part of the culture most easily admired or exhibited. Dancing in France has a colonial history; the fact that Paris has become a major dance capital is due not only to its central place in the history of French dance but also to its showcasing colonial and exotic dance forms, its embrace of many forms of dance by an appreciative dance public (not unlike foreign foods, music, and visual arts), and the public subvention of dance performance. Artaud's revelation at seeing the Balinese dancers in Paris is one of the best known of many.

In two examples drawn here from recent critical texts in francophone studies, dance becomes a marker or even model for a concept of authenticity, one that, in the domains of literature or language, is often critiqued. One example is to be found in Ronnie Scharfmann's "Nubile (in) Morocco" in the collection *Remembering Africa*.[33] In an essay recounting her first trip at an impressionable age, the author describes a moment of cultural fusion or enlightenment that happens when she is able to dance with Moroccan women at a premarriage party in a small village. The narrative is a classic one of a traveler granted access to a collective space in which the dancing constitutes a community—temporary or illusory—that is physically grounded. Dancing (*guerba*) allows the author to give up herself and become "other," in touch with these "others"; she writes:

I too am taken over by the dance.
I am pure presence, I am only body, I am only woman, I am all these women.

While the naivete of this young traveler is rendered charming by the author, it authorizes the use of dance to slide into notions of an "authentic" culture that in language the same author is far more wary of.[34] Furthermore, while defining the difference of this authentic "other" culture, the dance in this example permits its almost immediate accessibility. This passage emphasizes the contradiction between the enigmatic quality of the dance described, which gives access to the exotic—its mystery, which allows it to work such magic (erasure of identity and of difference, identification with the other, universal bonding, sisterhood, rhythmic union in the universal language of the music and dance, etc.)—and its translation into writing. That the author can say so easily what the dance is doing so miraculously or completely is the problem: a discourse that constructs dance as a magic unifier, creating a wordless bond, even as it—as an academic discourse about dance—participates in undoing and deconstructing the very "mystique" it is creating: discovering an "ineffable" that is then recounted in the text. In other words, if in dancing we are all one, then what is all the bother about the specificity and mystery of certain other cultures? How can the dance represent both a very precise, inaccessible, and ineffable cultural content and a glorious sublime available to all comers?

In a second example, dancing (here represented via a photographic image rather than a travel narrative) does a lot of "critical" work without, itself, being theorized.

I wonder what those "African dancers" in the cover photograph are doing on the cover of Christopher Miller's *Nationalists and Nomads*—aside of course from selling the book. The volume critiques the context of their live production at the Exposition Coloniale of 1931, as well as the exposition's manufacture of images (deconstructed via Césaire's critique: "in the image, it's not A or non-A…").[35] Miller does consider the exposition's manipulation of such images and its creation of hallucinatory spaces for performance, but not specifically that of these dancers. They stand in a strange relation to the title above them: presumably this image of dancers on the cover represents (more than the dancers in the picture did themselves) a critique of the nationalists who produced the exposition? Or does it represent the dancers as cultural nomads, performing "authentic" African culture in Paris, against the manipulated images created by/for the political leadership of the event? To what extent are they serving the exposition's ends and to what extent are they successfully resisting them? The gap between the image and the living performer gets erased, and the dancers in the picture become the mute *temoins* of an idea rather than the articulate spokespeople they were for a particular culture, here being made into Africa with a capital A. Because we do not have access to the dance other than through the archive, Miller's text, then, ironically like the exhibition it so articulately critiques, ultimately elides these pictured dancers, if not into "Africa," then into its exhibition. This happens every time we want to discuss dance via still images reproduced in books. In these two examples, dance is performing a "performance" of otherness or authenticity even as it is being mediated and tamed, translated while deemed untranslatable, used as a (silent) critique. Pictured on the spine of this book, hip hopper Jean-Charles Zambo, dancing in Compagnie LosAnges's *Zou*,(discussed in chapter 1), represents a self-taught dancer symbolically participating in the French movement for renewable energy identifiable in the abstracted wind turbines behind him, but also physically participating in the national cultural system which produced the choreography. When he dances, I see him as an active and eloquent participant rather than passive representative of these systems, whereas the photo can tend to reduce his performance to a more passive promotion.

In these cases, we see that we can only get at dance or dancers through their representations—their writing, their photographs—even as we expect them to represent a certain "liveness" or "presence," an incorruptible essence of culture, that defies representation or reveals its political stakes, which is what they are used for in the two examples I've commented on here. Such representations of dance, as well as the representation that the dance itself is, remain here unproblematized as dance is performing a certain function: keeping exotic others in place even as it allows us access to their otherness, guaranteeing the existence of an "ineffable" unsayable even while giving us a short-cut to its analysis. In spite of our formidable critical baggage, dance does something to us—as experience, as image—that offers a model very tempting for us as critics. Perhaps this is not so different from, say, the use that Aimé Cesaire puts dance to at the end of the *Cahier d'un retour au pays natal* or Assia Djebar in the "Transes" chapter of *L'Amour, la fantasia*. We say that dance and mime say what cannot be said: the intolerable history of slavery, the unspeakable wrongs never righted. But Aimé Cesaire speaks them in the *Cahier* and thus the dance of conclusion must play another role in the text. Ultimately, dance performs a different function in the critical texts than it does in these literary texts, constituting an "otherness" to be analyzed and guaranteeing that such analysis will fail. Yet "colonial"-era dancing was already mediatized, and cultural "authenticity" has also been produced through mechanical reproductions. It is worth emphasizing, again, that discussions of hip hop's "authenticity" are linked to the idea of an "old school," US hip hop movement rather than to an idea of "primitive" dance or a history of dance primitivism.

In these two examples, we are dealing with traditional dances danced in different contexts by colonial or postcolonial "others," but indeed hip hop as a postcolonial form is seen, in France, as a dance of (descendants of) colonial "others." For a French public, *le hip hop* taps into these dance traditions both through the bodies it mobilizes and through the diasporic dance forms it integrates into its choreographies, reflecting—nuancing—the quite recent development of a public discourse about the colonial era. Only since passage of the 2005 *loi du 23 février* requiring teaching of the positive side of colonial history (the so-called *bienfaits du colonialisme*)—sparking immediate protest and subsequently overturned—did French debates focus more clearly on the "postcolonial" situation of a majority of immigrants, even though the body of postcolonial theory in French is well known and much of it is now a half-century old.

FROM ARMADA TO EXODUS

Like many *hip hoppeurs,* dancer/choreographer Farid Berki began his training outside the dance establishment, in the urban-suburban environment of hip hop, and also came to extend his training into modern dance and other movement forms, to work with dancers from other countries, and to explore identity through dance's figural language, often in reference to experiences of colonization and exile other than his own. Choreographies by Farid Berki, one of the so-called pioneers of French hip hop, illustrate the way in which hip hop choreographies have referred to alterity represented in and by dance, to the colonial and postcolonial history of dance, and to dance's representation of exile, migration, and north-south relations. Two major works, *Invisible Armada* (2000; premiered at la Villette) and *Exodust* (2006; Suresnes Cités Danse festival 2007) explore the different faces of the interrelated themes of travel, colonization, and immigration.

Described as an autodidact who completed his dance education by studying modern, African, tap, and other forms, Farid Berki was the first to lead hip hop workshops at the Théâtre Contemporain de la Danse; for both of these reasons, he has come to be associated with *la danse contemporaine.* *Invisible Armada* premiered at the 2000 Rencontres festival at la Villette in Paris and was presented at the Brest Antipodes Festival '01. Berki choreographed and danced in this piece, first presented at the space called *la Nef* at la Villette on November 8. As opposed to the huge "Charlie Parker" stage, with its long rows of benches on risers filled with shouting hip hoppers, this more intimate space, also installed in the shell of la Villette, is arguably more comfortable, and programming full-length choreographies or plays (sometimes two pieces sharing the program), it attracted a different audience. The program announced *Invisible Armada* as "a piece that tracks the origins of the conquest of the New World to better interrogate its foundations" using two choreographic elements, hip hop and capoiera, "both artistic movements with important links to the exploration of identity."[36]

Farid had given an interview shortly before in which he emphasized that, although he had done modern dance, that was not what he wanted to do, nor did it describe what he does. The interviewer remarked that Farid, in espousing the concept of a *pure et dure* hip hop, seemed to be locating himself at the antipodes of his choreographies. But Farid justified his rhetoric in saying that he didn't want others to speak for hip hop; he wanted to continue to speak for it. Choreographers' descriptions of what they are doing can often be seen as complementary to their practice, not necessarily misleading, but important to consider along with the work.

In Jean-Pierre Thorn's film *On n'est pas des marques de vélo (2003),* Farid speaks about his earliest hip hop activities: training at the Paco Rabanne Center that had opened the doors to its building for dancers. When defending his hip hop roots or origin, Farid is clearly thinking of the small group of dancers who trained there with him (he names Bouda and Junior, among others). Hip hop is his language, he says: "I didn't want anyone else to speak for hip hop—I wanted to be heard."

But indeed, *Invisible Armada* reads as a modern dance choreography, one which fruitfully develops the hip hop idiom. The piece develops a story, a "ballet" in the spirit of the movement and with its basic steps as the vocabulary, with a clear storyline and a logical relation between these steps and the story being told. While the first version I saw suffered from a lack of rehearsal, it went further in this direction than any other full-length choreography presented at that Rencontres that year, with the exception of *Drop It!* to be discussed in the next chapter.

Onstage we see an abstract ship, rendered as a mast, prow, the sail on a screen, and a bound man being whipped by the capoiera-esque kicks given him by another. It is one in a series of master–slave or subjugation scenes presenting one of the themes of the piece. The dancers, however, are dressed similarly—beige or white pants and shirts, with sashes around their waists, and the woman dancing with them is dressed in the same way; the choreography here does not take account of gender. (See Figure 3.1) Later in the piece there will be redingotes and jabots to represent the colonizers.

Onstage also is a DJ and a musician playing African drums, a keyboard, and other instruments. Two men take the oars and row off on a reconnaissance mission to an unknown coast. They dance with these poles, exploring their possible choreographic and metaphorical significance: oars, weapons, connectors; sailor dances, folk dances, modern dance, martial arts moves. Landing on the coast, perhaps an island, one of the men goes offstage and is brought back on by watchmen or inhabitants. In a scene where we lose the narrative thread, the DJ plays music

Figure 3.1
Invisible Armada choreography by Farid Berki. Photo by Eric Legrand. Reprinted with permission.

that includes the words "go black boy," and some of the dancers bound together at the ankle, others at the wrists, dance some Latin-inflected dances, almost in the style of musical comedy. The reference is clearly to African diasporic dance forms and slavery, but the specific story being told here is somewhat abstract.

Onstage now a long rope hangs, and the music recalls the ocean, the beach, the desert isle, far from the world of hip hop. The lighting represents the blue skies, the orange and violet sunset of the antipodes, a morning on the beach or a night of a full moon. The setting recalls *Robinson Crusoe* or the *Tempest*. Yet the choreographer attempts to integrate recognizable movements from the hip hop vocabulary into the story. The woman, witch or seductress, turns away dancers who come onstage to watch the action, grabbing them by the head; one of them continues this movement down to the ground, where his head touches the ground and he launches into a head spin. The woman is playing the seductress, drawing the troop of men with exaggerated feminine hip movement, subjugating and then rejecting them—she is now the master.

Under a full moon, the men now seem possessed. An invisible force drives them; they fall and turn into dogs on all fours—or Circe's swine. We hear the cries of monkeys, and the woman, now climbing, transforms into a monkey. One dancer swings on the cord, entering and leaving the stage. Another arrives with a sack of gold. He sets himself up in the back, upstage, next to the musician, playing the "rainstick" and then inserting it in between the knees of a dancer doing a handstand, taking it back. He enters into a duo with this dancer, making music with his body—bodily percussion. This dancer's movement vocabulary is recognizably drawn from modern dance: arabesques, arm movements describing arcs in space, recalling Merce Cunningham's abstractions or even the more dramatic moves of his teacher, Martha Graham. This is very different from hip hop energy; barrel leaps, for example, draw a line in space beyond the body. In another figure, a dancer develops the *coupole* into a modern dance move: from the *coupole* he pops up to standing just long enough to then fall forward onto his arms, with his leg up, extended to the back, as in a Graham fall. Later he will do an *entrechat* jump where he beats the feet together while in the air, with legs stretched straight behind, and then a *glissé* or sliding step to move backward, with a sweeping arm movement—almost a ballet move, but informed by modern dance's re-energizing these steps.

A scene of "encounter" rounds out the story before a final revels and curtain call. Four dancers plus one in the middle dance together in duos reminiscent of capoiera. Two dancers arrive in the back covering one eye and then both eyes. Four more dancers dance holding long poses (more than eight counts, for example, for a headstand), and at the end we hear trumpeting. The musician plays piano, a form of jazz.

Onstage there is a commanding "master." Two dancers enter in aristo-cratic European costumes, perhaps from a ship. And using the small hops and hand movements of baroque dance, they bring greetings to the gover-nor. The musician sings "Invisible Armada," and one of the dancers, lying across the prow of the boat, also begins to sing, a song clearly known to the audience: "Salvador. . . ." The public joins in to sing with him and the musi-cian. He falls from his perch and the scene ends; he goes to play percussions next to the musician.

The concluding scene uses two long ropes hanging across the stage; with orange lighting, people in the back are lit while those in the front are seen in silhouette. A musical collaboration between the percussionist and the DJ scratching albums provides the accompaniment for a barefoot dancer doing a capoiera-inspired solo, and other dancers come on stage to play with the long sticks or the ropes. The orange turns to purple and the danc-ers seem to swim and dive. With dancers on the sides of the stage popping and locking, the other dancers continue with more fluid movements closer to the energy of modern dance; each dancer finds his or her own style. In the center, Farid Berki dances a solo that ends with held poses. After the bow, marking the end of the piece, there is a choreographed curtain call: three minutes of recorded music, a sort of classical pop accompanied by the drummer. Three dancers together dance a "hype" influenced by salsa, but recognizably hip hop. Then, the other dancers dive into acrobatics and break dance. Once again the choreography finishes in held poses.

While the choreography in the early performances showed some rough edges resulting from lack of rehearsal, it manifested a thoughtful choreographic process: a narrative reinterpretation of a certain history, with historical references for movements and clothing, abstracted on stage, and a collaborative process with dancers contributing to the construction of the various "characters" they play and styles they dance. Shortly after the opening, the manager of Berki's company Melting Spot told me that the piece was getting better with each rehearsal and each performance. This is quite honest for an agent charged with publicizing and selling the show; he seems to be acknowledging, at least to a knowledgeable audience member, that the work is not yet completely finished or needs some polishing.

Administrative support and audience respect for this company were evident at the 2000 Rencontres, and in spite of the choreographer's self-taught, street dance background, its public was quite different from the hooting fan clubs on the benches in the big auditorium called the "Charlie Parker" stage. I noticed that several small groups of two or three, possibly dancers, left during the show; but rather than interpreting their departure as a critique of the choreography, I guessed that they had to leave for a rehearsal or performance but that they thought it important to come and see, for whatever amount of time they could spare, what this company was doing. In 2000, it struck me as one of the touch points, anchor points, for the la Villette festival for its more selective dance audience, but also for its dancers.

In more recent work, Farid Berki has developed the notion of an "invisible heritage" that was already being explored in *Invisible Armada*. In his 2006 *Exodust* presented at the 2007 Suresnes Cités Danse festival, he continues to explore the confrontation of different dance vocabularies by linking them to cultural heritage, diaspora, and exile. Significantly, Berki also continues to dance and to teach, completing the teacher training for "jazz dance" in France and mastering many forms under its rubric. While other French "pioneers" such as Franck II Louise have chosen to focus on music and movie projects, Berki remains much closer to choreographic explorations of movement innovation and dance's metaphorical potential to tell stories linked to hip hop communities, with historical and geographic cultural depth.

In *Exodust*, working with different dancers, including Yiphun Chiem, to explore the topic of immigration, Berki emphasizes that this is not a dance about exile, but rather a choreography that takes exile as its starting point ("Ce n'est pas une pièce sur l'exil mais à partir de l'exil" http://www.theatre-online.com). When the piece tours, for example, to Warsaw, it is announced as a French choreographer's take on the theme of migration and, more specifically, "illegal immigrants." The choreography is said to represent their "hope, difficulty and disappointment" in a new society. Again we are twice removed from the situation of the hip hop generation in France: as a French company touring in Eastern Europe, but also as a choreography treating not the colonial or postcolonial migrations but the topic of illegal immigration. Here the broader approach to the subject, applicable across Europe, serves to anchor the dance's abstractions, rather than the specifics of the French history or actuality. In the same way, Berki describes the movement vocabulary drawn from hip hop but moving out of its circulation within the body, elaborating it out into space, a description that serves also for the choreography: moving beyond the closed circuit of vernacular hip hop into the realm of concert dance.

What sort of citizenship, what sort of identity, is posited in Farid Berki's dances? Layered onto a radical individualism rooted in hip hop (wanting to "speak" for hip hop, not wanting that job/duty to fall to anyone else) is an awareness of the historical syncretism of dance traditions. A state diploma crowns but is not incompatible with the individual training and search for a choreographic voice. With an "Arabic" North African name and Maghrebian *dominante culturelle*, the dancer/choreographer chooses in his art to speak of other colonizations and broad approaches to the question of migrations.

Berki's travels and commissions, his work with Chinese and Russian dancers, for example, have influenced the elaboration of his movement vocabulary, his creation of pieces for dancers with different origins and training and his restaging of classic modernist pieces such as *Petrouchka*. Entering onto dance's world stage, with its diverse historical and ethnic traditions, Berki moves into territory familiar to "French" choreographers—many of diverse ethnic origins. As a French choreographer he moves beyond the suburbs and the call for Maghrebian immigrant self-representation. Significantly, while sounding the foreign, the exotic, the multiple dance traditions, and the questions of travel, colonization, and migration, the moves become French.

PART TWO

Techniques and Technologies

CHAPTER 4

Dancing in and out of the Box

Franck II Louise's Drop It! *and*

Compagnie Choream's Epsilon

French hip hop dance's insistence on the presence of bodies represent-ing difference in choreographies that move beyond such differences have been facilitated not only by cultural politics, dance institutions, and choreographic development but also by new technologies. The rise of new technologies in general and new media in particular created the condi-tions for the embrace and development of a French hip hop dance across Mitterand's fourteen-year presidency. New public and state technologies, computer-based new media, and telecommunications, especially early access to the Internet, changed bodily experience and ultimately the way bodies communicated and signified in the public spaces of the republic.

In choreographies getting beyond the *banlieue*, technological modernity has been a major theme, and the development of a choreographic language for hip hop was accompanied by new digital means of production. Hip hop choreographies described in this chapter focus on both the fascination with new technologies that have marked modernity and an understanding of its pathologies. In the age of mechanical reproduction, dance has embodied a disappearing "aura" idealistically associated with the premodern and ideo-logically associated with the so-called third world. As live performance, it is often connected to the "aura" that Benjamin famously noted was wither-ing in modernity and associated with cultural traditions or "authenticity" thought to be at odds with mechanical reproduction. Equally idealized as a wordless art form, dance has been imagined as transcending linguistic and cultural barriers. But such idealizations of a premodern or prelinguistic form associated with an authenticity of traditional cultures more often reveal a two-edged image of dancers: first, as cultural agents preserving local live performance traditions in a heavily mediatized world, but also as illiterates or colonials, resisting linguistic universalism and globalizing technologies. In the face of a French history of dance as an exotic form, a nostalgic or idealized view of dance as a pretechnological form, francophone hip hop dancers manifest their "first-world" belonging in a dance form that is a commentary on modernity and modernization: in the last chapter's example, the "I Kiffe NY" festival, hip hoppers Pockemon Crew can use "traditional Arabic music" and are influenced by "multiple traditions" but brand themselves as the globally familiar video game.

If hip hop dance began as a critique or mockery of modernity, aping a mechanization gone to extremes in steps like the "electric boogaloo," in France it was part of the socialist modernization of the 1980s and 1990s. While these dance steps, at another moment in history, might have suggested the "wired" energy of electricity, they now represent the "wired," or *branché* (connected, well-informed), life of contemporary France, which "caught up" and in the '90s surpassed other countries in its implementation of new technologies. Dancing that began in the era of vinyl records and television has followed the shift to CDs and MP3s and the shrinking of the personal computer from desktop to laptop, refocusing from broadcast or from *audiovisuel* (multimedia) to the Internet; now with PDAs and smartphones allowing mobile connectivity, the climate for bodies moving in France and their access to information has radically changed. Even as dance holds the place of an "old" form, historically important and valorized in France, it carves out new bodies and new moves. It would be hard to miss the impact of the new technologies on daily life in France: urban and social mobility, communication and connectivity, and even French bodies and ways of moving though space have visibly changed. In 1996, in the opening moments of Jean-Pierre Thorn's film, *Faire Kiffer les Anges*, the young hip hopper navigating the margins of Lyon announces the look, the walk, and the language of a new generation of French.

Hip hop arrived in a France arguably less technologically modern than the United States, but its development reflected the technology boom that socialism espoused along with a support for urban cultures. By 2007, France led the world in the number of subscribers to Internet TV, and Paul Krugman argued that in spite of its "Americanness," the Internet has been better regulated in France. Krugman points out that "the world may look flat once you're in cyberspace—but to get there you need to go through a narrow passageway, down your phone line or down your TV cable."[1] This narrow passageway to the global superhighway is, he writes, controlled in the United States by "robber barrons." While French concern about pirated media, reflected in new laws, and about US-based projects such as the digitization of library collections, launched in 2005 by Jean-Noël Jeanneney, then director of the French National Library,[2] may suggest French fears and stricter control of the Internet, the influence of new technologies and new media in the transformation of the lives and art of the hip hop generation in France cannot be discounted. While the form may have started as a critique of modernity, and the two hip hop choreographies to be analyzed in this chapter extend that critique, it is also a form that has partnered with new technologies and the new bodies and groups it helps to form.

There is no doubt that access to information and images that new technologies have made possible have changed hip hoppers' lives, as well as their art: on YouTube, on social networking sites, and even on the omnipresent cell phone, there is greater access to the means of production of one's own image in particular and images in general, to musical creation and diffusion, and to the local and global communities of dance in general and the hip hop movement in particular, previously controlled by institutions difficult for many to approach. The mobility permitted by new devices, the availability of information even away from a home base, changes the very notion of circulating in public space in France and, on a larger scale, can facilitate links to the transnational community. In particular, free Internet e-mail and international calling programs such as the "Free Box" and now Internet video-phone services have changed communication networks within the country and with other countries. The freedom of movement that a smartphone can give, for example, in navigating a city, could translate on a larger scale to a freedom of movement within the French Republic. As French institutions have been both inaccessible and intimidating to a certain class of citizens, and as a certain appearance and accent often impossible for many to acquire have been an important part of public personas, the virtual space and speed of the Internet can indeed promise greater mobility and accessibility.

With the increased use of the Internet for everything from job applications to vacation planning, formality in self-presentation, like mastery of formal French and the handwritten letter, have fallen off as national measuring sticks for "character." Ownership and mastery of new technologies may well be part of new ways of measuring competency and judging character. But how much freedom—how much accessibility—has there been for the hip hop generation from the suburbs? While the mobile phone is now omnipresent, the high-tech plans of socialism have not been equally implemented everywhere. In Mathieu Kassovitz's 1995 beacon film *La Haine*, the suburban youth are still using the phone in a café in Paris, paying a high price for a drink and use of the phone rather than getting access to the high-tech card-controlled phone booths. One of their buddies in the housing project, nicknamed *Darty* ("Wal-Mart") for a big French merchandiser, runs a black market in appliances and other goods out of his small apartment. The gap between access to technology in the suburbs and in Paris is made clear in the film. Dancing hip hop may be a positive thing, as it has come to fill a void in the suburbs, but it is not a substitute for an education and a computer. In 2010, I noticed that card-operated public phone booths have all but disappeared in most neighborhoods in Paris, on the assumption that everyone owns a cell phone; the global number is now estimated at more than 4 billion.

A modernization that was not entirely an Americanization, linked as it was to a Socialist political and social agenda, marked Mitterand's programs. With the *Grands Projets,* the arts and high tech were teamed together: the Cité des sciences et de l'industrie at la Villette, the Pyramide at the Nouveau Louvre, the Opéra de la Bastille, the Institut du Monde Arabe, and finally the so-called TGB ("très grande bibliothèque," a pun on the high-speed train TGV), the Bibliothèque Nationale de France (BNF). These landmarks of the Socialist presidency, some launched as projects earlier, reshaped Paris, linking culture (of all kinds—performing arts, foreign culture, science) to modern spaces, with the goal of increased public access.[3]

One day when renewing my old reader's card from the old Bibliothèque Nationale at the new BNF shortly after it opened, I approached one of the windows where a staff member sat behind a computer screen. I waited for the person to finish what he was doing on screen and look up before beginning my request. When he did not do so, I risked being rude by beginning the conversation. On the contrary: the person remarked that he had been waiting for my greeting before paying attention to me. This exchange made me understand one way in which the presence of the new technology had changed normal behaviors and polite interactions in speech and gesture in France. At the old Bibliothèque, readers had to present a formal letter of introduction and were interviewed by staff who tried to send them elsewhere. Now the ongoing presence of the computer, the screen's hum, took priority for the BNF worker, who took notice of clients only when they interjected themselves over (beside) the screen. While the new library houses significant public access spaces, the computer—rather than the researcher—has become the heart of the institution. Renewing my reader's card again in 2012, I found that the BNF computer had no record of me.

Such a gesture reveals the modernization typical everywhere; but in France, the availability and accessibility of information were notoriously limited; when the United States had already switched to full-time telephone availability or messaging, French telecommunications (aside from the Minitel) were not broadly effective. In the early 1980s it was often difficult to get information by phone in France and impossible to leave a message requesting information in public and private domains. Going in person, passing by and presenting oneself, was still necessary for information gathering and communicating. High-tech socialism arguably changed bodiliness and bodily behaviors in cities such as Paris.

Automated machines appeared everywhere in Paris: *cabines* operated by *télécartes*. Entrance to the new Louvre, via the Pyramide rather than the overloaded sidewalk next to the Seine, was facilitated by a machine in which an entrance fee could be paid and ticket obtained by inserting a credit card. There were the so-called *Chirac-ettes,* coin-operated toilets with super self-cleaning systems. For a time, in Paris, it seemed as if France had bypassed systems available in most places in the United States. The rapid growth of technology was pervasive and effective. Businesses including cultural institutions that had not been available by phone moved quickly to solidify telecommunications and then Internet access. A place at the BNF, for which one had previously to wait, in person, in the hallway of the old library, in the Rue de Richelieu, could be reserved via Internet the night before. Even books could be called up and would sit ready for the reader at her place on arrival. At that place, there were outlets for plugging in a computer and the architect, Dominique Perrault, spoke of "leaving room" for plugs for the things yet to be invented. The idea of saving time and space, manipulating both via technology, vanquished the idea of passing by in person, stopping at the information window—for a train reservation, for a theater or concert ticket, or for a professional appointment. In this way the computer, and more precisely the Internet, changed physical life for many Parisians and has now changed the physical existence of a generation.

Yet technologies only work for those with access: credit card, information, transportation. In this history, it is important to factor in class considerations. A new generation of users developed around this high-tech presence, but not necessarily with the expectation that it would work. The first hip hoppers didn't have computers but faced a computerizing administration and culture. But a second generation of hip hoppers has now come from *cités* where the new technologies were already not working in an otherwise high-tech modern state, and where failure of technologies and infrastructure represents and repeats what in 2005 was labeled as the state's failure to take care of its citizens in the *banlieues*.

Rather than a purely euphoric, idealist, or highly functioning technology, then—a vestige of the success of a socialist state—technology in France has now become the subject of a discourse of pathology. Digital means of production, and self-production, are no longer viewed in entirely positive terms. Perhaps via discussions of bodily presence, situatedness, and materiality, via a new politics of identity, the virtual and cyber potential for digital technologies and new media is now producing debates about the illnesses caused by addiction to them. Bernard Stiegler's multivolume major study of technology, the most recent *Prendre Soin: de la jeunesse et des générations*, argues that juvenile addiction and adult irresponsibility are produced not simply by "cybernetics" but by marketing and *psychopouvoir*—elaborating on Michel Foucault's *biopouvoir*, engineered in part by the state, as well as industry. Mobilizing everything to produce consumers and creating consumers young and old, this industrial service economy causes the disappearance of *savoir-vivre*, poisoning youth and adults and making cure impossible without a reversal of this *psychopouvoir*.[4]

There is also a tendency in technology studies, even when based on case studies, to imagine that "we are already there" when a technology exists—as if its mere viability signifies complete accessibility and future pathology. Paul Virilio, for example, theorizes potential negative effects from the mere existence of a technology rather than its widespread implementation.[5] Yet the French suburbs are a good example of the fissure between theory and practice: a modernizing nation may put in place technologies of access, but in practice they are not really accessible to all. In France the problem is less one of technological literacy, even baseline economics, but rather a social problem: those who haven't had access to institutions continue to believe they do not, regardless of change in access. As discussed in the introduction, Etienne Balibar has noted how the *banlieusards* do not effectively have access to the very system they are part of.

In this way, in spite of the use of moves that critique high tech or pathologize modern urban life (the robotlike moves of popping and locking, for example), French hip hop might be described as the fulfillment of a socialist modernization plan for the arts in tandem with high tech. Hip hop largely developed in spaces that were already "safe"—"low-tech" public spaces—and slowly took over less familiar territory: the dance studios and stages of the big cities and, most significantly, the virtual space for the publicity and diffusion of their choreographies. The work of young cultural agents, computer-savvy managers, and a new generation for whom technology has never really posed a problem of access have finally made hip hop fully wired.

While dance performance has often staged dominant thinking about bodies and the technologies that shape them, I have argued in my previous work that dancing also comments on and can at times lead or shape this thinking. I will argue here that while being advertised as a dance of "the suburbs" or "old-school authenticity" or "multiple traditions," not only have French hip hoppers used the technology to which there has been (for the most part) broad access in France to gain access to institutions, to power, and to self-representation, but also their dance is responding to the machines that change life in bodies; they are anticipating and reflecting on the significance of new technologies for bodily practices and bodily knowledge.

Surely the most significant component in French hip hop's use of new media is the end of an opposition between live and recorded performance. For some of the dances or dancers studied here, film and video, now available on the Internet, are integral to live performance. But this is only the most recent step in a long process in which the performing and recording arts, the arts of "mechanical reproduction," nourished one another. At the same time, the increasingly present "net" of technologies has created the concept of a world characterized no longer by machines or industry but by concepts of virtuality, instantaneity, and the end of work. While dancing can use, even inspire, technologies, it also reminds us that we still have bodies. Hip hop choreographies studied in this chapter and the next suggest not a stark separation of life and recorded art but new ways to integrate movement traditions into new forms, the thrills and dangers of mechanization—and new technologies beyond mechanization—shaping not only our bodies but also our experience of time and space.

IMAGING TECHNOLOGIES

Historically, dance performance has been in dialogue with the picture-making technologies of its time, furnishing images for them and arguably inspiring them, lending content but also the idea of seriality to cinematography, for example. Dance has challenged modes of pictorial representation and influenced the technologies developed to create new kinds of images.[6] In previous work, I have explored how industrial modernity, the rise of mechanized maximum productivity and its essential coded gesture, looked to dance for its metaphors and linked its Taylorist choreography of labor to dance's diversion. In this exploratory connecting (or reconnecting) machines to dance, I returned to a moment in which physiological experimentation produced cinema. I proposed that alternative histories of the invention of cinema, such as Deleuze's, make us see the cinematographic image not as an absence, a screen veiling an absence or an inaccessible "imaginary signifier," but as a grounded, indexical icon. Taking its inspiration from dance—one of Deleuze's ideas—cinema first represented the tracing of movement in Marey's labs as much as it created a mimetic picture. The presence thus coded on the screen in the filmic image, beyond iconic resemblance to the image in motion photographed, also signals an indexical proximity (to use Peircean terms) of movement recorded by the machine in a space contiguous to it.

But modern dance—like Marey himself—would eventually find cinema too mechanistic, and popular cinema chose to keep a very different, mechanized dance form in the camera's and public's eye. While live dance performance came, through mainstream modern dance, to be associated with the natural, the mythic, and the exotic—a danced "authenticity" seemingly at odds with recorded film—this was, I have argued, an authenticity conferred by film. Some dance forms were seen in Europe only thanks to the cinema. Film, however, even when moving far afield—following the Lumière camera operators who did so during cinema's first seasons—remained somehow first world, its apparatus anchored in a technological modernity imagined as metropolitan even while modern dance was broadly seen as a critique of or counterpoint to that modernity. This history is significant for contemporary French hip hop.

The case of African dance in Europe is paradigmatic: often seen as an unchanging traditional form, it needs to be seen as a traditional form with contemporary dimensions of both live and recorded performance, a form in which dancers' "otherness" and exoticism are produced by the very mechanical and metropolitan modernity their presence seems to oppose. African dance was intimately bound up with the cinematic image (as well as exposition live performance) from its first appearances in Europe. Some dancing Africans made their first appearance in France in films by the Lumières and their operators at Paris expositions and other venues circa 1900; when Josephine Baker arrived with the Revue Nègre in the 1920s, her African-inspired dancing both brought these Lumière films to life and then, in the '30s, brought that liveliness to the films in which she starred. Josephine Baker's cinematic modernity, I have argued, followed a history of African dance being recorded and presented to European audiences on film. These traditional forms, then, were in European contexts inseparable from technology; their "naturalness" was produced and guaranteed by the cinematic frame.

Bringing together the liveness and authenticity ascribed to dancing with the technology often thought of as constructing artifice means reevaluating both cinema's role in dance performance and dance's haunting presence, even influence, on mechanical mass culture. My research has suggested that gesture and dance were in more complex collaboration with early cinema, in particular in its early and experimental phases. But the rise of cinema as the dominant form of mass culture in the twentieth century—while keeping a certain American show dancing on screen—sidelined another modern dance tradition, which only later reconnected to video and eventually digital arts.

In earlier chapters, this book has explored how France put its budget and its technologies at the service of developing a "French" profile in the arts. Exporting images of French bodies and a "French" identity around the world, cinema would seem to be the dominant form in creating and defining what scholars have referred to as "Frenchness." But significantly, it is the bodies in those films that might arguably be said to lead the concept of "Frenchness." Focusing on the 1950s, Vanessa Schwartz, in *It's so French! Hollywood, Paris, and the Making of Cosmopolitan Film Culture*, traces global media culture back to the mid-twentieth-century French cinema with its roots in the invention of cinema and *fin de siècle* entertainments described in her earlier work. In opposition to the recent history of the Bush era's rising tide of anti-Americanism (war in Iraq) and American dislike and disdain for France, the book emphasizes a two-way exchange of mass culture rather than a unidirectional "Americanization." The author's agenda is to show mass culture coming to Europe while looking beyond national history in studies of culture and especially the cultural history of cinema.[7]

Against the scholarship that argues that "mass culture isn't French" Schwartz emphasizes France embracing "leading-edge technology" from the nineteenth century on, especially in the realm of mass visual media, with cinema as the leading example.[8] She argues neither for a deterministic view of technology as the sole determining factor nor for a fatalistic view of US domination, but rather for a story of global media as contingent, and argues that global culture doesn't replace but adds onto local and national cultures. Following Pascale Casanova's elaboration of Braudel, she argues that cultural exchange and influence are not always a function of political or economic domination, that the history of cultural products must accept the disjunctures between politics and culture, and that cultural texts and experiences shape politics and economics as much as reflect them. For Schwartz, film culture fostered a cosmopolitan production and vision that grounds contemporary global media.[9]

The examples in *It's So French!* show how "Frenchness" was packaged for export in the form of films and film stars. Schwartz rightly remarks that midcentury films are often "selling" a touristic idea of *belle époque* France, one that still draws student exchange and overseas study programs, tourism, shopping, *gourmandise,* and armchair appreciations of French culture.

She explores in depth the image and images of the *fin de siècle* in these 1950s "Frenchness films," which often include can-can, music hall, *chanteuses*, and other references, and she sees these films mobilizing the early cinema culture and linking these films back to it through these references.

Schwartz focuses on how films such as *Gigi* and *An American in Paris* represent "Frenchness" through icons, visual images representing the nation, such as the Eiffel Tower (as a bourgeois rather than avant-garde building), or Technicolor in line with impressionist color palettes. Schwartz notes that these 1950s agents of French *fin de siècle* cultures such as Leslie Caron, who starred in both films, are often selling a tradition of live performance, stage, and *concert caf'* that fed into the cinema and separated from it, but her book does not concentrate on the cultural work they are doing as dancers, through dancing. How and why do their dancers communicate the *fin-de-siècle*? It is not through a choreographic concern for historical accuracy. Nothing is said about the choreographers, and the only mention of "choreography" is in descriptions that do not analyze it. How do these dancers refer to or reconstruct the visual culture of the *fin de siècle*? At the same time as there is a concern with location shooting, why use dance to evoke the poster and cinematic visual culture of the *belle époque*? Does dance have the same status as the built environment, or do dancers substitute for that "authenticity" when shooting on a set in California? What, then, is actually "so French" about them? Just as dance played a significant role in early cinema, it should be explored in greater depth in this narrative of global cosmopolitan cinema that features it; it is not a minor detail that for both Leslie Caron and Brigitte Bardot—key figures in this packaging of Frenchness for a US (global) film market, both trained as dancers— dancing is key to their "Frenchness." By mentioning that they both trained at the same school, that Bardot also "wanted first to be a dancer," Schwartz points toward a national (performance) narrative. *It's so French* accepts "Frenchness" as a debate without contesting its changing self-definitions, its definition vis à vis an Atlantic world and vis à vis a colonial or postcolonial global world. As a consumer and touristic concept, this national identity is of course far away from the concept of citizenship being contested at that time in the department of French Algeria and that had not found expression on the screen.

Rather, via its dancers, I would argue, this French cinema seems to be proposing something like a corporeal definition of Frenchness: more than a simple "look," more than a narrative about personal or sexual freedom, it is an identity that has to do with mobility and freedom of expression. While these freedoms are registered very differently in the bodies of Leslie Caron and Brigitte Bardot, their "packaging" is as much a use of their bodies not simply as consumables (for example, as pin-ups were consumed) but as inventors of new moves that, for whatever reason (and in spite of their origins or choreographers), are declared "French."

The choreographing of this bodily "Frenchness" in its various forms can be traced through to the development of French hip hop some thirty years later. French hip hop is also "so French"—recognizably French, as Bill T. Jones says in the quotation that opens chapter 2—but as dance, it is not only about what Schwartz calls "mass cultural visual clichés."[10] French hip hop could be analyzed in line with this earlier "packaged" Frenchness exported (to the United States) following Schwartz's outline of these earlier disparate actors, one particular "consul general," and some ministers and journalists—later solidified into the *politique culturelle*. French hip hop was critiquing US, capitalist, and global hip hop even while "selling" socialist high-tech and social programs. Hip hop as "French" ambassador in fact suggests the work that dance has always been doing in this regard, whether welcoming the more cutting-edge US companies, absorbing US forms (via their choreographers and performers), or receiving funding that brings a form like hip hop to the concert stage long before it gets there in the United States. *Le hip hop* has benefited from this cultural relation to the United States but turned its gaze sharply back onto France's role in the postcolonial world, a world globalized not via the United States but by postcolonial migrations. These hip hoppers, then, are the unlikely inheritors of this press kit promotion of French culture to the United States, mass culture marketed as (inevitably) French high culture and ultimately an *exception culturelle* for French cultural products on the market.

Indeed, the so-called cultural exception was created for a global cinema market, not for live performance. But it is important to think about cinema as the dominant medium in France while hip hop flowered. French hip hop must be "read," not only in the context of popular and concert dance, the context of live performance of theater and music, but also in the context of the media and media arts: from cinema to new kinds of television, music, and video production and consumption and, eventually, digital arts.

IMAGING TECHNOLOGIES

The "new" bodily Frenchness described earlier, the embrace of hip hop and its links to new media, arguably repeats this pattern that I analyzed in the machine ballets presented in Paris in the 1920s and that Schwartz finds in '50s cinema linked to dancers; Ginette Vincendeau finds it again in '90s cinema linked to the hip hop world. In "Designs on the *Banlieue*; Mathieu

Kassovitz' *La Haine* (1995)," already discussed in different contexts earlier, Vincendeau wonders how Kassovitz's film managed to use the stylish black-and-white high-production values atypical for the social realism usually expressed via "naturalism" or low-production values in other *banlieue* films. She points out that some critics "queried *La Haine*'s 'authenticity' on the grounds that its seductive *mise-en-scène* was evidence of a lack of political rigour."[11] She considers the film's *mise-en-scène* as both supporting and contradicting its social project; "it aims to shock and please", she argues, showing an interest in the sociological problems of the *cité* but also staging a stylistic distancing from it. The extended and edited shots of French dancers breaking and head spinning on the glossy floor of a building in the *cité* surely refer to US culture but already also to the French hip hop finesse that Bill T. Jones described; ultimately, *La Haine* anticipates the failure of the cultural policies that were supposed to help the *cités*, the characters' "alienation from the romantic tradition of poetic rebellion which traditionally informed the figure of the French proletarian rebel."[12] Yet these characters certainly were romantic rebels in their own right, or at least received as such in the acclamation of the film. *La Haine* has thus become an allegory about how the arts of the *banlieue* have fared better than the *banlieues* themselves.

FROM CINEMA TO TELEVISION

The later development of dance films and videos plays an important role in the development of *le hip hop*: in France such films might be available in archives but became more broadly accessible through festivals and television. At major hip hop events such as the Rencontres at la Villette, large and small production films including dance documentaries showed aspects of dance history, archival footage, and interviews that create a historical documentation for the rise of popular, concert, and diasporic dance forms. Such films can also be seen regularly on the television channel *Arte*. Although the American pioneers of hip hop are revered and were invited to dance in France, these dance documentaries suggest a broader base for what is now called hip hop in France and offer a broad dance history education to self-taught dancers.

For the first generation of hip hoppers in the 1980s, a TV generation, there was no incompatibility between a danced "authenticity" and televisual technologies. In the early days of hip hop in France, moves were learned from television, and then video, just as they are today via Internet. French hip hoppers embroidered on moves from TV and video, diffused via the French popular television program H.I.P.-H.O.P. starring Sidney in the 1980s. In work on so-called *beur* culture in France, television has been critiqued for its creation of passive consumers but also recuperated as a site for the active renegotiation of identity and breaking down stereotypes that Mireille Rosello has called *départenance*. Studying what she calls a "reappropriation of the television show" in contemporary novels by Maghrebian French writers, Mireille Rosello remarks on "an active and conflictual practice of re-interpretation": "the meaning of belonging to a minority community will be renegotiated through the television, as will the components of ethnic or sexual identity. These programs are the pretext for a redefinition of the role and the status of the 'foreigner.'"[13]

While the ideas of a positive recuperation of a denigrated medium, a younger generation of spectators thought to be more sophisticated because they are more experienced in TV viewing, and an older generation having a presumed lack of such sophistication due to language differences all announce a model quite different from the United States, Rosello's conclusions about the television can be applied to *la danse urbaine*. French hip hoppers' use of media images, of all kinds, for the elaboration of a new choreographic form reveals an active rather than passive consumption of television: French TV (including cultural programming), French dubs of US programs, and the recontextualization or reinterpretation of such cultural material, high and low, American and "French," live and animated, by dancers rejecting the passivity of spectatorship for active performance and production. The tone of "H.I.P.-H.O.P." was that cool could be learned: Sidney could be cool while telling you, and often showing you, how to perform a particular step.

This civic approach to "learning" hip hop has marked the adoption of the form and the pedagogy that spread its transmission in France and will be discussed with examples in chapter 6. Children's books on hip hop have the similar tone of a manual and come with a CD to practice to, even instructions on how to choose clothing. A children's book published by the Cité de la Musique in a series called "Carnets de Danse" that includes titles on classical, modern, and jazz dance furnishes an address book for finding the nearest hip hop dance class and recommends—although only as a backup—televised rediffusions of performances or dance documentaries (by stations that *défendent la danse*): "As it isn't always easy to get out [to the theater for a performance], one can always rely on those few television stations that program previously recorded dance performances or dance documentaries. Even though such programs often come on late, the VCR can happily resolve this problem."[14] The important detail here is that the television serves not only to constitute a community but also can be used as a cultural tool and a pedagogical tool: dance steps can be learned from it, and watching it can enrich one's culture, not only as an observer but also as a practitioner.

From US music videos to the Cinemathèque and from Sidney on TV to the live concert stage may seem like a huge leap, but it is precisely that leap that hip hop dance in France has made in its genesis; choreographers such as Franck II Louise, whose work is staged in the big national theaters and tours, first danced on H.I.P.-H.O.P. as a teen. It might not have been TV that pushed Fred Bendongue or Farid Berki to go to modern dance class, but it may have been the accessibility of all kinds of dance images on TV, video, and recorded and live performance. French television developed cultural programming, including dance performances and documentaries, second to none.

TO THE DIGITAL

In a 2006 commentary on his 1999 book *Liveness*, Philip Auslander revises his thesis away from the dominance of the television and toward the digital. Auslander emphasizes that the media are "not equal"[15] and that audience perception is influenced by the "dominant media" of any given time in a "cultural economy." Technological change, he argues, "the appearance of new media...produces shifts in this economy in terms of which media are dominant and which dominated." The digital, he argues, is now the dominant form.[16] Whether or not it is "visible" in the choreographies onstage, I would argue that French hip hop dance performance reflects a nation reorganizing around digital media and redefining bodily identity through and with new technologies: from the television to the VCR to the digital to the mobile.

Usually digital performance (like virtual subjects) suggests the suppression of distance, of class difference, geographical and economic divides.[17] In his recent work on performance and technology, Chris Salter focuses on "situatedness" and skips the "digital performance," "cyber performance," and "cyber theater" of MOOS, MUDs, CD-ROMS, solo-based computer gaming, Internet-based performance, online meta-verses, and virtual communities such as Second Life that he identifies as *"anytime, anyplace simulation."*[18] None of these have been used extensively in any hip hop I have seen, even though access to digital media is widespread in Europe. For Salter, the "euphoria for the simulated and the virtual that marked the end of the twentieth century" has subsided and given way to discussions of "embodiment, situatedness, presence, and materiality."[19] Salter sees the 1990s' ocular obsession with screens and data shifting now to a recovery of "felt experience, situated context and polysensory affect that simply cannot be reduced to text, code, or photons aimlessly floating on the screen."[20]

Indeed, much digital performance now focuses not on an idealized transnational or virtual subject but on the question of embodiment itself. Recent work trends toward human experience and bodiliness, sensory and emotive. In their collection of essays, *Performance and Technology: Practices of Virtual Embodiment and Interactivity,* editors Susan Broadhurst and Josephine Machon propose readings that stress "the emotive, the intuitive, the ludic, and the sensate"[21] in performance work using digital media. Far from the machinic or the technique of technology, digital performance forms focus on the body and bodily sensation and re-create and rethink affect and audience reception of moving forms.

In a similar vein, Laura Marks writes about "tactile epistemologies" that "conceive of knowledge as something gained not on the model of vision but through physical contact." In spite of a literature of "unrigorous, romantic, or downright spooky" sources, "viewed askance by many academics," she attempts to "describe a form of cinematic representation based on the sense of touch." In *The Skin of the Film,* Marks theorizes that beyond visuality, and in addition to its indexical function, recent avant-garde cinema has explored the senses, representing skin as a reservoir of memory and location of cultural differences and displacements that arise in immigration: "many of these works evoke memories both individual and cultural, through an appeal to non-visual knowledge, embodied knowledge and experiences of the senses, such as touch, smell, and taste." Marks focuses in one section on what she calls "haptic images" that "appeal to a haptic, or tactile, visuality" and that "invite the viewer to respond to the image in an intimate, embodied way."[22]

French hip hop is neither only about skin nor simply about virtuality. While France is an image-conscious nation and its residents bombarded with images, the digital can be understood not simply as a space saturated by images and manipulating images, but also giving the potential to free users from certain kinds of images.

In the early days, hip hop "associations" were run with public funding, and later hip hop dance companies were run by someone with a cell phone, and then a website. After dancers became known, a cultural agent or manager with funding rather than funds per se would run the publicity and technical side of the dancers' or companies' careers; while all members of the *mouv'* now have computer access and e-mail and receive and send images, the high-tech side of the hip hop scene has been in part accomplished through the community that makes it up as an "art world." Hip hop dance and its idea of community respond to the new technologies' isolation and screen fixation even while hip hoppers use these technologies.

While this book has argued for the centrality of dance in French culture and French cultural politics—a historical situation that is still the case perhaps only in France—in the age of global media and information, dance performance has moved to the margins. While it remains a powerful image as the last vestige of traditional cultures that are imagined as resisting technological modernization or as the future of cybernetic, wired bodies freed from work, dance itself is marginalized in a culture that Regis Debray has named the "videosphere." It is difficult to account for its continued popularity as concert dance in France, especially when we consider the marginalization of dance simultaneously with the massive media attention to sports and entertainment and the insignificance of any dance next to the broadest worldwide spectatorship for a soccer player's single head gesture. Just as dance stages the double bind of expressivity within constraint, of poetics along with a certain pedestrianism, it also raises questions about what might be called the surplus value of certain bodily gestures in an economy in which dance itself is largely valueless. Yet perhaps an exploration of the role of dance in the age of global media, or a look at dance gestures in their French context, can tell us something more about the meaning of French soccer star Zidane's gesture in the 2006 World Cup final. While wondering why dance has become a largely insignificant cultural product, removed from the center stage it occupied (e.g., in France) in the nineteenth and into the early twentieth century, I am hoping to show what dance offers the information age; this chapter concludes with a reflection on what dance brings to our thinking about new technologies.

Dance performance serves as material or inspiration for some of the very technologies that are arguably killing it off, figuring the bodily freedom of the outside-the-box iPod users into the advertisement. Such technologies are also implicated in performance practices that imagine or deploy mobile, portable, semiprosthetic [body-worn] technologies such as MP3 headphones/cell phones. While animating the body with machines, these technologies also create a certain disembodiment; in *L'art du moteur*, Paul Virilio likens this amplified, technologized body, in the work of Stelarc, for example, to the Nietzschean "superman." The reduction of gesture to minimum effort and maximum efficiency that characterized the machine age continues in the age of information and evolves in forms of new media, descendants of the technologies that dance, I have argued, helped to make possible. The repeated and minimal gestures of modernity evolve—from the assembly line to data entry, from pushbutton to click or voice command. Yet while we are being declared a society of consumption, not production, beyond work and beyond bodies, we know that for most people in the world this theory does not describe their experience. Production is simply displaced from the center of "our" societies to the margins, outsourced to the developing world. These chapters, rather than exploring the work that explicitly stages technologies joined to bodies, consider how, even while using recording, imaging, and communication technologies, dance continues to represent both some pretechnological cultural form that speaks of the daily experience of working, moving bodies and the universal bodily transcendence and apparently out-of-the-box feeling of the iPod dancers.

If dance offers the new technologies an image, the new technologies in return offer hip hoppers another way out. Metaphors of network and community continue to dominate in the digital world in spite of the massive consumer manipulation and commercialization it manifests. But more significant, it seems, is the distance or potential anonymity that the digital world can afford in a society that emphasized presence and appearance and that claimed to ignore visible difference while excluding it.

Drop It!

The fascination with what technologies make possible for bodies, and how they limit them, has been explored in many hip hop choreographies in the past decade: choreographies to be analyzed here serve as illustrations of hip hop's *mise-en-scene* of the wonders and horrors of technologies, offering different choreographic demonstrations of being boxed in and thinking "out of the box": first Franck II Louise's *Drop It!* and second Compagnie Choream's *Epsilon*. Both premiered during the 2000–2001 season and both received public funding; both were signed for longer seasons, the first at the prestigious national stage of Chaillot.

At the Rencontres in fall 2000, the full-length piece *Drop It!* was the first to explore the possibilities for hip hop images and movements while remaining within the spirit and the idiom of hip hop. The choreography revealed that time had been taken to explore and develop movement ideas as well as a story: it manifested both a great deal of time spent in hip hop, learning all the moves, but also a great deal of time spent with the dancers as they learned to develop their own language for the stage. The piece is a *ballet mécanique* with certain resemblances to those of the 1920s and '30s, performed in particular by the Ballets Suédois in Paris, both idealizing the culture of the machine and, at the same time, warning of its dangers.

The human machine is a natural subject for hip hop choreography, with the fragmented forms of popping and locking recalling mechanical and industrial machines and assembly-line work. In the opening passages of the piece, we see such human machines, robots, dressed in an armor that suggests that of both the knight and the futurist automaton. Trapped inside the pools of their spotlights, in their armor and their restricted movements, these "robots" slide mechanically across the ground; we do not see the humans inside. (See Figure 4.1) But one of them, isolated, takes hold of his helmet and begins to extricate himself from his suit of armor.

We wonder about the people hidden inside this armor: Who are they? What do they look like? This one reappears in a red track suit and dances a solo accompanied by music including a loop in English, "feels so good inside." It is a solo of self-discovery and bodily freedom, using movements on and with the floor to express the illusion of being blown by the wind or drawn by the force of gravity toward center stage. These are recognizably hip hop movements, yet they are performed in such a way as to extend the movement illusion to express something abstract, beyond the hip hop battle: rather, a body battling various forces, currents, and weights, and a body taken in by these forces.

The music composed for this choreography, pieces of music that follow one another seamlessly, provide their own narrative thread and take us to a third section. Following the human machine, the half man/half machine, and the man liberated from the machine, we arrive at the moment of combat between those who are free and those who remain mechanized. These one-on-

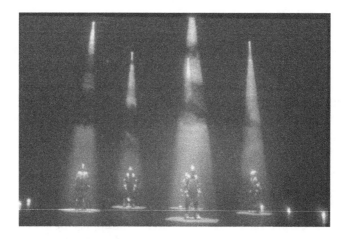

Figure 4.1
Robotic dancers before their metamorphosis in *Drop it!* (2000). Choreography by Franck II Louise.
Photo Credit: Bill Akwa Betote. Photothèque la Villette, Rencontres Urbaines, 2000.

one combats finish with the victory of the "men" over the automata and then their transformation into men in a successive stripping off of armor.

It is the in-between stages here that are the most interesting, showing the dancers' transformation and suggesting the dance form's fascination with mechanization. At one point, one of the men masters one of the machines as a horse, riding him; at another moment, one of the transforming robots reappears wearing only one of the heavy mechanical shoes and sheds it, dancing with it to the soundtrack of birdsong. Perhaps the strongest moment of the choreography comes when, after the victory of "men" and the liberation and stripping of the automata, one of the men, alone on stage, goes and takes back a part of the metal shell and, fascinated, drapes it over his shoulders like a cape, remembering a past that threatens to resurge.

A final long scene stages the freedom of these dancers, in standing forms and break dancing on the ground, who become tired, who seem to deflate and then reinflate with the same song playing the lyrics "feel so good inside" to a disco rhythm. The piece ends with the men in the same spots as in the beginning, but with each dancing his own style and the one in the center spinning on his head. It is clearly no longer the same world, even if in some ways it is still recognizably the same dance, used to express human mechanization and human freedom.

In a discussion with the choreographer, I asked about the title, and Franck's response suggested a different resonance for *Drop It!* in French. He understood the phrase to suggest the relaxation and exploration made possible by hip hop dance—to my mind, symbolically expressed through the stripping off of the armor. "Let it go" might be a better phrase to interpret this easygoing generational response to the political intensity of the preceding generation of 1968. Significantly, Franck did not choose the French verlan *laisse bé-tombe* (for *laisse tomber*, "let it drop," "let it be," "get over it"). His English is not good, but he clearly felt the English communicated this concept better than the French, as did the English words to the song that opened and closed the second section of the choreography.

At the audition for dancers to play in the touring version of the choreography, Franck also spoke about this positive good feeling in hip hop that he sought in the "complete" (well-rounded) dancers he needed for the piece. After an audition sequence that dancers had to learn and execute, a circle formed on stage and music was played, during which dancers stepped into the circle to improvise, with Franck standing onstage with them. "On kiffait," he remarked later ("we were having fun"), and dancers who did not participate could not be considered for the roles.

In a conversation with the dancers for this show—not so much a company as a young group assembled by Franck for the show—we discussed the "best" dancers. While each had his specialization, all agreed on the expertise of certain young colleagues. Many elements of their discussion surprised me: they described the advantages and disadvantages of a hip hop diploma (having to find a vocabulary), wished to be *agrées* rather than *diplômés* (qualified without having a program of study), and accepted without any difficulty the informal interviewing of a researcher backed by the Ministry of Culture. Most surprising for me, as *intermittents du spectacle,* they seemed far from struggling; one was leaving on a ski vacation, and all of them had advantageous touring contracts that included backstage snacks and excellent terms.

Meeting the dancers who had been hidden by the armor made me think about the role of this disguise, the mechanization in the choreography as a metaphor for the loss of individual and ethnic identity in automatized anonymity. The choreography suggests that what one man does alone, a moonwalk—can be seen as crazy, but when a group does it together, it becomes mechanization and seems organized. Isn't this true about the dancing in general? The piece shows dance as a kind of misguided, marginal activity, but when a group does it, it becomes mainstream, industrial, and impressive. Suddenly it has the force of a machine.

Drop It! suggests both an ease that comes from technology and the ease that comes from letting go, the seductions of machine culture and the individualism that it can erase. A more critical view of the ways modernization has shaped bodies, space, and time and a broader exploration of the magic and mechanization of embodiment emerge in Choream's *Epsilon,* commissioned in the same season.

Epsilon

Another choreographic highlight of the 2000–2001 season was the premiere of Choream's *Epsilon,* originally a 1999 la Villette commission, which also had extended engagements and went on tour. Co-choreographed by the company cofounders, Stéphanie Nataf (who also performed in the piece) and José Bertogal (who did not), *Epsilon* was presented at La Cigale in March 2001 at a soirée organized for programmers, cultural agents, and performers from the world of hip hop. Waiting in line with my invitation outside La Cigale, I met young television show hosts, dancers, and choreographers. After the show, a reception was held in the bar of the beautiful old theater, where I saw all the most visible festival programmers, managers, and choreographers. I was struck at that time by the presence of a majority of French of African descent. Most hip hop events I had attended, I realized, had had a majority white public.

The choreographic collaboration between Nataf and Bertogal, which ended with Stéphanie establishing her own company, Los Anges, a few years later, created an identifiable style of stage spectacle based on a concrete hip hop movement vocabulary elaborated in abstractions. In *Epsilon*, there is not so much a story as a movement story; hip hop is at the service not of a historical or cultural tale, but used and developed in a movement exploration of the concept of development itself, time or evolution. (See Figure 4.2) In this way it follows precisely the compositional structures of modern dance choreographies, exploring abstract ideas through movement that makes logical sense and constructing its own narrative.

This exploration of the base of hip hop, extension into the elaboration of new steps, and development into evening-length choreography (what some critics call "ballets") lasting about an hour is what has distinguished the French situation from the original US form, and it required dancers to extricate themselves from their dance in order to see their dance from the choreographer's or audience's point of view. In an interview, I asked Stéphanie for confirmation that José had stopped performing in order to focus on choreography. She explained that "we really needed one of us to stay outside" in order to see the choreography. Before that, she said, they had had to relay one another, not dance at the same time. José had knee problems and made the choice to focus on choreography, she said, "which he adores." At the presentation of *Epsilon*, when I asked José about his choreographic process, he described keeping a composition journal next to his bed and making notes whenever they came to him, even during the night.

Epsilon, in fact, resembled a dream, incarnating the flux of time: animal time, wind and light, and the modern mania of organized time. It admirably combined the two choreographers' very different styles: José's fluid exploration and Stéphanie's spectacular precision. In the convulsions of organisms in the primordial slime, as in the beating of the human heart, time becomes localized and takes shape in the movements of individuals and groups. But later on, such convulsions or contractions become mechanized and create a world ordered by enslavement to the clock, to work, and to the idea of time as money.

The hip hop movement vocabulary lends itself perfectly to this critique of modernity, especially exaggerated in Stéphanie's danced contraction of time and money to a rushing, complex rhythm with a chiming cash register and the constant, ringing refrain of "work, work!" Group dances using locking and pointing imitate the clockwise movement of the hands of a timepiece. But going even deeper, this company pushes hip hop further to find its potential onstage, merging with elements of African or modern dance, never individually presented as such, but as part of the dance language. It is

Figure 4.2
Hip hop moves in a choreographic reflection on the nature of time: *Epsilon* (1999). Choreography by José Bertogal and Stéphanie Nataf. Compagnie Choream publicity poster.

the same with the costumes, uniformly gray but permitting the individual expression of each dancer, just as the choreography variously presents an unformed mass of bodies at the beginning, the anonymity of primordial time or of modernity's "full time," as well as the particularity of lived time.

The omnipresent "wave" of hip hop—performed by bodies lying down or kneeling—here becomes the wings of birds, ocean waves, and even metaphorically the subtle alternation of perception and experience. The moves are full of meaning but never weighed down by an explicit message—they signify suggestively. This choreography contrasts the illogic of daily life with the *durée* of prehistory, of the unconscious, and of relativity and seems to opt for the more difficult but more powerful logic of this "other" world. Choream's choreography demonstrated that dance signifies and is enriched by movement's suggestiveness, which allows it to express for example, abstractions like time.

Epsilon was received, for example, by the young dancer sitting next to me at La Cigale, as "aesthetic." In this context "aesthetic" might mean that the choreography took place before us but not "for" us; it was for a public but not addressed to them; and it contained elements that went beyond the here and now, addressing a larger (invisible) public. Its dancers know why and for whom they dace and, internalized, this fuels the power of their performances. While giving us their all, they are not for sale. They are not dancing in time; they are time itself; they create it. They do not follow the rhythm of the music; they are rhythm themselves. They do not execute the gestures and moves of a choreography that has been imposed on them; rather, they reshape space itself with their bodies. This is dance's theatrical power, in particular modern dance's, but it is still surprising in the hip hop idiom. This aestheticized representation offers a different way to speak about cultural diversity, a different lived experience of time and space.

Neither *Drop it!* nor *Epsilon* used elaborate stage technologies or new media in their choreography. But in her more recent work with her new company, Los Anges, Stéphanie Nataf has pushed choreographic experimentation toward the use of computer projections in the hour-long *Zou,* discussed in the first chapter. She is now exploring improvisational exchange between live dancing and recorded digital images in her current work, *Pixelle*. While in the first chapter I described *Zou* as representing and in some ways marking the end of a certain politics of technological modernization in France, *Pixelle* promises to enter the digital performance world, referred to as "anytime, anyplace," that seems largely disconnected from national-industrial technology politics. But the first-worldliness of some technologies, and the continuation of states of exile in spite of global access, continues to fire the hip hop choreography discussed in the next chapter.

CHAPTER 5

Breaking History

Hélène Cixous' L'histoire terrible mais inachevée de Norodom Sihanouk, Roi du Cambodge *and Yiphun Chiem's* Apsara

This chapter will consider the theater practice of two francophone women, focusing on their work on the relation between dance, language, exile, and immigration. The title heading of this next section is taken from a play by Helène Cixous, underlining the parallel or equivalence between "our *language*" and "our *dance*," and also the "our"—of ownership and of community. In *The Terrible but Unfinished History of Norodom Sihanouk, King of Cambodia* first performed in Paris in 1984, Cixous raises important questions about language and dance as they create and disperse identity. Fulfilling the prediction about the future of Cambodian dance in the diaspora in the play's concluding lines, contemporary Cambodian-born dancer Yiphun Chiem's performance piece *Apsara* (2007) represents the genocide and her family's exile by integrating traditional Cambodian dance into contemporary urban dance. One of the few women break dancers in European dance, Yiphun learned both the Cambodian traditional dances and hip hop growing up in Brussels.

Hip hop in Europe has absorbed steps and movements from the source cultures of its dancers, as well as the forms of dance visible in cultural venues in the cities—classical forms and popular forms that have become concert forms—and even other movement forms such as the broad range of martial arts. Arguably many of these forms filtered into hip hop in its making, but concert urban dance in Europe has brought them out more fully, using music, costuming, and choreography that summon many dance traditions. Yiphun's solo *Apsara* anchors the multiculturalism of hip hop into a story about origins—her family's nation—and about transnational exile. It also manages to "speak," without words, of the horrors of the nation's and the family's past.

In her careful choice to "speak" of the genocide without speaking, Yiphun uses her mastery of two dance forms to create a performance with a deep dramatic and political content. The solo demonstrates the rage carried by the survivors of the genocide and the national "confusion" about what happened only now being addressed by the international tribunal within Cambodia.[1] But it also weighs the place of tradition in the forging of new generations in exile and the ability of new forms, such as hip hop, to allow immigrants to belong somewhere else.

Yiphun's choreography stages, along with this shift from the traditional to the modern, a shift in gendered identity: from the femininity of the classical form to the universal androgeneity or even machismo of hip hop. The piece thus suggests the difference that place and space make in gendered identity, the freedom that break dancing can offer a girl from a traditional culture, and the challenge of learning new ways to move while preserving the old ways. *Apsara* enacts traditions even as it moves beyond them.

Significantly, the performance piece fills in the very gap that Cixous' play left open: the unspoken plight of the many victims of the Khmer Rouge. Only now coming into public discourse in Europe and the United States, through published books and memoirs; research centers and study groups, such as the Cambodia Genocide Project based at Yale University; and widespread journalistic coverage of the tribunals, this chapter of recent Cambodian history is explored in the francophone public sphere by Yiphun's piece, which serves as a next-generation response to Cixous' earlier work: both communicating through a witnessing that is a result of travel not toward but away from Cambodia. Twenty-four years after Cixous' play brought what she had witnessed in Cambodia to Paris, Yiphun Chiem's performance at la Villette in Paris brings a different set of answers to the questions posed by Cixous at the end of her play.

"OUR LANGUAGE, OUR DANCE"

Dance performs identity or its dispersal across eras and cultures in ways that we usually attribute to language as it performs nationhood, or global citizenship. The discourse of nation and language is old: the idea that a people define themselves by their language (e.g., Gaelic), or the idea that if you want to found a nation you must suppress the linguistic variation of minority groups, slang, code, and so forth, and create a standard form—often this is accomplished via radio, television, and so on (French, Italian). The discourse of colonialism also depends on language—the colonizer imposes a language through empire and the colonized resist by keeping, sometimes secretly, their own language. The oral tradition meets the print tradition and the traditional arts meet new inventions, and the history of colonialism and the postcolonial recounts these sometimes violent meetings.

In earlier chapters of this book, dancing has been identified—in some ways of thinking—as close to ethnicity, to nation, and "borrowed" to transmit a notion of cultural authenticity. Two examples considered in this chapter blur these distinctions and illustrate movement in two senses: first, in a local or punctual sense—gesture that is specific to a time and a place. We often say that gesture is the universal language that everyone understands, that we all share a body and we all speak its language or languages, but body language is very culturally rooted, varies from place to place, and is quite specific.

How do we decode gesture? There is a range of disciplines dedicated to the decoding of gesture's precise meaning: semiotics, cultural history, psychoanalysis, rhetoric, and even dance scholarship, because in many ways dancing belongs to this kind of movement even if it is more carefully prepared or performed. In the introduction to *A Cultural History of Gesture*, historian Keith Thomas notes that just as historians reach contradictory conclusions when studying the past, scholars who study gesture realize that the meaning of many gestures and postures remains constant: "Contemporary experience thus confirms the moral which is to be drawn from these studies of the past: namely, that behind the apparently most trivial differences of gesture and comportment there lie fundamental differences of social relationship and attitude. To interpret and account for a gesture is to unlock the whole social and cultural system of which it is a part."[2] Or, as he says, gesture illuminates what in French is called *mentalité*, the "fundamental values and assumptions underlying any particular society."[3] In other words, states of bodies reveal states of mind: not as default or shortcut communication, but rather showing the complexity of mental and linguistic structures. In fact, it has been argued by philosopher Giorgio Agamben that states themselves—nations, communities, the ethnic and linguistic communities that make and unmake nations—function politically as a kind of gestuality, to be discussed later in this chapter.

The second kind of movement illustrated in these examples is global, the movement across continents, emigrations, and exiles, which take these gestures out of their usual contexts and bring them into new ones. Here the disciplines of anthropology and history help us decode these movements through comparison that calculates translation and displacement in space and time. We often think the local movements and meanings get lost in these displacements. It is important to think, for example, how different communities might receive or interpret the gestures of a young woman, deprived of her voice in her family life, deprived of the means to publish her writing in a print culture controlled by the taste and power of people who belittle her, and forced to express herself in some other way, for example, in illness.[4] Examples such as the case of Freud's patient Dora, I have argued, help us to consider movement not as a default but as a choice to go beyond the limits of language or the linguistic differences that separate us.

Cixous' work offers two avenues for connecting dance to literary theory: first, through a theory and practice of writing the body, from the body, with the body, and so forth (linked to psychoanalysis and feminism), and second, by staging questions of dance within theater, bringing text and movement together. How did Cixous get from the first, a writing of the interior, a writing practice epitomized by the title of her first novel, *Dedans* ("Within"), to the "without" or outside of theater?

In an essay called "From the Scene of the Unconscious to the Scene of History: The Path of a Writing," Cixous explains that, searching for ways to write the other, in the "feminine writing" (*écriture féminine*) that she defines as not simply the province of women but seeking to explore all the differences—the many differences—that sexual difference founds or summarizes, she arrived at the theater. She said she found in the theater a way to write the multiple and the other that had often eluded her in fiction, essentially to give voice to characters and let them speak, and to use actors' bodies, with actors giving themselves and lending their bodies in an almost religious way to these characters.

In *Portrait of Dora*, one of her first plays, Cixous stages this discovery of the difference of the feminine. In this play, we see that theater gives us another chance at history, because although the case and its characters are one hundred years old, theater exists "in the present," as Cixous says.[5] In her play, Dora gets to tell her story to a wider audience, to speak for herself, and the meaning of Dora's words and gestures can be reopened to interpretation. In the final lines of this play Cixous links the key words of Dora's analysis together in a kind of free-association poem that suggests a multiple resonant reading that Freud missed. Dora comes alive not just as a character but as a person who now has her own text. She is given a body—lent a body by an actress and a voice by Cixous, who hears her differently and expands her text.

Cixous' staging of Dora's case shows that what had to be repressed and expressed physically as a symptom can now echo in the poetry of freer association. The body is no longer the site of a default or short-circuited expression of an idea that fails to take shape as language, but the very source of language. A feminist practice of psychoanalysis and of theater suggest that both the private space of the analysis (the "Scene of the Unconscious," which Anna O called her "internal theater") and the public space of the stage can be spaces of creative, healing expression rather than symptomatic repressed expression.

For Cixous, it is a different matter when creating characters in her writing who are Cambodian peasants who cannot themselves write, which she does in *The Terrible but Unfinished History*. She is writing for people whose entire country is lost and has become reduced to their language: "At a certain moment, for those who have lost everything, a being or a country, it is language that becomes their homeland."[6] She asks, "How do I write about those who don't know how to write?...How do I not put my language before theirs?"[7] She found that theater allowed her to let them speak. And to come to this point of writing for them, she had to work on losing herself: "How does one manage to make theater...when one is a writer of fictions? I have to make the journey in myself outside of myself. In the theater, one can only do it with an 'I' that has practically volatilized, that has been transformed into space."[8]

So if writing allows Cixous to be multiple, interestingly, by writing for the theater, she loses her body: "I the author, have to disappear so that you, so other, can appear. My answer has come through writing for the theater. On the stage I, the author, am no longer there, but there is the other."[9] The actors give their bodies, too: "the gift that theater gives is incarnation." The result is a group that elsewhere Cixous metaphorically calls a dance: the "I that is multiple" is "an intense pseudonymic activity, a dance of individualities which traces the open group that is No one."[10]

At the same time that theater is multiple, its writing must be "zen"—that is, violently condensed, it must not waste our time or our eyes.[11] Cixous describes theater as "a place for the immediacy of the desire of the other, the desire of all others." She explains this by citing a fourteenth-century theoretician of No, Zeami.[12] The No interests Cixous because it is played, says Zeami, according to the feeling of the audience. The No implicates the spectator in an intense way: the art of the spectator is also part of the drama. That's what theater is, Cixous confirms: it is the desire of all "others"—of all characters, of the public, of the actors, of the director, of us, ourselves. To be able to stage this, "you have to arrive at this state of 'de-ego-ification', this state of no-ego, of dispossession of the ego, which will make it possible for the characters to possess the author....Writing a play, *The Terrible but Unfinished History* ... all of a sudden I was invaded by a people and by very precise individuals whom I did not know at all and who became my family permanently."[13]

The history of Sihanouk represented for Cixous a significant shift from her earlier work to the global stage of history and politics, from the punctual gesture of Dora, for example, to the global movements of peoples. Cixous says she was asked often why she was writing about Cambodia and not *des femmes*? Her first response seems Orientalist: she says her favorite poets told her life is oriental. But she also links the word "Orient" to Orian and to Oran, the city she grew up in, underlining how her position both within and outside Algeria puts her in the middle of both Western and so-called non-Western cultures.[14]

But her second answer as to why she came to write about Cambodia is because its existence is precarious, and the examples she gives of what is in danger of extinction (around 1987) include dance. She describes the very precarious existence of Cambodian exiles in huts near the border of Thailand, which she calls "de vraies maisons de l'amour et de la danse." She went in the 1980s to visit camps where Cambodians facing guns and death "fight for an art and a culture that are threatened with extinction, where the khmer children born in the refugee camps who have never known anything but its prison learn the eternal dance."[15] They are "saving" the Cambodian national dance.

In *The Terrible but Unfinished History*, there are several mentions of "dancing" as a metaphor for ritual community or celebration, and the entire play, as performed at the Cartoucherie by Ariane Mnouchkine's troupe Théâtre du Soleil in 1985, was choreographed around the music of composer musician Jean-Jacques Lemêtre, who plays the royal musician onstage. These metaphors suggest that dancing is very present in the thinking and living of the Cambodian court, but none is as powerful as this idea of the love that preserves the "eternal dance" of the ancient Khmer culture in the refugee camps, and this more important dance is invoked in the play's final scene from which I take this section's title.

Cixous' play references in many ways the Shakespeare history plays, as well as the tragedies, and its production at the Théâtre du Soleil followed the company's Shakespeare cycle. *The Terrible but Unfinished History*, often performed in two halves (or "epochs") two nights in a row, follows the fall of a king and his exile from his homeland, across Europe and Asia, in an unending and precarious dance in which he has to negotiate on one side with Americans and on the other with the Khmer Rouge, both of whom want to wage destructive war on the people who call him "Monseigneur

Papa." As in a Shakespeare play, Cixous shows us not only the life at court, the king's thoughts, but also those of the peasants who love him and the various members of the opposition, including the Khmer Rouge, who court him first and later chase him out of the country. It is important to note that Cixous was criticized for the play's representation of Sihanouk, who was present at the premiere of the play, as an entirely sympathetic character (when in fact, because of his relations with the Khmer Rouge, he is often blamed for some part of the extermination) and also for seeming to glorify a living politician. Aspects of the play's production attempted to address this: most significantly, the presence of stuffed figures ringing the performance space seemed to bear witness for the silenced victims of the Khmer Rouge.

In the play's final scene, Queen Kossomak (Sihanouk's mother), who has died, and her best friend, Mom Savay, the ex-premiere danseuse of the Cambodian royal dance troupe, appear as ghosts before the peasants fleeing the Khmer Rouge and send them forth with an injunction to preserve the Khmer culture. They are not the only ghosts in the play; Sihanouk's father, Suramarit, has been from the beginning present in certain scenes, intervening in various projects with the extremely superstitious peasants, Khieu Samnol and Mme. Lamné, her Vietnamese friend. The ghost of Suramarit, the former king, says to those on the road, including the boy Yukanthor: "Wherever you end up living abroad, do not forget our language, our gentle Khmer language. Speak it every day. Don't let it disappear." The queen adds: "Because our language is the water of the Mekong, it is our wellspring, our freedom, our sublime ground, our survival, our memory and our pride. So as long as our river runs through the world through our people, all our people living and dead will all remain unforgotten." And Mom Savay, the dancer, continues: "And the second source is the dance. Our royal dance. We must save our dance." The young boy Yukanthor exclaims: "Ah, Bouddha, the royal danse! How will we do that?" And Mom Savay replies: "There is my little niece Sihamino. You know her; she was my pupil. She lives in Vancouver, Canada...."

The final lines of this political play about more or less contemporary times suggest some hypotheses about political and ethnic identity and dance and the diaspora: first, that dance can encode culture in a way that makes it a "source" of self-definition for a people, like language the bearer of a precise ethnic content and thus in danger in certain political situations. In fact, as carriers of a cultural tradition, the dancers of the so-called Cambodian Royal Ballet were among the targeted victims of the Khmer Rouge exterminations. It is estimated that 90 percent of them were killed.

Touring in France in 1998, dancers from the newly reorganized ballet saw clips from a tour thirty years earlier made by a French television crew. One of the former dancers, Mr. Proeung Chhien, now a teacher and dean at the company school, "was deeply moved to see not only his younger self, but also many colleagues who were among the estimated one million people who died under the Khmer Rouge. A few dancers brought into the reborn dance company as orphans in the early 1980s even saw the faces of dead relatives on the screen."[16] This dance, then, in some way has become a dance of ghosts.

In this case, dancers were seen as transmitters of a cultural code that needed to be erased. The fact that this dancing survived, in and through bodies that were and are more vulnerable than texts, less mobile, and more visible, is remarkable. Indeed, it was preserved through exile and distance and mobility, in a tradition that valued the dances and taught them even in less than professional conditions, in the refugee camps, and also in the court in exile. It was thus also preserved by politics, by the kind of political strategy that Sihanouk is engaged in throughout the play, trying to play each side—Khmer Communists and American capitalists—off of the other.

In fact, it was this court that had revived the classical dance in the first place: it was Queen Kossomak, Sihanouk's mother, who "played a central role in reviving Cambodian classical dance after an earlier decline."[17] Her granddaughter, Princess Buppha Devi, Sihanouk's eldest daughter who joined the company at age six, returned with her father from exile in 1991 and began teaching immediately. In 2000, she was the minister of culture and, among other duties, oversaw the dancers' training—nine years of morning classes, at the end of which dancers become employees of the state.

In some ways the Royal Ballet represented first a pro-European sensibility: reflecting in its own way the heritage of French colonialism by referencing the court origins of ballet, but also, eventually, an anti-European politics championing indigenous art rather than adopting European ballet as some so-called third world countries have done. But in spite of this ethnic and national pride in the dance, and in spite of the fact that many of the leaders of the Khmer Rouge studied in Paris, a thorough rejection of all things French, especially cultural, marked their revolutionary regime. Thus, although it is possible to imagine many political uses or positions for a national dance company, its mere existence represented the monarchy that the Khmer Rouge eventually—if temporarily—displaced.

If, then, dancing has a specific content and a specific location (in bodies and in a country), how can it be preserved, and how can it travel and transcend the politics of extermination, exile, and globalization? How and what does it speak to its global audience? Dancer/choreographer Yiphun Chiem produces dance that is traditional and modern at the same time, sampling both "authentic" old forms and present-day innovations, and thus refers to the dance pieced together from fragments and mechanical reproduction as able to represent some kind of authenticity and wholeness—at least for some people.

Television clips from 1969 also revealed how much has still to be recovered:

> Until 1975, the classical dances had been preserved through living memory: court dancers became teachers who passed along their experience to new generations of dancers who in turn became teachers. When it came to rebuilding the tradition after 1979, everything depended on the traumatized memories of the twenty or so dancers and five teachers who had survived. 'I'd remember something; someone else would remember something else' recalled Mr. Proeung Chhien. '...We also found some films and recordings from abroad, and we'd remember more. But there is still a lot missing....'"[18]

Now some invention is taking place, elaborating choreographies from mythic subjects or creating new dances for some characters from the repertory. It is clear that these dances, reconstructed following trauma and television, serve to refound this community.

If gesture, or dance, is a universal language, something we share universally, then it would seem that we cannot own our dances. It is also said that without bodies the dances do not live. But this example seems to illustrate the contrary: dance is both local and global, both punctual, belonging to bodies, and transcendent, living without them—sometimes. Movement is a local language that also signifies globally, often with some kind of translation. Movement can constitute a people or nation as language does, it has cultural roots, and it is political.

Cixous argues that we are born in language and that it shapes us; it even shapes our bodies. It's not that we don't have the words to say what we need to say, she argues, it's that we don't have the body; we are too disciplined or unable to speak with it: "it's that right away we rush towards clichés. It is not because we do not have the language, but because we do not have the body. The language is there, one can do what one wants with it. But it is our bodies: right away we are disciplined, straitjacketed."[19] For Cixous, we do not let ourselves be worked in our bodies by language. She imagines reading the book of the world with one's body, liberating ourselves from internal despots, receiving the million things that happen to us every day.[20]

Cixous asserts that language is a country: "At a certain moment, for those who have lost everything, whether a being or a country, it is language that becomes their homeland." While this is different from using a language to define a homeland or to colonize someone else's homeland, we can see why, in migrations and other mobilizations in the modern world, the link is important. Agamben argues that we are not so determined by language, that we are not born into it, that it does not so shape or control us. Linguists base their work on the simple *factum loquendi*, the fact that people speak to and understand one another, a fact that remains inaccessible to science. In an essay entitled "Languages and Peoples," he points out the intimate connection that has been made by historians between slang and gypsies in Europe (and between slang words in many countries and the gypsy language rom): "just as slang isn't properly speaking a language, but a jargon, so the Gypsies are not a people, but the last descendants of a class of out-laws from another era."[21] But on a closer look we can understand that all languages, he argues, are essentially slang spoken by a group that is in its own way a kind of gypsy band. He writes that "essentially we don't have the least idea of what is a people nor what is a language."[22] And our task is not to construct grammars of these slangs nor to recodify people into nation-identities but rather to "break at some point the chain: existence-of-a-language-grammar (tongue)-people-State. . . ."[23] For Agamben, it is as if every language is already an exile, not a homeland—or rather, a mobile homeland.

In "Notes on Gesture," Agamben wonders what happens when a culture loses its gestures. He considers the example of the bourgeoisie at the end of the nineteenth century, losing its masterful grip on its gestural code and succumbing to interiority, psychology, and cinema.[24] Agamben sees a culture's gestures as a crucial part of its political and intellectual, or philosophical, identity. Gesture is a language that is a "means" without an end, and it shows the character of our being-in-language that Agamben believes is also our political state.

Agamben writes:

What characterizes gesture is that it is no longer a question of producing or doing something, but of taking something on and getting on with it ("*assumer et supporter*"). In other words, gesture opens up the sphere of ethos (ethics) as the sphere where humans belong. . . . If dance is a gesture, it is . . . because it consists entirely of shoring up and showing the medial character of corporal movements. Gesture consists in exhibiting a médialité, in making visible the means, as what they are.[25]

Opposing those who think of dance as an aesthetic gesture with its end in itself, Agamben argues that it illustrates not an end in itself but simply the means: "like mime in which the gestures subordinated to the most familiar ends are exhibited as such and held there in suspense 'between desire and accomplishment, perpetration and memory' in what Mallarme calls a 'milieu pur': in the same way, in gesture, it is a sphere not of an end in itself but of a pure médialité without end that opens up for humans."[26]

Mallarme's famous text on the mime ("Mimique") and Derrida's reading of it in "La Double Séance" (in *Dissemination*) are important here, but Agamben takes the discussion to a somewhat different conclusion. It is not that language eternally defers its meaning or differs from meaning (as does *écriture*), but that there is an essential *mutisme* or aporia on which philosophy rests that is acted out by the mime and by the cinema:

> [G]esture has nothing to say because what it shows is human being-in-language as pure *medialité*. But since being-in-language is not something that can be announced in propositions, gesture is in its essence always a gesture of not finding oneself in language, always a "gag" in the full meaning of the term, which in its dictionary definition is what one puts in the mouth to block speech, and then becomes what the actor improvises to fill a memory gap or the impossibility of speaking. Thus the proximity not only between gesture and philosophy but between philosophy and cinema. The essential "muteness" of cinema (which has nothing to do with the presence or absence of sound), like the muteness of philosophy, is an exposition of human being-in-language: pure gestuality.... Every great philosophical text is the gag that language itself exhibits, being-in-language itself as a huge memory gap or incurable failure of speech.[27]

It is not a question here of lacking the precise words, but of language itself as a short circuit of communication. Like Cixous, though in a different way, Agamben would argue that it's not that we don't have the words, but that we don't have the body, to say—not because we are born into language, but because, from his perspective, we are a culture that has lost its gestures.

Agamben concludes these notes on the gesture: "Politics is the sphere of pure means; in other words, of the absolute, integral gestuality of humans."[28] Here, then, are at least two options: to see dancing as similar to language, organizing and rooting social and political identity, or to understand linguistic and political existence, like gesture, as a means without an end. In both of these perspectives, we do not need to oppose politics or language to dance; and we can understand not simply that dance is political (that it can have a political content) but that linguistic and political identity can be understood as profoundly gestural, even choreographic. Agamben's perspective is an alternative to the idea of a residual bodily "truth" in gesture discussed in chapters 1 and 2 in theories of embodied agency such as Judith Butler's. Yiphun Chiem's dancing, along with the Cambodian Royal Ballet's, challenges the idea of "lost" gestures through their reanimation of Cambodian classical dance.

Yiphun Chiem's *Apsara*, named for the dancing goddesses in classical Cambodian cosmology, revives some of the sequences from the traditional dances while recontextualizing them in a performance piece commenting on the genocide, on Cambodian identity in European exile, and on the hip hop generation seeking a universal code of assimilation or integration.

Yiphun clearly separates the two geographical components of her culture—her Cambodian roots and her European formation—and imagines herself spanning them as two people; in her dancing, she says, she is most able to move between them. Her dance vocabulary, in this piece, is both "Cambodian" (the gestures and steps from the traditional forms she learned in exile in Belgium) and "French" (i.e., the contemporary urban dance that is described as "francophone" but that is clearly, for Yiphun, a global dance form). Across the sections of this dance, Yiphun's moves refer to Asian forms, martial arts, video games, and US break dance and invent new twists and spins on the classic six-step and other floor work. In her opening sequence, hand gestures and steps from Cambodian dance are woven into movements on the floor, spinning and kicking with a quickness and a fluidity, hair and skirt flying in the wind, that make it seem as if we are seeing her image through a scrim or blurred on a screen. (See Figure 5.1)

Yiphun describes the last thirty years of Cambodia's history as enraging; her motivation for dancing (at least in this choreography) is this rage, which she speaks about with tears in her eyes but represents onstage symbolically with both a certain *sang froid* and a tremendous humanist (rather than simply personal) empathy. Yiphun's "rage for dancing" is both a political, contestatory performance and the breaker's drive to show off interesting, inventive moves, to be the fastest or the coolest, in the competitive atmosphere of battles and "high performance" matches or showcases. She describes learning how to break dance at age twenty, seeing and imitating dancers in Brussels, and then training for six months until they declared her ready to tour with them. Yet as she performs them, these are more than "power moves," adding nuances of culture, race, gender, and performance traditions. In Europe, break dancing remains male territory, and in France and Belgium the majority of hip hop dancers are of African and North African origin. Yiphun came to hip hop with only her training in

Figure 5.1
Yiphun Chiem, *Apsara* (2007).
Photo Credit: Carlos Casanova, Dies Da Danza Festival, Barcelona, 2007.

Cambodian classical dance but acquired the movement language of the breakers and invented her own language within the form, a recognizable style, very quickly.

One section of *Apsara* recounts, with humor and insight, the transformation of its female performer—wearing a dress and dancing as a female goddess—into a masculine, macho hip hopper. Using the audience as her mirror, Yiphun dons the baggy clothes, track suit, and backward baseball cap and perfectly mimes the swagger and loose gestures of her generation of dancers. Gently mocking the studied nonchalance of this world, this section also allows Yiphun to mock her own conversion to hip hop, as she pretends to check every look and every move in the mirror and flops as she practices her first break dance moves. In this section, we see not only the ambition of a young adult discovering hip hop and wanting to belong to the *mouv'* but also the universal and very specific desire of immigrants to disappear into the dominant culture—even one that has been seen as a counterculture. The hip hopper who stares back at us as if we are the mirror loses her Cambodian identity and assumes the identity of all migrants signing up for a global cultural identity. Yiphun's scenario here shows that one way for youths to integrate after emigrating is to lock into the global circulation of certain images.

But in the section just preceding this, Yiphun recounts the Cambodian genocide from which her family fled when she was a small child. The episode is framed by the arrival of Yiphun holding a chair in front of her. She speaks two lines to the audience, with a voice quiet but full of emotion: "Bonjour, je m'appelle Yiphun, et je voudrais vous raconter mon histoire." She sets the chair down in front of her, downstage, and sits in it. But the story then pours out in gestures rather than words, and the telling is masterful, not hesitant as the few spoken words were. In this gestural language, Yiphun manages to show the great sweep of the war in her country, the absolute cruelty of the genocide; in a repeated gesture, the dancer shows the unflinching terror imposed by the executioners on people of all ages— women, children—and the breadth of the destruction. Without varying the pace or the gesture, she shows both individual slaughter and the historic dimensions of the genocide. In an interview with me, she mentions that there is a word, in Cambodian, for this killing, and that her family, for example, uses this word specifically to describe the genocide they fled.[29]

Interjected into this story of political terror, imprisonment and execution, and fear and flight are several precise moves from the vocabulary of the Cambodian dances we have seen the dancer performing in the opening sequence of the piece. The fingers appear to hold and pluck a flower. They insist on the specificity of this flower or this moment; they create a spark, marking a precise moment in time and space—that is the specificity of Cambodian culture. As the dancer repeats this gesture, its very precision overwhelms its ambiguity, its meaning; even if we do not know the gesture or speak the language, we understand very well what is being marked here.

While it is tempting to see spoken lines onstage as rehearsed or repeated and thus somehow false or "staged" (regardless of the quality of their performance), even rehearsed and repeated gestures, in this case, suggest that language's impasse has been resolved; these gestures seem somehow truer to experience, closer to a lived bodily truth—because they do not use words. Yiphun's request to tell her story, pronounced and then allowing her to fall silent, suggests that only *without* words can this story be told, that the tragedy is in some ways beyond words, beyond speaking. The symbolic value of the gestures, and the dance that frames them, suggests the effect of the genocide on this particular witness and its retelling in this symbolic language as profoundly cathartic.

The section of the girl's transformation into a hip hopper, following after this horrifying sequence of storytelling, can now better be understood: as providing necessary comic relief to the tragedy of the catharsis, and also chronologically following the family's flight from Cambodia to Europe. It allows us to see the young hip hopper channeling the rage following the genocide, deflecting the anger into creative energy in a dance that is itself warriorlike, that adapts pugilistic moves into dances. Yiphun talks about shedding femininity in this dance, as opposed to the Cambodian dance, which is a definition of the feminine. In the macho stance of the young, androgynous break dancer, all the world's problems are being taken on and all manner of battles are being fought—not simply the search for an immigrant identity.

While representing what happened in another time and place, at the limit of the dancer's memory and yet permeating her family's daily life, this dance also suggests the rage that nothing can be done about such world events. The means of global communication make it possible to remain in contact with the living but can do little for the dying. The sensory overload of global information—pictures and testimonials made available on the Internet, rapidly and widely circulating—needs its own form of catharsis to address the cognitive overflow syndrome that has developed in response to it. Even King Sihanouk, in 2004, announced his abdication (for a second time) online.[30]

Yiphun Chiem's *Apsara* breaks down superficial barriers between classical and new forms, between new technologies and traditions, between live performance and recordings. In this sense it is of its time—it could not have been possible twenty years before—and it speaks in the language coinage of its time, the global vernacular of hip hop. Yiphun continues Cambodian history, at a distance, by modernizing it and by representing what it is to be Cambodian today, not for all time, and in Europe, in French. Significantly the birth, in 2009, of her second child is not keeping her from training and touring. Passing on life and dance, in the diaspora, are not incompatible.

For Yiphun, performing live and performing on YouTube are also not incompatible. Her MySpace page contains information about her upcoming shows, her blog, a full profile/history, pictures, videos, and a link to a review article. Her private Facebook page contains images of her on tour and with friends and family. Combining her training in Cambodian classical dance with her passion for hip hop, Yiphun has moved on to next-generation technology, posting and watching moves on the Internet.

In these two examples of Cambodian classical dancers using French film, after the fact, for the reconstruction of their cultural heritage and French-francophone hip hoppers using archived images not simply to reconstruct but to elaborate a new form, we see dance forms intimately linked to technologies, a dissolution of the categories of local and global forms, traditional and new forms, and even the private lives and public performances of dancers. The fact that technology gives another life to choreography, and brings it "back to live" via the archive, demonstrates that it serves to re-create rather than simply destroy live performance. It deserves a greater place in our theorization of the relations between the "first" and "third" worlds; it offers a model of greater complexity in technology transfer and transculturation. In this way, imaging technologies, like the French language, somewhat ironically facilitate the survival of "francophone" cultural forms, not only offering a "market" for those ready to exploit it, but also offering an opportunity for continued existence and circulation. Technologies accessed via francophonies extend local, threatened, or restricted performances into global performances, preserving something of the original even while mediatizing them, preserving gestures via the same technologies that also—globally—erase them.

CHAPTER 6

Techniques

French Urban Dance in Intellectual Context

The opening chapter of this book sketched the history of the *politique culturelle* responsible for the unique situation of hip hop in France and in the European Union. In this final chapter, I consider the theories of culture that made possible a ministerial valorization of hip hop as an art practice, as pedagogy, and as popular culture worthy of the national stages. Beyond the funding—or before it—what made possible this positive view of hip hop and its choreographic elaboration? This chapter reads several key French texts in the theory of practice, broadly studied in France and now canonical, that prepared the way for thinking about hip hop dance as more than imitative of US culture and for seeing it as a creative space of representation.

MIMESIS, "HIGH" AND "LOW"

At the intersection of global culture and local realities, the art of hip hop dance could be seen as doubly mimetic: imitating everyday life or televisual or video images and expanding on an imitative global youth culture, influenced by first-world consumerism and media as much as by its critique in urban countercultures around the globe. An art of the age of mechanical reproduction—or postmechanical, virtual reproducibility—its gestures parody machines as robots, time clocks and TV, splicing and fragments, instant replays and photo finishes. Elaborated and coded, they are then diffused by the very media they mock. In the United States, as discussed in chapter 2, this double mimetism made hip hop the target of a right-wing critique focusing on rap music: condemning it as not realist but imitative, vulgar, or extremist; not community based, but linked to gang behaviors and ghetto violence; not reflecting the residue of centuries of racism but racist in itself. As has been pointed out, this critique has been promulgated by the conservative Right even as large-scale corporations market hip hop music, clothing, and culture to a young middle-class audience, those who can afford its products.[1] Contemporary critics trace mimetic exchanges now in the circulation of persons, goods, and ideas in the global culture of immigration and mediatization, and in patterns established during colonialism, continued during ethnographic encounter, and currently reinforced via the omnipresent screens of global media and transnational capital.[2] This book has suggested that within this generational global circulation, French hip hop dance remained something of an exception. This chapter explores hip hop's imitative pull and its global reach within the specific intellectual background that accorded agency rather than mindless mimicry to its dancers, that helped make it possible to respect their practice as constitutive of community rather than destructive, and as an inclusive response to their exclusion.

In France, hip hop is a *forme populaire*: meaning not only "popular" in the English sense but also *working class*, "of the people." The chapters of this book sketch how the form has been championed by Socialist cultural ministers and left-wing groups because of its multicultural American, neighborhood community and minority origins, as it has been, in France, danced by minority populations mostly from the African and North African diasporas. But if its success as an art form reaching the "national stages" in France is in part due to a political strategy openly referred to as "recuperation," it is also dependent upon an intellectual climate that permits a view of dance as something other than counterculture or as positive cultural production through contestation. While hip hop in France poses questions about the representation and representability of class and color, it also responds to questions asked by theorists about the role of the body in everyday practice, bodily identity, and the possibility of bodily signification of the unconscious. Dance has participated in discussions shifting the definition of "culture" over to practice, to a focus on the "everyday" or popular forms of "what people do" led by the work of Pierre Bourdieu, Michel de Certeau, and others.

In the history of the plastic and performing arts, ranging from high to low, admirable to negligible, clever to copycat, imitation has been seen as both an art and art's enemy. In the performing arts, imitation is as often praised as it is critiqued: a performer's representation may move audiences with its realism or amuse with a parodic copy. From Plato and Aristotle to the present, mimesis has been understood in the Western theatrical tradition as both crucial to performance art and a dangerous talent: responsible for the emotional lure of the theatrical illusion, the actor's "lie" in playing someone who is not himself, the "contagion" that is imitation.[3]

Surrounded by the rhetoric of romanticism or modernism, discourses of individual expression and invention, of originality and abstraction, dance forms performed onstage are not always associated with the mimesis of the stage: most modern dance forms moved away from ballet's narratives and toward abstraction. Yet for Walter Benjamin dance was the example par excellence of the "mimetic faculty," an imitative art, like child's play, and similarly disconnected from a necessarily human content: the child's imitation of a windmill or train (an abstraction, like a dancer's) is as mimetic as ancient dance's cultic imitations of astrological wonders.[4] Benjamin historicizes the "mimetic faculty" informing most of our "higher functions," emphasizing that it changes over time: "neither mimetic powers nor mimetic objects remain the same in the course of thousands of years." His history of mimesis, then, charts a shift away from dance— away from "reading what was never written, such as stars or dances"—and toward reading what is written. In this draining away of the magic powers from earlier forms of mimetic production and comprehension, language use becomes the highest level of mimetic behavior, fusing semiotic and mimetic elements. In print culture, dance isn't what it used to be: though its ritual or traditional forms may refer to its old mimetic magic, which Barbara Browning sees as one option for the capoiera circle in contemporary Brazil;[5] I have argued that forms such as ballet or early modern dance can be seen as reflecting a new status for gesture in industrial modernity: as an excessive gesture expressing somatically—wordlessly—resembling the symptom in pathology or as a minimum gesture expressing mechanically, both imitating and inspiring the choreographing of labor by scientific management. Hip hop dance, while far removed from the domains of medicine or industry, arguably does both: miming and mocking the machinery of industrial production and of the televised image, our culture's sickness, as well as its pathological productivity.

If we are interested, still, in mimesis, it must be because of its perceived dangers: threatening the enduring modernist (and romantic) myth of the artist's originality; threatening the release of representation from imitation, as explored in the work of Philippe Lacoue-Labarthe;[6] threatening the idea of individual freedom of expression and desire, as sketched out in the work of René Girard; threatening the idea of an "original," as well as originality itself. If anthropologists, ethnographers, and literary theorists have emphasized that humans are ultimately imitative beings, modern art theory has more than once pronounced mimesis "dead."[7] Against the formalist and abstract arts of twentieth-century modernism, those arts of popular culture that stage everyday life, whose performances are integrated into everyday practices and whose culture is part of the street and the stage, are representational, or "mimetic," in what has often been seen as a negative sense. The contemporary arts of hip hop, including hip hop dance, have fallen into this category.

The first two chapters of this book outlined French hip hop's most significant difference from the United States in its adoption by state agencies, cultural actors, and the *Maisons de jeunes et de la culture* across France where it was promoted as a way to channel creative energy within the populations of the ZUP (*zones d'urbanisation prioritaire*). Hip hop, from early days in France, was seen as a pedagogy: something to be taught to young people, a challenge to be taken on by them and a battle to be fought in a cultural arena. While at the beginning, this dance form represented everything that was not French (ways of moving, styles of living, musical rhythms, etc.)—but also represented the sort of cultural product that French artists and publics admire and absorb—it became French through the work of ethnically diverse dancers, as the chapters of this book have described, and also through their recruitment into a pedagogical and art establishment. But it also became French or *francophone* through the operation of a cultural-intellectual elite giving credit to dancers' cultural work and establishing a theoretical foundation for it and, perhaps most significantly, a forum in which to talk about it, as a historic and semiotic form of expression more complex than its appearance. The French *sciences humaines* of the last half century have located dance both close to culture and close to technology, to the very idea of *techne*, body techniques or embodied knowledge. From the mid-1960s into the 1990s, for theorists who are not necessarily writing about dance but who are nevertheless thinking about it, dance provides a link to the past as far back as prehistorians can trace and a model for a cyber future, as a bodily practice manifesting a form of technique. Marcel Mauss's 1935 essay "The Techniques of the Body," in which he identifies cultural and national learned movement styles, was foundational for the works I will explore here: describing the "habitus" of bodies with a triple analysis—biological (also described as mechanical/physical), sociological, and psychological—to understand the "total man."[8] Through the development of sociological studies of bodily practice, influenced by and influencing philosophy, a corpus of now-canonical work has made it possible for students in many disciplines to look at dance differently and for culture ministers to argue for the importance of learning to spin on one's head as a civic activity.

While the three French thinkers—André Leroi-Gourhan, Michel de Certeau, and Pierre Bourdieu—discussed in this chapter might seem somewhat disconnected from the hip hop material that is my focus in this book, their work participated in an intellectual climate in which even intellectuals not writing about dance per se can be seen thinking through its questions in their discussions of practice. There have been, of course, many other theorists whose writings are closer to the question of bodily technique and discipline, invoked often in contemporary dance theory or performance studies, and elsewhere I have emphasized the importance of works by Foucault and other French historians considering intellectual and material histories of bodies. Here I am focusing on those whose work has made it possible to imagine culture as practice, or more specifically, to see bodily practices as culture—not simply in traditional ethnographic terrain, but also in modern big cities, and not only as a nonverbal or pre-verbal form, but closely in sync with speech, writing, and new technologies. Leroi-Gourhan assumes a very early starting point and a long development of dance as performance; de Certeau and Bourdieu flesh out the individual and community development of these practices in transmission and pedagogy. I am focusing on works published in French that would have been read by those who would come to constitute the bourgeois audience for hip hop, facilitating its development from the near ritual of the "battle" into a form of concert dance. All three of these authors, publishing in French, were part of the curriculum in the French context before becoming canonical texts in anthropology, sociology, or theory programs around the world. While there is much to be drawn from their work on the history of culture, on the individual's relation to the state or power hierarchies, and on modern urban life, this chapter will focus specifically on texts that link techniques or *techne* to bodies.

It is significant for my study that paleontologists working on primitive humans do not identify dance as a "primitive" form but as a highly technical one, elaborated with tool use and language and not separate from it; similarly, sociologists do not identify dance as a nonlinguistic or illiterate art form, but one close to language and writing. While acknowledging the role that class plays in this popular form, sociology, for example, can give us a framework for understanding even popular forms of dance in terms of bodily practices that are "savant" or knowing, rather than the opposite of forms seen as professional or highly technical such as ballet.[9] Dance like hip hop can be seen as simultaneously carnival-esque and as deeply disciplined, requiring the mastery of movement technique. A historical perspective allows us to see hip hop developing as modern dance did in France, also from an arguably American model, and with help from state funding, choreographic subventions, and unemployment compensation for artists with the status of *intermittent du spectacle,* remaining a central cultural product.

While these theoretical texts do not reflect the same kind of *politique culturelle,* "recuperating" cultural products or cultural actors, they also helped create the climate that facilitated the institutionalization of hip hop in France, that made it possible for ministers of culture to see dancing like a robot or a crab as culture and—eventually—as art. Given the climate surrounding hip hop events with state funding, the official "discourse" of hip hop (to use Foucault's term) makes more sense when considered in context with these other discourses, which define dance as a technique, both high tech and literate, a bodily practice producing complex self-expression in a highly articulate yet alternate mode, created by bodily discipline and anti-disciplinary at the same time.

FROM PREHISTORY TO *EPSILON*

In his classic study *Le Geste et la parole* published in 1964, prehistorian and ethnologist André Leroi-Gourhan speculated that the cybernetic age would change the human bodies that have remained essentially the same for forty thousand years. Following on the hybrid machine and the Taylorization of gesture, the *déculturation technique* of the assembly line, Leroi-Gourhan wondered about the slow evolution, in tandem with technologies permitting sitting and button pushing, of something other than *Homo sapiens.* There had already been, he noted, certain irreversible changes (*sans retour*) linked to technology and *planétarisation* that humans would accommodate and elaborate in the next century; he wondered in particular about the influence of the media and the consumption of what we would now call "new media": "Curiously enough, we can wonder if audio-visual technologies really do change the traditional behavior of *anthropiens.*"[10]

Arguably, bodies or their practices do change; the developments of the most recent technologies follow in the wake of relations between tools and bodies that began in human prehistory. But what difference does it make—historically—how people stood or sat, or their bodily comportment in different situations in, for example, *belle époque* France? Can daily gestures, stylized or simple, restore some lost piece of economic history or class relations? Does reviving these lost gestures restore some importance to the people who performed them that is rightly theirs, that the greater strokes of historiography have minimized or marginalized?

In the last half century, many disciplines across the humanities and social sciences, the *sciences humaines*, have been attempting to trace the everyday gesture in history, anthropology, literature, and ethnography. In addition to iconography, it is often literature that has archived these gestures in their psychological, social, and historical contexts for us, and it can be an idea from science as often as social etiquette that shapes how bodies are educated or how they are seen to signify.

For historian Alain Corbin, after a period of rigorous remodeling of bodies, the *attitudes imposées* on school children, pensioners, soldiers, prisoners, and workers in the *belle epoque* manifested a great desire for the liberation of bodies (of course, with class differences).[11] Physical education shifted from a concept of *modelage* or molding bodies to an emphasis on training that for Corbin, as for Georges Vigarello—historians who have focused on the French history of the body and its training—is linked to thermodynamics and the idea of the motor: "During the first half of the century, mechanics, and then after 1850, the model of thermodynamic energy made images of bodies evolve. The body appeared to be a network of forces, then a motor: the important thing is no longer to mold it, but to train it."[12]

In this history in France, as I have tried to show, dancers play a major part. Corbin identifies the new thermodynamic conception of the body within the French reception of Americana dancer Isadora Duncan, Isadora as representative of a new idea: "the experience of a body that we no longer perceive as external to ourselves."[13] As I discussed in *Dancing Machines*, Isadora herself used the vocabulary of thermodynamics and confessed to reading and admiring biologists of her time. Now in a culture of global information, thought to have put bodies into new virtual realities and to have ended work, we are following the prehistorians and the historians imagining new conceptions, experiences, and perceptions of bodies.

Yet in spite of the changes brought to bodies by technologies, which must be historicized and theorized, Leroi-Gourhan emphasizes how little the human body has changed since prehistory. The human adventure has been a long slow slog toward an upright spine, a hand freed by an upright stance, and speech made possible by the hand freeing the mouth from its sole occupation with food. In Leroi-Gourhan's crystalline formulation, humanity begins at our feet: "l'humanisation commence par les pieds."[14] Standing upright constitutes the major stakes of humanity; in this balance that is unique to humans, the freed hand makes possible both the use of tools and language, "le geste et la parole," instrumentation and social relation, technology and speech. Central to this conception of *Homo sapiens* is of course not only the feet but also the brain, whose development is also made possible by the upright stance. Yet for Leroi-Gourhan, much of what makes us human was in place long before the brain developed to its current state, a development still in process. Rather than opposing cerebral and motor functions, the brain and the hand, paleontology sees them in parallel: "The two poles of creative activity, the face and the hand, in language and technique" ("Les deux pôles de l'activité créatrice, la face et la main, dans la technique et le langage").[15]

Le Geste et la parole emphasizes that human bodies have been recognizable for roughly forty thousand years and have remained more or less unchanged across the rise of civilizations, even into the electronic age: "the entire history of the rise of civilizations was accomplished by the same physical and intellectual human who hunted the mammoth and our electronic culture, barely fifty years old, is built on a physiological apparatus that is forty thousand years old."[16] For Leroi-Gourhan, it is not just the brain but all the human characteristics created by the upright stance—the hand using tools, the mouth using language, the senses developing an aesthetic—that constitute the starting point for a humanism insisting on the universality of human thought across temporal and geographic divides; while respecting cultural and historical differences, he emphasizes a (zoological and paleontological) "equivalence of human thoughts."[17]

Against the background of this prehistoric bodily humanity, and the universality and stability of the human body over the long haul, the other "universal languages" fall into place: a zoological or paleontological unity of human thought over millennia and around the globe, the broad presence of human language as a common language linked to human bodiliness, and the universality of the discourse in which it is studied, the discourse of science. The universality of the human body, crucial to a reflection on the origins and evolution of a shared humanity, has an echo in the natural and human sciences that have studied it: just as there is one science, there is one body for all the world's peoples, even though it is the task of the so-called human sciences to explore its many expressions and variations.

What does it mean to sit down at the computer with a body more or less unchanged from those early humans who hunted the woolly mammoth? Are we still driven by the same bodily needs, hunger, and fatigue? For Leroi-Gourhan, the computer is just one more step in the long "externalization" of our gestures taken over by specialization or mechanization, in particular in relation to the practices of the arts. There must be, he argues, intermediate steps in the evolution of human practices from survival to the creation of "rhythmic" art forms to their consumption, in the elaboration of aesthetics from eating to dancing to watching dance in a theater: "from the full stomach to the beautiful tool, to dancing to music, to dance spectatorship in the theatre, there would be the same phenomenon of externalization" ("de la satisfaction digestive au bel outil, à la musique dansée, à la danse regardée dans un fauteuil, il y aurait le même phénomène d'exteriorisation").[18]

And rather than opposing language and action, speech and motor locomotion, or even figuration, he sees them flowing from these same biological and zoological sources: "Given what we know about the make-up of humans...figuration takes the same paths as technique and language; the body and the hand, the eye and the ear. What we distinguish as dance, mime, theater, music, visual and plastic arts comes thus from the same source as the other manifestations."[19]

Relying on paleontological evidence as well as ethnography (with a brief nod to psychoanalysis), Leroi-Gourhan links technology to the arts via the concept of "rhythm," a repeated and thus patterned marking; for dance and music there is little material evidence, but much inspiration from both the biological and the ethnological findings. Rather than opposing speech and movement (or imagining, as De Certeau does in performance art such as opera, sounds "irreducible to meaning"), Leroi-Gourhan argues that the arts come from the same sources as technology and language: "Tool, language and rhythmic creation are consequently three contiguous aspects of the same process;"[20] the roots of language and rhythm (*comportement figuratif* including dance as "figuration motrice"), he argues, go as deep as those of technology.[21] This view from prehistory, via biology and ethnology, reveals a fundamental unity of gesture and speech, even in the arts: "the inseparable character of motor activity (whose most perfect agent is the hand) and verbal activity."[22] The body biological—and thus universal—shared by humankind for tens of thousands of years constitutes a human bodily archive ("fonds corporel de l'humanité") and the corporeal foundation of art and of values: "les fondements corporels des valeurs et des rythmes."[23]

Leroi-Gourhan's extraordinary summary of tens of thousands of years of prehistory, as well as the scientific history of the past few centuries, makes the human adventure into a seamless choreography, described as a series of "liberations": the upright stance frees the hand to become the organ of relation; this hand then frees the mouth and face for language, the brain for thought ("la main qui libère la parole"); technologies have freed us—not unproblematically—from certain duties of *Homo sapiens*.

But is this hand really free? Parallel to the *histoires des techniques* or histories of the body inspired by Foucault, Corbin, and Vigarello that detail the rigorous and specific forms of training developed over the course of the past centuries, Leroi-Gourhan speaks of much earlier "chaines opératoires machinales"—series of gestures of survival inculcated in the body even as its operations are externalized. Neither automatic, unconscious, nor purely instinctual, these are the gestures of daily life that even in modernity are not entirely reinvented each day, yet reveal a high level of "disponibilité cérébrale"—they do not require complete lucidity but cannot operate without it either.[24] If, for Leroi-Gourhan, the body "knows" or its gestures reveal what it knows, it is not only in the "rhythmic" processes but also in these sequences that he traces back over human history.

Such gestures get codified as professional or social only much later and are transmitted through families and institutions. In a process of externalizing our functions into technology, a certain "manual regression" takes place, for example, in the "déculturation technique" of assembly-line work and eventually in white-collar work that requires no hands-on knowledge in a "technicité démanualisée."[25] For Leroi-Gourhan, the emphasis is not on the tool, but on movement: the tool only exists in the gesture that makes it useful.[26] If the tool gets separated from the hand, externalized in a machine, as the word is separate from the object, he argues, it is part of the same detachment that allows humans symbolic formations, a detachment permitting self-scrutiny. Now, with the "externalization" of even higher human functions into thinking machines, another "manual regression" presents itself, possibly freeing us (some of us) from the depersonalizing work of globalized industry.[27] While wondering what changes will be brought—were already being brought—by "audio-visual" technologies in the 1960s, with the likely disappearance of writing into visual popular media, Leroi-Gourhan wonders if new technologies might constitute a "regression manuelle" that is a "new liberation" ("nouvelle 'libération'"—with 'libération' in quotes) or rather a "transposition of the technical field" ("transposition du champ technique") where the power of those who do not work with their hands is guaranteed (often through their access to and mastery of writing).[28] In this regard, he deems it necessary to imagine a *Homo sapiens* "complètement transposé;" he suggests that in the next century humans may look for a new label to attach to "homo" rather than "sapiens," as we spontaneously seek the equilibrium that made us human in the first place.[29]

In *Agency and Embodiment: Performing Gestures/Producing Culture,* Carrie Noland has also found in Leroi-Gourhan's volumes a key to understanding the history of gesture as well as the practice and theory of kinesthetic experience, "the somatic attention accorded to the lived sensation of movement, that allows the subject to become an agent in the making of herself."[30] Under the rubric of "gesture," the book studies many kinds of movement, performances, acts, and behaviors, arguing that "it is specifically through gesturing that human beings embody culture while simultaneously submitting it to transformative variation." The book's major intervention is in the history of the disciplines, the context of the elaboration of poststructuralism in the French *sciences humaines*, and the availability of such problems as bodily knowledge (agency and embodiment) to a range of disciplinary explorations. Its project is to recall the significance of the work of Mauss and Leroi-Gourhan on bodily knowledge and techniques to a generation of critics who don't see them as foundational; they are described as its two pillars—with, to a lesser extent, Merleau-Ponty. On a second tier, the book addresses current theory debates on poststructuralist bodily identity, questions raised by concepts of virtuality and gender, posed via performance and technology (new media) studies.

In some ways, then, this adventure of life-in-bodies has irrevocably changed. While bodies have barely changed in terms of phyletic evolution, in terms of what Leroi-Gourhan calls our "ethnic" evolution, the externalization of many of our capacities in machines was already, in 1964, recognized for its rapid global spread.[31] While imagining a future at least as long as humans' past, this long-standing human physiological structure, which in turn shapes human social structure, may yet be inflected, Leroi-Gourhan imagines, by new technologies, especially those externalizing the brain's capacity for counting, judging, and reasoning. Against the background of a long-stable physical structure, for this paleo-historian, the pivotal moment will be this century. Something major in the history of bodies is about to happen—is happening already.

E = *EPSILON*

Compagnie Choream's 2001 choreography *Epsilon*, discussed in chapter 4, seems a perfect illustration of Leroi-Gourhan's paleo-history and predictions about techno-theory. Tracing the concept of time from the primeval sludge to the punch clock, from animals to the beating of the human heart, the piece explores how time shaped humans and how, drastically, humans have shaped time. What Leroi-Gourhan calls "externalization," however, the building up of machines with human skills, is also traced in the piece via a particular "internalization" of mechanisms into human bodies. When Stéphanie Nataf dances, in a particular sequence with a tape loop repeating the words "work, work!" (illustrating the frenzy of time equals money), it is hard to say if the movement represents the body turned into an automaton or the anthropomorphic convulsions of the machine itself.

Leroi-Gourhan's reading of the history of the human body gives us a structure for imagining it not simply embodying knowledge but putting it into action, and understanding bodies not so much as loci of knowledge—embedded or embodied *techne*—but as vehicles: mobilizing the tool in the gesture, in the same way that language will mobilize objects. Locating language use with tool use, technology and expression, together, Leroi-Gourhan suggests a different approach to the question of dance's "primitiveness." While dancing is ancient, it is far from an undeveloped form of expression; rather, with the other "rhythmic" forms, it is figural movement (*motricité figurative*), collaborating with technology and language from human origins rather than opposing them.

For Leroi-Gourhan, the challenge is to find an intermediate stage, for practices such as dance, from these *chaines opératoires* to the development of an aesthetic, following the elaboration of tools into machines and speech into writing—to find for dance, for example, the transition from participatory danced rituals to the appreciation of concert dance onstage:

> We can adopt the hypothesis that, just as technique and language are two aspects of the same phenomenon, the aesthetic might be a third. In this case, there would be a guiding thread; if the tool and the word moved toward the machine and toward writing by the same steps and almost synchronously, the same phenomenon must have been produced for the aesthetic: from eating one's fill to the beautiful tool, to music that is danced to, to dance watched from a theater seat, there would be the same phenomenon of externalization. We should locate, in history, the aesthetic phases comparable to the passage from the myth to writing and from the manual tool to the automatic machine, an "artisanal" or "preindustrial" period of the aesthetic in which the arts, a social aesthetic, and technical mastery would have attained the maximum individual absorption, then a threshold of specialization marked by the disproportion between producers of aesthetic matter and the ever-growing mass of consumers of pre-made or pre-imagined art.[32]

Once participatory forms such as dance are elaborated as aesthetic forms, they have a common architecture and individual variation: "In figural practices such as music, dance, poetry or plastic art a clear separation is produced between the general pool of material and the individual variations"—individuals can develop their own style without changing the fundamental architecture of the form.[33] Yet in spite of what is called dance "technique"—institutionalized, professionalized, and transmitted—dance continues to be considered an "illiterate" form. It takes seeing dance as a figural language and a bodily poetics—as well as a technique—to understand it as a form of knowledge close to the "literate," as Leroi-Gourhan liberates it as a form of rhythmic expression close to both *techne* and *poesis*.

WHERE BODIES KNOW

The later history of Leroi-Gourhan's *chaines opératoires* movement sequences is traced in the intermediate terrain of socialization and institutionalization under the rubric of what de Certeau calls *les arts de faire*. For de Certeau, these are localizable, analyzable practices, knowledge located in the body. As the practice of a kind of nonwritten, nondiscursive knowledge—the locus of a bodily knowledge that recalls the marking gestures of writing, graffiti—gesture reveals a certain *savoir-faire* and models a certain way of knowing that de Certeau reads as operating another version of the condensation and displacement that is the dream work and then poetics of metaphoric displacement. Gesture is itself *techne* as well as poetics, establishing the embodiedness of knowledge and situatedness of knowing.

The many disciplines devoted to the theory and study of gesture consider it not only as a discourse, nor as a picture—fixed or moving—but as practice. In the French text, de Certeau frequently uses the word *danse* or *danseur* to describe all kinds of practices: the graffiti in New York marking territory are "graphes danseurs" of an urban "practice" of space; there is a homology between verbal figures (rhetoric) and the figures of walking or using urban space, also already stylized, says de Certeau, in dance figures.[34] This metamorphosis of space, "styling" space, takes shape as gestures.

Similarly for de Certeau, a popular oral literature, voices of the people, mostly silenced by a modern economy focused on writing, can be found circulating there, "danseuses et passantes, dans le champ de l'autre."[35] In the same way, reading practices, far from showing passive consumers, reveal "danses ephémères", a "danse entre lecteurs et textes" that suggests active reader reception, the inseparability of texts from their reading and readers.[36] De Certeau rarely focuses on dance itself, except in one or two historical contexts of authors themselves using dance as a metaphor for a certain kind of knowledge in practice: Kant, on the cord dancer in *Kritik der Urteilskraft*, and the ancient Greeks analyzed by Marcel Detienne and Jean-Pierre Vernant in *Les Ruses de l'intelligence*; and he does not explain what exactly is dancelike in these practices, which he often refers to as "silent" and "knowing," never elite or elitist and always popular. Without saying it explicitly, his text emphasizes that dancing models the bodily knowledge of its time, the "where" people know. But explaining a practice, in particular a historical one, requires not simply a description; it requires entering "into the dance." For de Certeau the theory of practice is itself an invitation to "dance" those practices.[37]

In his analysis of everyday practices, *arts de faire,* and their theorization, de Certeau situates his own work vis à vis that of his contemporaries Foucault and Bourdieu, as well as historians Detienne and Vernant. For de Certeau, such practices are significantly language-less ("silencieux" as in "ruses silencieuses"), because in his practices, "l'homme ordinaire se soustrait en silence"; these are "les arts de faire depourvus de langage,"[38] yet they can and must also be understood via the structures that Foucault names *discourse* and its organizing "gestures."

De Certeau focuses on the mobility of such practices in the face of the organizing structures Foucault's early work puts under the emblem of *discour*s.[39] After the "geste qui a organisé l'espace du discours" explored in *Les mots et les choses* and "le geste, minuscule de quadriller un lieu . . ." of *Surveiller et Punir* follows the establishment of a discourse, in the so-called human sciences, that then allows Foucault to identify a nondiscursive gesture in a contemporary concept of such *science*—one that needs to be explained. Foucault speaks of the nondiscursive gesture of the scientific. ("*un geste non discursif* qui, privilégié pour des raisons historiques et sociales à expliquer, s'articule dans le discours de la scientificité contemporaine").[40]

De Certeau is interested precisely in these practices that Foucault does not trace, the ones that do not constitute discourse or are left out of discussion: "What is the status of so many other sequences that, following their silent itineraries, did not give way to a discursive formulation, nor to a technological systematization?" They constitute a reserve: "in this multiple, silent 'reserve' of procedures that consumer practices would be seeking out . . ." ("dans cette multiple et silencieuse 'réserve' de procédures que les pratiques consommatrices seraient à chercher . . ."). For de Certeau, this "silence" of the practices out of reach of language can also be thought of in relation to Bourdieu's notion of a *docte ignorance* that cannot say what it knows.[41]

In de Certeau's summary, Bourdieu speaks of distinction as two operations: one of them discursive and the other without a discourse: "l'une discursive (dans et par le langage) et l'autre sans discours." What is the status of the "savoir-faire without a discourse, essentially without writing"? With the rise of methodology, practices not yet articulated as/in discourse are classed in relation to those that already are. Soon the "savoir-faire sans discours, essentiellement sans écriture" begins to follow the logic not of discourse but of the laws first of "physiocrate," and then capitalist, production.[42]

For de Certeau, in spite of their differences in methodology, these theories of practice, and of gestures, are themselves gestural: *decoupage* and *retournement*.[43] They bring practice into discussion and into texts, project language onto them or draw language out from them, and listen to their stories, as well as use them to tell stories. While praising their work, de Certeau also critiques these thinkers' interventions: for example, emphasizing that *la docte ignorance*—savant precisely in that it knows too well (without being aware of it) what it does not or cannot say—depends on a sociologist who is then implicitly in the position of he who knows, a position no ethnographer or sociologist would want to occupy today: "It then followed that we needed an ethnologist to know what it was without itself knowing. Today no ethnologist would dare say so (or even think so)" ("d'où le corollaire: il fallait un ethnologue pour savoir ce qu'elle était sans le savoir. Aujourd'hui l'ethnologue n'oserait plus le dire [sinon le penser]").[44]

For de Certeau, there is a point at which the *savoir-faire* carried in the gestures of *arts de faire* parallels the psychoanalytic concept of an unconscious storing away and forgetting or denying its knowledge; and it points to an unconscious knowledge located in the body—somewhere:

> About these clients—and about all the others as well—the analyst will often say: "Somewhere they know this." "Somewhere: but where?" It is their practices that know—gestures, behaviors, manners of speech or walking, etc. There is a knowledge there, but to whom/to what does it belong? It is so rigorous and precise that all the scientific values seem to be mobilized, with all their arms and equipment, on the side of this unconscious, in such a way that to consciousness are left only the fragments and effects of this knowledge, ruses and tactics analogous to those that previously characterized "art."[45]

In this reversal, it is the non-thinking and non-speaking (*l'insu* and *l'infans*) that are "right" whereas "enlightened" consciousness is only the "borrowed" language of this particular knowledge. Individual knowledge, unconscious and yet in constant practice, and the gestures of *arts de faire* instantiate a precise and rigorous knowledge that is un-self-reflective, "unknown" to itself (*insu*) and nonverbal or "unspeaking" (*infans*). Yet far from illiterate, such "unconscious" bodily knowledge is the "true" or "proper" language of knowledge, while "enlightened" consciousness is its improper, false language.

The idea that the body or practice *knows* and—often—doesn't *know* that it knows, as the proverb goes, makes it possible to understand bodies assimilating cultural elements from other cultures and elaborating them into something else. In French hip hop, the debt owed and homage paid to African American culture is evident, yet it is also clear that French hip hop is more than mimesis, not a copy of the various US forms. Between the carnivalesque freedom and the intense training, the counterculture revolution and the pedagogical manuals teaching children how to spin, some part of the *chaînes opératoires* developing hip hop in France must be imitation and some part must be training, facilitating creation. As hip hop is now considered global culture, deeply imitative, the French "exception" or "innovation" must be, in part, the result of a pedagogical approach. If hip hop dance classes are now taught all over the United States, it is worth asking whether this is also not, at least in part, due to the French success in teaching hip hop to broad publics, in dance studios, and to children. These reflections on the teaching and learning of hip hop are drawn from my section of the collaborative report to the Mission du Patrimoine Ethnologique and the Ministère de la Culture et de la Communication, "La danse hip hop: Apprentissage, Transmission, Socialisation," authored by Roberta Shapiro, Isabelle Kauffmann, and myself, and submitted in October 2002.

TEACHING COOL

While a certain hip hop is developed and diffused in dance studios welcoming a paying public of mostly amateur dancers—and young children of bourgeois "hip" parents—it is quite different from the self-educated athletic dancers who have practiced in the stairwells of their lower-income housing estates and in the hallways of building complexes or shopping centers, such as the Paco Rabane lobby or Les Halles in Paris. These forms of training and their link to the formalized "soirees" or evening parties held in halls or bars, where dancers challenge each other in the circles of "battles" (*défis*), have been studied by Isabelle Kauffmann; some of these dancers such as the company BBB, which she has followed for a decade, have become teachers, and some companies are formed by dancers moving from such informal to more formal rehearsal spaces. But the dance studio shapes hip hop in a particular way, contributing to the phenomenon of "aestheticization" and "institutionalization" of this popular form, and the different forms classes take make a difference in the kind of dancers, and hip hop, they produce.

The phenomenon of hip hop dance classes taught at modern dance studios, African dance studios, and studios where everything from tai chi to ballet is taught is a significant part of this "successful" rendering of hip hop accessible to the mainstream public. It is significant that in the United States this phase of institutionalization of this dance did not become widespread until later—well after its popularization in Paris, for example. While hip hop classes could be found in dance studios on university campuses in the United States a decade ago, I did not see them everywhere, nor did I see such courses available to children as they were in France. While forms of jazz dance close to hip hop were taught in dance studios in the United States in the 1970s, aerobics classes might have used hip hop music or taught dance moves, or modern dance companies included hip hop dancers or movements, the rise of hip hop happened much faster in France and may well have influenced the situation in the United States.

In the studios, hip hop teachers who are often themselves the product of self-training but who have turned professional teach amateurs who are impressed by the moves but will never fully choose the lifestyle. The dance is taught with a vocabulary that in essence translates the essence of hip hop into steps to be attacked and accomplished. But the teachers clearly despair of ever communicating to these paying clients what it takes to enter into the *mouv'* or fully embrace the form.

One popular hip hop dancer and teacher who works at various studios in Paris, whom we call in our report "Gabriel," uses a precise vocabulary and attempts to teach both the discipline necessary to master the moves and the spirit of the *mouv'* in classes taught at dance centers and studios. Gabriel always give the name of a step he is teaching, explains where the name comes from, and shows the step's possible variations. In one ninety-minute class, for example, we learned:

> le "pimp walk"
> le "scoobeedoo"
> le "chamadoo"
> le "pace" (punching the time clock)
> le "scoobot" (one hand sets the scooter going; the other stops it)
> le "stop and go"

Gabriel insists on the drill, and on the vocabulary: you must learn the names of the steps, he says, "and not forget them" because "that will allow you to pick up choreography quickly without too much reflection."[46]

In the studio format, the class does not leave much time for internal reflection or self-expression: the rhythm is aggressive and the teacher uses terms such as "il faut" ("you've got to...") or "toujours" ("every time...") or "jamais" ("don't ever...") without giving many personal corrections. The course depends on sequences repeatedly performed before the mirror, with loud music. In one class, Gabriel explains that although "locking" is generally danced to "funk music" and thus very fast, he managed to find a slower tune exceptionally appropriate for our practice: Aretha Franklin's "Rock Steady." He encourages the students, insisting that if the feet do not fly in the air, "it isn't dance." But there is no significant transmission possible in this context: courses in dance studios are organized by hours and space that limit and define the class. While this teacher, in other classes, is deeply engaged in the music and spirit of the dance, he often seems tired or defeated with students at the beginning level.

Yet in a different context, teachers can teach not only the moves but also the essence of the *mouv'*—even and especially to young people, beginners who can indeed go on to become dedicated professionals. An example would be the class that was taught by the company cofounders of Choream, in Montreuil, and their coaching of young dancers forming the company 109 (pronounced *Sang neuf*, New Blood). In between the two extremes of passionate self-organized training in public spaces and the private bourgeois dance class, this might be described as a master class; although it attracts students from other neighborhoods and those students pay for class, it is community based.

The Choream class taught by Stéphanie Nataf and José Bertogal in the 2000–2001 season took place once a week in the *salle polyvalente* of a housing block across from the Mairie de Montreuil metro, the end of the Parisian metro line, the bus terminal, and an ugly shopping mall destroyed in 2007 for improved city planning. During the town's and metro's reconstruction, the surroundings were bleak, recalling that Montreuil has long been a working-class and Communist suburb, although now a sought-after destination for Parisians fleeing high prices, and with the country's first Green party mayor. The course is given in a warm setting, a studio used for many programs, workshops, dance and theater groups, and yoga and literacy courses and is also used by residents of the block including a women's group for immigrants. This "Centre Picasso" occupies two basement rooms, a hallway with lockers next to the open space at the center of the housing block, including a soccer field.

Stéphanie welcomes the students, most of whom she knows already; takes the money (about $5); and uses the "tu" form with everyone. One of the students, "Aïcha," arrives from the other side of Paris, sent by her cousin, also from a Malian family, who lives in Montreuil, which has the largest concentration of Malians living outside Mali, mentioned in the opening pages of this book. The setting and the ambience encourage much more self-expression, exploration, and elaboration of moves. Class often begins late and runs late, but it is far from the "dancing to the beat" in front of the mirror, the series of repeated steps, that is the format in the dance studios in Paris. This setting, by contrast, seems to make possible the *socialisation* of hip hop, its accessibility to and absorption by young people.

The young company coached by Choream, "109" rehearses here,[47] sometimes before the class. During some nights, they stay on to rehearse in the neighboring smaller room, and there is some contact between these young dancers just starting to stage their own works in 2000–2001 and the beginning pupils. On one occasion, I watch them informally practicing in the space before our class begins, sketching standing sequences with interesting, fluid variations they watch in the mirror, or, with their backs to the mirror or heads toward the floor, breaking, doing handstands, cartwheels, and so forth. There are several young women of African origin in the company, all of them good dancers, and as I look at the group I don't see any white members at all. They are clearly an inspiration for Jesse, a young man around seventeen years old from an African family, who learned to do the *coupole* or headspin in class with me several months earlier and has improved rapidly.

The goal in this space is learning moves but also acquiring what in modern dance is called a movement vocabulary, making the movement one's own and expressing oneself through it. In this Choream class, the moment where people start "dancing"—after an initial warm-up—comes much earlier than in studio classes. I find often that we would start dancing even during the exercises—at any rate, earlier than in studios where one learns bits of a routine that only come together, danced, at the end of a memorization process. The Choream teachers take a different approach, closer to a workshop or master class: instead of teaching sequences that one repeats blindly, they give students the working elements of a move, shown in great detail. They put on some music that serves as a background (although it is often loud) and they allow the students to practice the movement to the music, together or on their own, digging in and figuring it out. They circulate through the room to give help to each dancer. The teaching is thus at a very high level, as in a master class, yet personalized. The explanations given are both physical and metaphoric: how to do the move as well as how it feels, images to conjure up in order to do it. While allowing each student to practice and develop, the teachers are also demanding. One evening, for example, we are taught in careful steps how to spin on the head. José shows each step and gives students hands-on help. But students are expected to work hard at it, and when I give up, both teachers come to work on me, encouraging me—they think—by speaking to me in English, as if the move, an "American" move, is best explained in English. As José had earlier said to me, discovering that I was American: "this dance comes from there" ("cette danse vient de là").

This context also allows students to understand the choreographic process that by 2000 was replacing the emphasis on "authenticity" or "old school" performance. Even when demonstrating a classic step, José takes time and uses the space and the mirror to explore the "inside" of the movements—their origin in the body, cause, direction, and motivation—and to push them to the "outside," to follow a movement where it leads, and take it to the floor or wherever it leads, rather than stopping the movement as a well-defined unit with a name. I almost never hear the names of steps in the Choream class, although once Stéphanie used a ballet term, "première"—she corrects José; instead, they are working with the basic movement vocabulary but exploring its choreographic possibilities, developing it, stretching it, varying it by looking both inward (to the movement's impulses) and outward (using the mirror, thinking about the theater and the audience for this dance).

Stéphanie's dancing, even in a beginning class, is clearly on a theatrical level; it anticipates the proscenium and the audience. While this is true for many teachers—all excellent dancers—here I am even able to see, in spite of the great differences in rhythm and energy, as well as weight and shape of the movements, links to modern dance techniques, for example, Martha Graham's use of the floor, which uses similar abdominal force in a very different way. There is thus less emphasis on the language or vocabulary, the transmission of precise steps, and more emphasis on teaching dancers how to find their own style, to do movements but also develop them. José makes us work but never calls out "5–6–7–8" as an order—rather as an invitation. There is no sense, in this class, that knowing the name of a step is crucial to being able to perform it; and already in 2001, the teacher/choreographers described that they no longer cared if the label "hip hop" was attached to their work.

In her in-depth analysis of the institutionalization of hip hop as a professionalized art form in France, Roberta Shapiro emphasizes the "academic" form of ballet as the standard: in developing an aesthetic vocabulary for hip hop choreographies, journalists and the dance public are casting hip hop in the mold of ballets performed on big proscenium stages. In "La Danse à l'envers," she points to several examples of hip hop choreographies openly addressing the confrontation with ballet as a high art, part of the cultural and national patrimony, and also arriving at a point where concert versions of hip hop choreographies are treated in the same category as "ballets."

Yet, in fact, in between the "high" form and the popular form is a historical tradition that troubles this distinction, one in which dancers have been seen as lower class in spite of their actual background or even stardom in ballet. In between ballet and hip hop, there is also the important precedent of modern dance forms, arriving in France from the United States and also institutionalized. In the regional CNC dance and choreography centers and on the big dance stages, at festivals and in dance studios, it is modern dance rather than ballet companies that have gained the biggest audience and that have become the norm for "academic" dance, even reaching out over the last decade to forms of world dance and now to hip hop. The institutionalization of modern dance, in particular the variety shaped by Merce Cunningham and members of his troupe teaching in France, is a significant contributor to the "aestheticization" and "institutionalization" of hip hop in France. I would argue that now many hip hop choreographies are indistinguishable from modern dance and that the (concert version of the) forms will continue to merge in future choreographies.

The teaching of modern dance also serves as an important precursor to the socialization and transmission of hip hop. In studios that modern dance opened up to the many forms influencing it, including African dance, Indian dance, and many popular forms, hip hop took hold and has become accessible to dancers even as children. Modern dance, in its brash American experimental forms, adopting, adapting, distorting, and renaming steps from the classical corpus, paved the way for hip hop in France. While it was never a "popular" form per se, modern dancers were subject to the same marginalization as *corps de ballet* members, even when idolized, associated with physical labor and with the backstage world of the theater. *La danse contemporaine* also struggled for legitimacy, diplomas, a vocabulary, and an audience, even if its path to aestheticization and institutionalization were guaranteed. Like avant-garde theater, it worked its way to the center from a marginal position, and in many cases its dancers and productions were poor in contrast to well-supported ballet companies, even those doing modern-inflected pieces such as Maurice Bejart's.

The success of a company like Choream, and its dancers and choreographers, is clearly built not only on a history of hip hop as a popular form but also on modern dance as a revolutionary form opening up the world of concert dance in France.[48] With the expansion of hip hop out of housing projects and malls, reaching a dance public in theaters and studios, a language had to be developed to teach hip hop. Children were "recruited" into hip hop in France under a label of "cool" but at the service of multiculturalism; in addition to the rhetoric of the *mouv'* and its cultural agents, a language had to be found to train young dancers or teach those who had some classical or contemporary dance training. In this process, after local cultural agents and the state, ultimately the regional dance centers and private studios, their teachers, and their students have played a role.

Even books have played a role in hip hop pedagogy. One striking example is the children's book by Vernay published by the Cité de la Musique in a series called "Carnets de Danse," which furnishes an address book for finding the nearest hip hop dance class and recommends starting at the local city hall. As discussed earlier, the guide then goes on to suggest—only as a backup—televised rediffusions of performances or dance documentaries with the goal of encouraging the freedom of movement and social participation that dance class offers. Vernay also emphasizes that hip hop would be something to learn about from a book or in a library. This manual for children reminds us how different hip hop's story is in France, of the importance of state-funded local centers and cultural agents in the growth of hip hop dance as a participatory civic form, that has taken it far from its counterculture origins. For much of the past decade, my position has been not simply to laud such programs but also to emphasize, in France, the lack of a US parallel, the poverty and marginalization of the dancers so admired for having created the form. Our US artists have little hope of being "recuperated" by a national arts program and in the past, under conservative governments, have been vilified by it; in the United States the art form is valorized when it makes money. Only now and perhaps in part because of its French success is hip hop dancing featured in television advertisements for back-to-school clothing and supplies, are hip hop dance classes being offered in degree dance programs, and are choreographers who have been using hip hop vocabulary being recognized as among the most interesting.

Pedagogy relies on imitation; but can "cool" be taught? As Sidney's H.I.P.-H.O.P. and the children's *carnet de danse* suggest, can the resistance coded into hip hop counterculture become itself an instrument of pedagogy, inculcating a taste for nonviolent—danced—rebellion? Usually a site of imitation par excellence, one we would not associate with hip hop's tradition of freestyles, practice sessions, and parties, the dance class has become a major site for transmission of the form, an intermediary space where individual style can be developed even while "correct" ways to perform moves are learned, and a movement vocabulary is developed that can support choreographies for the national stages.

In French hip hop pedagogy one stereotypically "American" model does persist: one that generates images and performers to be marketed via video and film; but there has also developed a school of teaching hip hop that remains "truer" to its US origins of diaspora and melting pot, to social harmony and other ideals, and has moved beyond a notion of "old school" authenticity or a single antecedent. That this form should be seen as good for children and should derive elements from modern dance class, master class, and composition, developing within institutions but escaping the restraints of orthodoxy, is a French success story. Such an idealization of the situation in France, echoed by US dancers who seek funding and programming there, may well be as naïve as French idealization of an "America" that originates such arts and artists. Both views are emblematic of the misunderstandings on both sides in the ongoing debate about French universalism and US particularism, discussed in relation to hip hop in the first chapters. Defenders of US culture might argue that French hip hop misses the point, imitates without understanding, and capitalizes on US black culture's rich mix without taking into consideration the particularity of its sociopolitical realities. Defenders of French culture might argue that universalism has been the means by which minority cultures such as African American have been valorized, and that French hip hop permits multicultural expression that reflects issues of a postcolonial and immigrant society quite different from today's United States. It is in response to such debates that my work considers hip hop as mimetic in more than a negative sense and French hip hop as more than simply imitating an "American original."

It can only be something more than imitation when a French hip hop professor insists on the accuracy of Uncle Sam's "I WANT YOU!" gesture, teaching—in front of a dance studio mirror—how to perform properly a gesture that signs and mocks authority's call to arms, even if one considers that the professor represents an immigrant minority in France, even one of those called upon several generations ago to bear arms for the republic. For students and teachers alike, it is one thing to perform the gesture mocking mastery and another to *learn* to master the gesture through self-correction in the dance studio mirror. The mirror is used not only to integrate an external image but also to elaborate an identity in danced self-expression; it plays an important role in teaching, and learning, hip hop. While the analysis of this movement (and the *mouv'* of which it is a part) from this "postcolonial" perspective might have remained somewhat abstract, far removed from the concerns of the dancers dancing it, notes and images published in the review of the Ministry of Culture and Communication, *Terrain*, are offered as an alternative to such abstractions.

HIP HOP PEDAGOGY

If the headspin at its invention in New York signified a "cosmic" turn, reflecting the folly of a world turned upside down, it also represents a comic turn, laughing at the world from its underbelly. In a different context, at least twice removed, what does it mean to spin on one's head in a dance studio in Paris? To pay a teacher in order to *learn to spin* on one's head? To study upside-down-ness in a hip hop dance class in France? What brings "Aïcha," a young student whose family moved to France from Mali, all the way across Paris for a Monday night dance class with Compagnie Choream, in addition to the classes she can take at her university and instead of training in the lobbies or hallways of public buildings? (Our research team assigned her this pseudonym in our report.)

In the photos accompanying this chapter, we see the hip hop class for beginners that Aïcha and other dancers, ranging in age from eighteen to thirty-something, take in the arts center of a housing project in a Paris suburb. From an American perspective, this looks like a dance class taught in a dance studio; with the personal attention of professional dancer/choreographers Stéphanie Nataf and José Bertogal, it looks more like a "master class," and the mirror is being used both for pedagogical purposes and for the creative development of a movement style.

What does this mirror reflect? The formalization of a dance form and its teaching, as well as reference to a culture of imitation and the imitation of moves from that culture, but also the elaboration of a danced cultural identity, a classical dance heritage, and the idea of self-expression in movement. Within the imitative matrix of pedagogy, students are also being taught to tap into inner motivation and to expand movements into theatrical dimensions. The mirror becomes not only the tool for insertion of one's own image, or one's own body, into a discipline but also a way to escape the confines of one's own self-image, even one's body, in movement images. The mirror reflects these individual and community formations, but they are not contained by it.

Aïcha comes to this class because it represents a challenge, and because it is a first step toward performance. In 2000–2001, she was a young college student who had been coming to the Choream class all year, and she naturally fell into discussion with me as we walked out together after class and ran to catch the shuttle bus back to the Paris metro. Aïcha walks and talks fast. She is around twenty, is studying for her *licence* degree in psychology at St. Denis, and plans next to do the training to be a high school teacher. On Mondays she takes another dance class at Nanterre that costs about half the price (around $30 per semester). But she finds the Choream course much more interesting.

She has never seen the company perform onstage and thus—from my perspective—does not yet fully see what makes them so special, but for the past five months, she has been coming all the way across Paris on a day when her only other class is another dance class. She says that it was a cousin who lives in Montreuil who first told her about the class and who was also taking it until quite recently. Aïcha comes to this class, in a sense, underground; although she lives at home, she does not tell her family about the class. It represents for her both an opportunity to join the *mouv'* and to find expression in a form that constitutes a form of rebellion, within a communitarian social context.

For Aïcha, tackling the headstand and headspin means crossing gender and social boundaries, moving away from religious and ethical strictures. It represents a different kind of revolution or rebellion, a citation of the freedom of an upside-down America but one that takes on added layers of signification in this context.

Aïcha says that her family is "strict" and that her father, or her family, would be against her taking such a dance class. In one of our conversations during the winter of 2001, I asked her: "Are your brothers and sisters, your family, happy that you are dancing hip hop?" She says that her parents are unaware that she does. I ask: "You just told them you are taking some dance class?" "No," she replies. "They don't know. They are very strict; they would be against it. My father…they are very strict." I ask: "For religious reasons?" She answers: "Yes." I ask if it would be possible to explain to them what she gets out of the course. She describes the hip hop class, the space of the dance, as a "space where you can express yourself." She repeats often that she is ready to do whatever it takes to continue, for example, work to pay for classes, but it is clear that she has no plan to discuss this with her family.[49]

She also sees class as a personal challenge; this year she has made real progress and is doing much better in the floor work. She confides: "I'll try a movement, I can't do it! But then you watch other people doing it and you say to yourself, if they can do it, I can do it. So I try it at home—first try, second try, and so on. And then, I get it! I really want to be able to keep on dancing." "Onstage—at la Villette?" I ask her. "Sure," she smiles, "wherever!"

Hip hop may look like fun, but it requires discipline, like every other form of dance; teaching *la coupole*, Stéphanie says, "afterwards, you have a big bruise, it's required" ("ensuite on a un grand bleu, c'est obligatoire"). Like other young *hip hoppeurs*, Aïcha complains about her *courbatures* but is proud of her bruises; they are the sign of a physical and artistic struggle to acquire this means of expression and make it hers. The bruises both symbolize metaphorically the violence that hip hop responded to in its invention and displace that violence in a figural, corporeal, choreographic language that speaks of something other than violence. Aïcha has a friend studying at Harvard who tells her it is violent in the United States; she says she is not interested in visiting. Hip hop means something more to her than the mythic but misunderstood struggle of African Americans in

US inner cities. *La danse urbaine* allows her to articulate her differences from her family's Malian culture, even if for now she must remain "underground." Between an African Islam she perceives as too strict, forbidding hip hop, and an African America she perceives as too violent, crucible of hip hop, Aïcha negotiates a place for herself in hip hop in France, accessing a certain freedom that one might imagine as "postcolonial" even within a matrix of mimesis.

Hip hoppers' relationship to the mirror is crucial for hip hop's transformation from an informal, participatory circle to a concert dance form taught in studios and performed on proscenium stages. In these images from fieldwork, I focus on the mirror as the multifaceted tool of mimesis: its different uses and importance within hip hop pedagogy, as well as its signal role in turning a street dance into a concert form via the studio, and within the studio, into both a standardized form and an individual form permitting a wide range of choreographic expression.

In hip hop dance class, teachers give—even to beginners—an idea of hip hop as a concert (stage) form, as a *spectacle*. Students receive this image differently, often depending on the class's framing and the teaching space. Two models were studied in fieldwork in the Paris area: the dance studio and the *salle polyvalente*, described in the preceding section. The use of the mirror differs in each and marks significant differences between the two. In the first model, dance classes fit into the framework of scheduling in a dance studio. In their classrooms, often rectangular, it is impossible to avoid the mirror that usually covers the entire length of one of the long walls. In hip hop classes, it is often used exactly as in ballet classes offered in the same room. Taught facing the mirror, hip hop becomes, in a certain way, a classical form of dance, with steps and gestures that the students try to reproduce with great precision. Teachers in such studios usually ask students to imitate their model without getting too involved with each dancer's own body. The expression offered in dance studios before a mirror is a self-presentation for the mirror, with a projected mirror ideal. In the second model, illustrated here, teachers give an idea of the theatrical possibilities of the form while taking a different approach. This type of dance class offers an interiority that can include play with the mirror as a choreographic tool but does not involve the same kind of idealized mirror image, projected or introjected. Here, we will consider specific examples that illustrate the development of personal style and individual expression within the imitative matrix of pedagogy.

Beyond the global gestures associated with hip hop that have been seen as imitative and rooted in the televisual, these examples from French urban dance pedagogy reveal that some teachers allow more room for variation and use the mirror for something other than copying, or show a greater ambition than that of rehearsing or diffusing favorite moves. These video stills suggest these variations at work in the pedagogical and choreographic practices of the cofounders of Compagnie Choréam of Montreuil.

Hip hop as a *forme populaire* depends, along with the elite support and public structures of hip hop that account for its development as a "French" form, on "people"—dancers like Aïcha. Hip hop pedagogy, teaching her to know in a *bodily* way, or teaching her how to use the knowledge of her body constitutes her both as a reflective individual and as communitarian, allowing her individual expression and the support of a group, participating not simply in consumerism but in a social movement of her time.

At the same time that Aïcha is digging into herself and bringing out hip hop moves, she is identifying with a global movement but also joining a generation of French youth asking for equal opportunity. For Aïcha, hip hop is no longer a US form but a French project, and it is a direct response to her Malian family and heritage. Keeping her dancing secret from her family, yet ambitious to be good enough to perform, Aïcha uses hip hop as a site of personal development and group belonging that proposes a strong civic alternative to family and religion—even if it must be segregated from them. Aïcha clearly feels enough support in the *mouv'*, whether from her cousin, her fellow dancers or teachers, or her school friends, to make it possible for her to break through and "become French" in this dance. That there is a French public for this dance, constituted at least in part by intellectual discourses thinking through the body and its knowledge, can only help. What Aïcha dances is counterculture from her family's perspective or from the perspective of heritage and tradition, but from an intellectual "French" perspective, it is cultural self-expression and "social" solidarity. Aïcha learning to spin on her head is both bodily training and physical freedom, participation in a discipline and countercultural revolution. (See Figure 6.1)

The setting is the multifunction room of the Centre d'Espoir Pablo Picasso in a housing block in Montreuil outside Paris but on the Paris metro line. This center houses projects and workshops in theater, dance, yoga, literacy, and women's immigrant solidarity groups. Rooms like these, used as dance studios by fledgling professional companies, as well as by beginners, have played a great role in the transmission of hip hop. The Choream hip hop dance class has a more relaxed rhythm but also resembles a master class; the teachers are communicating skills and techniques to the students, but they are also communicating something about choreography and performance, not simply depending on the mirror or on imitation.

Figure 6.1
Choream dance class, Montreuil, France. Company cofounder José Bertogal teaches a student to head-spin.
Photo Credit: Felicia McCarren.
First published in *Terrain* 44 *Imitation et Anthropologie* 2005 pp. 66–67 (copyright Maison des Sciences de l'Homme, Ministère de la Culture et de la Communication, Paris, 2005). Reprinted here with permission.

The space and the teaching here allow the expression of an interiority, a certain reflection that is not only that of the mirror. This room is big enough so that one can avoid looking in the mirror; during class, the teachers ask the students to change orientation, forcing them to find their motivation within. At times the teachers stop demonstrating and say, "Now I'm going to watch."

In this setting, José moves easily between teaching and discussing. (See Figure 6.2) He physically manipulates bodies and encourages and praises students without losing his perspective as a teacher and model. He does the same with the mirror. While the dance steps are clearly produced "from inside," he also checks in the mirror and isn't afraid to develop the movements, elaborating and linking them—across the space of the studio or the stage—to understand on a bodily level both the basis and the finish of these movements.

In the Choream class, students sometimes move in pairs or in the center and not facing the mirror. The personalized instruction of the teachers encourages the dancer to look inside herself for the sources of movement and the possibilities of expression, then to express herself in her own idiom. Discussion helps here, as does looking in the mirror and working with a partner.

Figure 6.2
Choream dance class. José demonstrates a move derived from the floorwork of break dance but not without connection to some forms of modern dance.
Photo Credit: Felicia McCarren.
First published in *Terrain* 44 *Imitation et Anthropologie* 2005 pp. 66–67 (copyright Maison des Sciences de l'Homme, Ministère de la Culture et de la Communication, Paris, 2005). Reprinted here with permission.

In spite of the significant differences between the forms of contemporary dance and hip hop, in spite of hip hop's different energy and movement quality, there are some parallels between the class process here and that of a modern dance master class. While the hip hop movements here seem less dramatic or emotive, dancers are more anchored in the floor and not completely resisting it, as in the bound-flow energy of much modern dance; there are some resemblances to the floor work developed by Graham and other modern choreographers. Drawing from modern dance and dance composition as much as from the street or *cité*, this pedagogy and choreography create a space for self-expression that both acknowledges the presence of a mirror and (implied) audience and knows that new moves come from somewhere other than the mirror.

AÏCHA, THROUGH THE LOOKING GLASS

In a global culture of signs and screens, it is tempting to see dance—and in particular an omnipresent dance form like hip hop—as a universal language, an internationally understood gestural code erasing local differences. But the French case suggests that even in a form like hip hop, diffused globally by the media, there remain significant local differences, gesture does not necessarily mean the same thing across cultures, and deep pockets of difference remain. While dancers on the two sides of the

Atlantic, or anywhere in the world, might choose to dance hip hop for the same reasons, the form articulates difference differently in its various locations. Aïcha chooses her revolution with the discipline of a dance form that has been adapted to classroom and stage. While for some, dance represents the world upside down, the carnival, the bodily liberation from bodiliness, for Aïcha, in this context it seems to represent a liberation through training and professionalization.

Perhaps dance attains something of its ancient power, the more positive mimesis referred to by Benjamin, when it finds itself positioned as, if not a cosmic, then a civic practice and permits citizens like Aïcha to situate themselves as actors in the French metropolis, within the *mouv'*, and within and beyond the mirror. In dance class, Aïcha learns both to look into herself—physically and psychically—for the sources of movement and to look at herself differently, as a hip hopper breaking the mold, overcoming obstacles, surpassing other people's, as well as her own, expectations. This individual and group potential are reflected in the dance studio mirror; they are formed through it and beyond it. In the mirror, she cannot help but see herself, not only as an image of movement—revolution, change—but also as part of a community.

In her 2007 doctoral dissertation, *Génération du hip hop. Danser au défi des assignations* (University of Nantes), sociologist Isabelle Kauffmann, who attended class with me as part of our research team, reached a similar conclusion.[50] Kauffmann writes: "hip hop dance practice constitutes a space of autonomy where the children of working-class neighborhoods can be free of assimilationist designations, which are a form of symbolic violence exercised by the State and the thinking of the State.[51] Hip hop, in fact, beginning from its importation into France, presents coupled oppositions (visibility/illegibility, mass media/small insider group, stigmatized population/aesthetic platform) that offer the image of a way out for young people oppressed by both stigmatization and the injunction to integrate." For Kauffmann, hip hoppers achieve the institutionalization of a collective "auto-validation": "This socialization is possible," she writes, "because it extends that of the neighborhood while moving beyond it, beyond the *cité* and into adulthood."[52] It is significant that for this sociologist, it is no longer a question of government subventions for hip hop but injunctions to integrate: with hip hop practice as a form offering a way out that is also a way forward for youth in the suburbs.

Conclusion

A few days after the epiphanies in the streets around Paris, described in this book's introduction, I was again US bound. In the airport magazine *Aéroports de Paris,* I found an article on dance centers set up in Paris's two major airports, Charles de Gaulle-Roissy and Orly. Hip hop dance classes can now be taken—free—by passengers who have already checked in. The promotional article reads in part: "... [passengers] can try out a few classic steps: samba, salsa, country, or more streetwise tecktonik and hip hop. Once they've checked in, dance fans glide onto the dance floors set up in the departure lounges. With the help of a teacher, they can practice the moves with headphones on, so as not to disturb other passengers."[1]

The Paris airport management's astute linking of dance to travel underlines a long, historical association. Dances have traveled—and continue to travel—around the world; in Siegfried Kracauer's 1925 essay "Travel and Dance," dancing is a form of travel and traveling, a form of dancing.

But travel is also the obverse of the immigration that is the legacy of colonialism and postwar labor recruiting. To associate dance with travel is to classify dance's connection to foreign places as one of tourism, pleasure, and French cultural absorption, not to see it as an expression of the foreignness erased within an assimilationist system or as a product of migrations. French hip hop dance is both: a foreign import (an embrace of black American music and dance forms) and a venue for expression taken up by immigrant communities or those youths described as *issus de l'immigration.*

To associate dance with travel is also to reconnect today's circulation of global information to earlier forms: global travel—the movement of bodies around the globe—for some theorists prefigures the flows of global capital and information. Dance, too, with its poetic expression coded into gestures that can be easily transmitted, like information, has historically circulated around the world.

It may be true, as Baudrillard and others have said, that information makes us sluggish,[2] and thus urban dance may be compensatory and cathartic; but it is also an elaboration of information in the public sphere, making archived movements come alive or drawing on dance's historic links to global migration, prefiguring the coding and transmission of information around the globe. Hip hop is a global form: it has traveled all over the world on the feet and in the arms of dancers taking airplanes; it is traveling all the time over the Internet. In the information age, freedom of movement through the world and freedom of movement of one's body parallel and intersect the global circulation of information. The dance moves of hip hop, invented in an era of video rewind and record spinning and elaborated across the decades of the rise of the personal computer and the Internet, symbolize a certain freedom of movement even as they critique the mechanics of an automated world. Technology theorists often argue that, with nearly worldwide access to information technology, bodies have changed, and work has changed; one could argue, with them, that now any move is possible. Circulating easily and (seemingly) infinitely, now via YouTube, dance moves move like information, but they also are information, reflecting and nuancing global networks.

In the global adventure of French urban dance, its absorption from across the Atlantic, its development in communities themselves displaced or diasporic, and its return back across on tour as French culture and around the world's francophone spaces, there is a response to two contradictory actualities: first, that the circulation of text and images around the globe in digital form is *liberating*, that it has perpetuated the dream of a universal language. In the culture of global information, dance suggests that our universal language is *gestural* at heart, rooted in our bodily humanity and transcending differences of language, culture, and religion, as well as the pathologies of attention deficit disorder and cognitive overflow syndrome created by this technology.

The second reality this dance confronts is that in spite of the global circulation of information, the global circulation of people has become entirely less free; with the closure of borders, restrictions on immigration, economic woes, the pressures of first-world consumer culture, and the politics of developing-world outsourcing, globalization is far from liberating. Against the background of global circulation and new obstacles to freedom of movement within and across nations, the gestural, bodily freedom of movement and of communication made possible by technology is now severely taxed.

THE MOVES: CIRCULATION OF FORMS AND PEOPLE

My discussions of the cultural transfer of hip hop from the United States focus on the French particulars and the mechanics of its teaching, staging, and choreographic development. How did these dance forms get to France? There is a colonial component of showcasing foreign performance forms in *Expositions Universelles*, a cultural pattern of absorbing circulating forms under the rubric of cultural superiority, and a historic domination in the dance world by some French forms, such as ballet, drawing foreign choreographers to its dance capitol. Hip hop arrived in Europe via television, video, and airplanes. Dancing is historically rooted in bodies and in places but has arguably played, with music, a special role in world travel that, some argue, foreshadowed globalization. Before Louis Lumière coined the phrase and the Lumière camera operators went out into the world to do it, dance was one of the forms "bringing the world to the world."

But while film technology, and later film distribution, moved unilaterally out from the *metropol* to the colonies, dance moved in all directions, with gestures and dances being imported and exported by European cities. Dance and music have long served as examples of mixing of cultures made possible by travel and exchange, historically syncretic, suggesting a global culture before airplanes. In "Travel and Dance," Seigfried Kracauer posited these as two distinct but similar options: dance and travel allow people access to spheres to which they have been denied access. But for Kracauer travel and dance are void of meaning: dancing marks time and travel marks space, but in both, technology becomes an end in itself. And of course, like everyone else, dancers get on planes, which make it possible for audiences far away to see "local" dance in the same way that film, television, or the Internet can. Pictures—certain kinds of pictures, now sent via the Internet—have come to follow air travel, and they, instead of airplanes, move ideas (and talking heads) around the globe.

Airplanes and the Internet, the two major agents of globalization, can be seen as the descendants of the trade routes and practices that Nayan Chanda suggests began the process long ago.[3] In their study *Empire*, Michael Hardt and Antonio Negri argue that airplanes and the Internet in fact erase the dichotomy between local and global in what they call the production of the local (and locality).[4] As a result of this production, they write, local differences are neither "natural" nor preexisting, and globalization is not a homogenization.[5] Yet the question of freedom of movement on the planet is now politicized and can no longer be discussed purely in terms of technology or even access to technology, as Hardt and Negri defined it before 2001: since the September 11th disaster, global movement has been massively restricted. While some potential flyers have chosen not to fly, others have been forced not to. In response to the closure of borders, clandestine traffic across the African and European continents shows no signs of slowing.

In his novel *Courrier Sud,* Antoine de Saint Exupéry relates his own experience in the 1920s and '30s as a mail pilot flying from France to Africa and South America. Airplanes take letters around the globe and pilots with them, to foreign places where people speak languages they don't understand, and so they communicate in gestures. But in this early parable of globalization and the airplane's role in it, the foreigners—those encountered by pilots on the ground—also gesture *in* their different language. The foreignness of the people on their own turf is constituted for the pilot, not only by the language difference, but also by gestures that he reads as their language.

Today, what we might call the culture of air travel has brought new gestural protocols that have forced us to confront the idea of local, symbolic, signifying practices researched by anthropologists and ethnographers. On the plane, it seems that everything for the past half century has been moving toward this idea of a universal language; Esperanto may have failed, but English, via the Internet, seems to be winning. Call it globalization, now; but it is the same thing that airplanes brought in *Courrier Sud* and that the push toward universal communicativity, a common language, attempted. The performance of the (now familiar) safety information gestures by flight attendants points to the same thing; on my flight from Brussels to Casablanca, there is a video with versions in Dutch, French, English, and so forth. It takes, however, more than one cabin person to perform the announcements in the several languages; and the Arabic version is on an audio tape.

In this contemporary culture of air travel, we see to what extent universal language depends on a picture, gesture, sign language, or technology. In the global circulation of ideas, Bruno Latour has traced a continuity from early map making to the age of information through the inscription of local details and their transmission to centers of power.[6] Even modern science, he argues, works this way: scientists dominate flat representations of data (charts, graphs, images produced by instruments and computers—all of this now available and transportable onscreen) and use them to convince others they are right. The map making of the atlas, de Certeau reminds us, was originally called "theater,"[7] but for Latour it is not simply the inscription but the performance of mastery of the data—flattened and transported to the new context—that is crucial for the convincing. The distribution of information of every type continues this process, flattening onto a screen even if modeled in three dimensions, translating into bits.

Has information, then, taken over the global movement that people, since September 2001, have been less free to perform? Does information freely go where and while people do not? The global politics of restrictions on freedom of movement are beyond the scope of this study, but this subtle but significant difference between sending something and going *oneself* is at its heart. It is important to keep in mind how information is the only movement around the globe that some people have, and that the practice of transmitting information (about oneself, for example, one's voice, one's face) offers to many the promise of real movement (through work or personal connections established via the Internet). Thus, information—word or picture, message or video—becomes the gesture of expression, of movement, launched and globally accessible. It is ironic, surely, that freedom of movement fills our screens around the globe, whereas going around the globe freely—sometimes even moving freely in one's own city—is impossible for many people. French hip hop adopts, adapts, and elaborates ways of moving that were new to the republic, enriched by local training and funding and highly visible on tour and via high-tech new media.

To the metaphors of travel and translation used for hip hop throughout this book can be added the metaphor of information. The description of hip hop as a poetic code, and as a movement, indeed aligns it with the constitutive elements of information. The conceptual framework for information—an encoding into bits that facilitates faster circulation—provides a background against which we can read the invention of new gestures and the new conceptions of the bodies making them. It is tempting to see dance as a proto form of the information that now dominates life in the so-called first world, and that will sooner or later reshape life in the developing world. Leroi-Gourhan wondered in the early 1960s about eventual evolutionary changes in behavior brought by *audio-visuel* media (film, television, video); but what has changed in our era of information, in which movement can be not only filmed and archived but also digitized and circulated; where a gesture can be, in a matter of moments, essentially globally accessible; and where computers no longer take up entire rooms or need to be programmed but can be worn on the body and manipulated with simple gestures?

The performers and choreographers of French urban dance for the most part grew up with the computer; moving from "audio-visual" to digital media, their "art world" may have been shaped by the spirit of the *mouv'*, but it exists thanks to imaging and networking. For the first generation of hip hoppers, computer access may have been limited, but it is now an essential part of being a choreographer or performer.

French urban dance raises questions about tradition and technology, and about dance's status as an "authentic" cultural source and as an urban crossing of cultures, for technologized global culture, virtual cyber culture, and quotidian embodied citizenship. Yet this dance is also seen as having its roots in the United States and in a global Anglophone culture now spread by the Internet. The case studies explored in this book suggest that live performance and "recorded" performance no longer stand in clear or complete opposition to one another; we must redefine our very notions of what is "live" and how the recorded archive functions along with and within it.[8] In the same way, performances can be simultaneously local and global, seen as a product of a modern, individual-glorifying culture, and staging the traditions that constitute a community, even one in diaspora. In the case studies explored here, the use of film archive and of television and the role of video and the Internet have been particularly important in bringing together traditional and new forms, global and local practices.

In the French *mouv'* all media forms—pedagogical television, movies, commercials, music videos, dance videos, digital, Internet, telecommunications—have provoked and produced live performance rather than swallowing it up. As a francophone dance form, French hip hop does show us that forms can be assimilated in a multidirectional transculturation: neither the mystical experience of universality nor the image of the exotic. For the new generation of hip hop dancers, YouTube naturally becomes the place for watching performances at dance battles or even showing off a new move filmed at home. New media has meant greater accessibility to dance institutions, to the means of production that such institutions once controlled, and to the source materials that they archived or exhibited.

Global information follows in the wake of the worldwide exploration, contact, and conquest, colonization whose history continues to be explored and that has become, in France, a matter of significant public debate. Just as dances revealed far-away origins, translated and traveled across cultures in earlier historical periods, now dance—like information—can tell you something about somewhere else. In French hip hop it brings the rage of inner-city America to a public that identifies with it and valorizes US black culture at a distance; it can bring the Cambodian genocide into the realm of discussion of human rights in Europe; it can make it possible for a young woman from Mali living in Paris to move beyond family or other constraints, to dance as if she were "somewhere else."

Profoundly local and historically global, untranslatable and yet caught up in translation, dance speaks with great cultural specificity of its place and time and yet has always traveled. While encoding bodily traditions and limitations, it suggests a link between the ancient and the technologically modern. As a form of bodily knowledge, a location of culture, and a poetics of movement, dance serves not as the antidote to, but as a model for, information itself: the globalized gesture that is both image and story, condensed *gestus* and narrative *geste*. The conclusions that are drawn here suggest that the body is much more implicated in technology and technology far more hybrid—linked to the body—than we think,[9] and that dance does not lose its essential quality in the face of technology but anticipates it as a *techne*—a way of knowing—in itself, as code that travels. Like information, dance has crossed the globe as code: encoded and diffused like information, and as information (on the Internet, for example). Yet as a bodily art, its form—its formatting—represents the richer experience of the body. So while dance may be seen as an ancestor of the kind of packaging and transmission of an idea that information now makes possible on a scale of global immediacy, it also represents the leftover meaning, what is *in-forme,* unformed or formatted, a bodily resistance to mediatization and diffusion. In spite of global media and globalized culture, gestures continue to mean different things, and mean differently, in different places.

In a passage on the practice of singing opera as "sons irréductibles à un sens," discussed in chapter 6, Michel de Certeau suggests the possibility of sound or gesture richer than meaning. In this view gesture would be not a simplified communication but rather a condensation of intents, effects, and even unconscious elements in communication that could not be reduced to its meanings. In this way, as I have argued elsewhere, gesture resembles somatization, expressing what is not said—what cannot be said *otherwise* than with the body because it is precisely to show the body also capable of language. This signifying in the gesture is not reductive but, in fact, richer in this form and irreducible to one meaning. In this sense, gesture in reaction to machine culture, to the simplification and orchestration of gestures in industry, can also be seen as a kind of somatization. As machines take over, and as we become mechanized, we still have bodies producing gestures, in a somatization that is now taken seriously.

As technologies come closer to modeling human intelligence, we seem to be returning to the kind of situation identified by Simon Schaffer in the tale of Babbage's dancer and the Difference Engine, which I discussed in *Dancing Machines*. A dancing automaton inspired the first proto-computer: in this inspirational influence, Schaffer claims Babbage discovers the cultural invisibility of the human skills accompanying machines, making them look intelligent, a discovery ultimately inspiring the industrial revolution.[10] In the information and communications technologies of the past thirty years, bodies disappear or are sublimated, aspirated, or floated into cyberspace and yet everywhere present, imaged, encoded, voiced, and reproduced.

Dance has now come to represent a pool of tradition yet it has also served as the image publicizing the iPod. The young consumers of technology dance to a drummer we cannot hear (they are wearing headphones) yet suggest that this device, so private, allows an extroverted expression, dancing not unlike the "thinking out of the box" that technological innovation privileges. Why use this low-tech "authentic" form—dance—to figure the most recent version of the computer? The silence of the image (it is a picture without sound) repeats the silence implied in the image; we cannot hear the music that motivates the dancers. But amidst this double internalization (of the music, of the sound) is the idea of externalization; expressing oneself in movement is both private (inner motivation) and public, visible rather than hidden.

The double-bind structure of this "dancing out loud" without noise also parallels the particular version of the double structure of information. While in information theory, everything appears to be working to produce total communication through homogenization and free exchange of information, and while information itself seems massively accessible, this creation and distribution of information works through encoding—or to be more precise, encryption. On the Internet, sending messages includes a degree of secrecy, via one-way processes of exchange (key exchange) and at the same time making public some information such as an address. This combination of encoding along with public release can be understood also as a description of what dance does: the public performance of a coded message.

While patterns of encryption and key exchange seem far from life in bodies, the use of biometrics for personal identification is now widespread—for example, in French passports. The ultimate guarantor of identity and secrecy is held in the body itself. Decryption thus far has been held at bay by the need for calculations that require too much time, far greater than one person's life or ambition, to accomplish.[11] While they may "disappear" in them, bodies are implicated in our new technologies. The principle of electronic forms is that wider diffusion is possible for the more condensed message; reduction to bits makes a message more easily diffused. Encoding and sending information can be seen as another variant of the condensation and displacement Freud identified as the dream work: the smallest, simplest translation or coding of the idea (as is gesture) and its launch. At the same time encoding and sending information can be seen as an age-old process that has also been called "globalization" and to which mobile forms of dance traditionally contributed. French urban dance, taking a form from somewhere else, performing it and sending it back out somewhere else, manifests dance's contribution to new technologies that both sustain and threaten to erase it. While I have shown how new media can free bodies in French contexts, and mobilize dancing and other subjects, new technologies used for surveillance can also limit movement in certain spaces.

More than ten years after beginning my research, and following the development of a discourse about immigration and integration in France—one of the many surrounding urban dance—the flow of traffic between Africa and France has far from abated and continues despite the perils brought by new restrictions and border closures. It could also be argued that the freedom of movement brought by the *mouv'* is at risk within France, not only for hip hoppers like "Bouda" subject to *la double peine* of extradition, but also for all those now threatened with exclusion from French territory. There are more and more extraditions from France, beginning on a major scale with the *roms* in 2010. Those immigrants known as *clandestins* attract more and more attention even as they attempt to "disappear" in Europe, and it is often through their appearance or behavior that they are identified, interpellated, and eventually repatriated. The more deeply we theorize leaving bodies behind in new technologies, the disembodiment and mobilization of new media, the end of work, the insignificance of bodily particulars, and the ineffectualness of categories of race or ethnicity, the deeper we are in danger of forgetting to take bodily experience into account. It is this book's contention that, as our theory—like our technology—supposedly "frees" us from our bodies, they have more to tell.

NOTES

INTRODUCTION

1. See Roberta Shapiro "Du smurf au ballet. L'invention de la danse hip hop" in Nathalie Heinrich and Roberta Shapiro, eds., *De l'artification; Enquêtes sur le passage à l'art* (Paris: Editions EHESS, 2012), 171–192.
2. "Envoyé spécial," TV5MONDE, July 24, 2010.
3. This comment about dancing "in the break" was made by dancer/choreographer Koosil-ja Hwang, who attended with me an anniversary event for the Rock Steady Crew in New York City, summer 2000.
4. Pap Ndiaye, "Pour une histoire des populations noires en France: préalables théoriques," *Le Mouvement Social* no. 213 (October-December 2005): 91–108.
5. Shayna Samuels, "Europe's Hip-Hop Isn't an Exact Copy," *The New York Times*, Arts section, October 10, 1999, 8.
6. Lisa Traiger, "Compagnie Käfig: Hip-Hop Goes Global", *Washington Post*, Style Section, October 11, 1999, C5.
7. Halifu Osumare, "Global Hip Hop and the African Diaspora," in *Black Cultural Traffic: Crossroads in Global Performance and Popular Culture*, ed. Harry J. Elam, Jr. and Kennell Jackson (Ann Arbor: University of Michigan Press, 2005), 266–288.
8. Tim'm T. West, "Keepin' It Real: Disidentification and Its Discontents," in Elam and Jackson, *Black Cultural Traffic*, 162–184.
9. See, for example, Diane Amans, ed., *An Introduction to Community Dance Practice* (London: Palgrave, 2008).
10. See, for example: H. S. Alim, "Translocal Style Communities: Hip Hop Youth as Cultural Theorists of Style, Language, and Globalization," *Pragmatics* 19, no. 1 (2009), 103–127. Alim argues that hip hop youth are both participants and theorists of their participation in the many translocal style communities that constitute the global hip hop nation and are engaging in the agentive act of theorizing the changes in the contemporary world as they attempt to locate themselves at the intersection of the local and the global. Jesse W. Shipley argues, in "Aesthetic of the Entrepreneur: Afro-Cosmopolitan Rap and Moral Circulation in Accra, Ghana," *Anthropological Quarterly* 82, no. 3 (2009), 631–668, that "the moral legitimacy of a microphone-wielding speaker is produced and contested in lyrics and critiques of politicians, pastors and the mundane struggles of daily life. Youth are produced as self-sovereign subjects who aspire to success through the structures of entrepreneurship. Hiplife reconfigures Pan-African liberation as an entrepreneurial project epitomized by the rap artist."

11. See, for example, Sujatha Fernandes, "Fear of a Black Nation: Local Rappers, Transnational Crossings, and State Power in Contemporary Cuba," *Anthropological Quarterly* 76, no. 4 (2003): 575–608. The abstract reads in part: "The essay explores how the Cuban state has harnessed the energy of the growing hip-hop movement as a way of bolstering its popularity; I highlight forms of appropriation and collaboration between transnational cultural forms and the nation-state that have generally been absent from accounts of cultural globalization. But I also suggest that Cuban rappers' participation in transnational networks allows these rappers some autonomy to continue promoting messages of racial egalitarianism and to develop alternative strategies in a moment of declining options for black youth."

12. See Dan Hancox, "Living Colour," *New Statesman* 136, no. 4839 (2007): 40–41, on French rap group TTC's leader Teki Latex.

13. Katy Khan, "Chinese Hip Hop Music: Negotiating for Cultural Freedoms in the 21st Century," *Muziki: Journal of Music Research in Africa* 6, no. 2 (2009), 232–240.

14. See Pancho McFarland, "Chicano Rap Roots: Black-Brown Cultural Exchange and the Making of a Genre," *Callaloo* 29, no. 3 (2006), 939–955.

15. *On n'est pas couché*, program anchored by Laurent Ruquier, aired on TV5MONDE, May 5, 2011.

16. Arjun Appadurai, *Modernity at Large: Cultural Dimensions of Globalization* (Minneapolis: University of Minnesota Press, 1996), 64.

17. Alison Fensterstock quoted in "New Orleans' Gender-Bending Rap," *New York Times Magazine,* July 25, 2010, http://www.nytimes.com/2010/07/25/magazine/25bounce. In looking "deep" rather than "wide," Fensterstock sees this new form within the long tradition of cross-dressing and gay mainstream performance in New Orleans.

18. Appadurai, *Modernity at Large,* 63.

19. Reportage Akram Khan, *Danser* no. 317, 2012.

20. Théâtre de la Ville Paris 2012–13 Programme, 43.

21. Rey Chow, *Ethics After Idealism: Theory, Culture, Ethnicity, Reading* (Bloomington: Indiana University Press, 1998), xiv.

22. Jean-Loup Amselle, *l'Ethnicisation de la France* (Paris: Nouvelles Editions Lignes, 2011), 33–34.

23. Mireille Rosello, "Tactical Universalism and new multiculturalist claims in postcolonial France" in ed. Charles Forsdick and David Murphy, *Francophone Post-colonial Studies. An Introduction*, (New York: Oxford University Press, 2003).

24. Thomas de Frantz, ed., *Dancing Many Drums, Excavations in African American Dance* (Madison: University of Wisconsin Press, 2002), 21.

25. Within concert dance forms developed in the United States, elements borrowed from African dance forms represent a range of movement possibilities, typifying an African American idiom in choreography by Alvin Ailey such as *Cry!* or composing an abstract movement vocabulary in choreography by Paul Taylor.

26. The term is Brenda Dixon Gottschild's, borrowed by Halifu Osumare, *The Africanist Aesthetic in Global Hip Hop: Power Moves* (New York: Palgrave Macmillan, 2007).

27. In this way, my analysis differs from that of Halifu Osumare, who focuses on break dancing's "power moves" and muscle, rhythm, and text: "Through the nonverbal expressivity of the body, breakdance brings the global and the local closer than we usually imagine. The centrality of the body in Africanist aesthetics privileges 'structures of feeling,' to use Raymond Williams' term, where the rhythm of hip hop is made visible literally through the muscles, apparent not only in the improvising b-boy or b-girl, but also in the emcee and deejay in his/her skilled delivery." *The Africanist*

Aesthetic in Global Hip Hop, 15. I hope to show here how the French case suggests a different model. I agree with her that the dancing is "philosophy in action."

28. While I hope that my work avoids what Eve Sedgwick described as "paranoid criticism"—separating pleasure from the study of the body—it has taken a different direction from much queer theory or gender/feminist work arguing for the skewing of institutions and upheaval of norms in performances.

29. New performance work uses visual, recording, and other digital technologies in a wide range of ways: from choreographic processes to recasting the audience's relation to the performers; from distance performance (telepresence) to the simultaneous use of stage and screen; from the triggering of movement via a sensor that then projects forms instantly onto a screen to biofeedback for performers. Johannes Birringer, choreographer and theorist, writes in *Dance and Media Technologies* 24, no. 1, a special issue on "intelligent stages" about computer-aided choreography done in a "lab-like" environment, or the creation of "environments"; or "virtual dancing": dancing across distances: "how might we dance with remote partners in real time" or in digital dancing environments in which "Dancers will not move through space but connectivity and its inputs will move (through) the dance." In comparison, the way hip hop "mobilizes" communities or changes dancers' environments must be understood as low tech indeed. In the same issue, Timothy Murray speaks of art addressing the "digital divide" using the latest software and best bandwidth but making work available on CD/DVD for those without. Even in the face of the "net condition," the German group he is writing about considers those "users in the most rudimentary of digital environments."

30. Georges Vigarello, *Le corps redressé* (Paris: Armand Colin,, 2001), first edition 1979.

CHAPTER 1

1. This was the case with a documentary film commissioned for the *Rencontres Urbaines* and screened during the festival at la Villette in 1999; see also Claudine Moïse, *Danseurs du Défi* (Montpellier: Indigènes, 1999). A 1995 film program organized by the Cinémathèque Française "Rythmes et Continents Noirs" (Cinémathèque de la Danse, January 13, 14, and 15, 1995) included films of African American dancers with ethnographic films of African dance. In this programming, as in documentaries linking African American jazz dance to African dance forms, the programmers seem to be influenced by the aesthetic of the French review *Documents*, whose two issues from the 1930s juxtaposed ethnographic documents from Africa with photographs, film stills, and reviews of the performances of African Americans. On Paris as a meeting point for African Americans and Africa throughout the twentieth century, see Tyler Stovall, *Paris Noir: African Americans in the City of Light* (New York: Houghton Mifflin, 1996).

2. Edgar Morin and Patrick Singaïny, *La France une et multiculturelle* (Paris: Fayard, 2012).

3. "What Is the European New Frontier," lecture by Mr. Renaud Donnedieu de Vabres, Tulane University, New Orleans, October 30, 2008.

4. Emphasizing the peaceful, communitarian tone of Afrika Bambaata at the foundation of hip hop, Joseph G. Schloss's 2009 work, *Foundation: B-boys, B-girls and Hip Hop Culture* (New York: Oxford University Press, 2009), describes in detail the dance steps and styles in a tone closer to French analyses and reviews of hip hop choreographies, although in France these are most often concert dance events. Carla Stalling Huntington refers to a recent "suburbanization" of hip hop in the United States and a shift to "feel-good" children's empowerment in hip hop dance,

leaving parents uneasy with the moves being taught even though visibly proud at the performances. See Carla Stalling Huntington, *Hip Hop Dance, Meanings and Messages* (Jefferson, NC: McFarland, 2007), 4.

5. Pap Ndiaye, *La condition noire: essai sur une minorite française* (Paris: Calman-Levy, 2007).

6. The http://www.sos-racisme.org website lists 30,000 such exclusions per year. "Anti-Semitism" and "Collaboration 1940–44" are two of the lexicon entries on the SOS-Racisme website.

7. Harlem Désir, interview, "On n'est pas couché," TV5MONDE, May 19, 2012.

8. On dance studies, see Randy Martin, *Critical Moves* (Durham, NC: Duke University Press, 1998); Naomi Jackson and Toni Shapiro-Phim, eds. *Dance, Human Rights and Social Justice: Dignity in Motion* (Lanham, MD: Scarecrow Press, 2008). The moving testimonies and analyses of this collection show how bodies remain vulnerable in political crises and how threatened dancing is in many contexts and across cultures.

9. Jacques Rancière, *Dissensus: On Politics and Aesthetics,* ed. and trans. Steven Corcoran (London: Continuum, 2010).

10. The hip hopper who goes by the name of Bouda, because he was subject to *la double peine* of extradition, was forced to go into hiding; he is interviewed in the film *On n'est pas une marque de vélo* by Jean-Pierre Thorn.

11. Roger Celestin and Eliane DalMolin, *France from 1851 to the Present: Universalism in Crisis* (New York: Palgrave/Macmillan, 2007), 3.

12. Quoted in Brian Rigby, *Popular Culture in Modern France: A Study of Cultural Discourse* (London: Routledge, 1991), 8.

13. Richard Derderian, *North Africans in Contemporary France: Becoming Visible* (London: Palgrave Macmillan, 2004), 2. See Michel Wievorka, "La Crise du modèle français d'intégration," *Regards sur l'actualité* (1990), 161; and "Culture, Société et démocratie," in *La Société Fragmentée? Le multiculturalisme en débat,* ed. M. Wieviorka (Paris: La Découverte, 1996), 33–38.

14. Derderian, *North Africans in Contemporary France,* 3.

15. Rigby, *Popular Culture in Modern France,* 6.

16. Ibid., 7.

17. Lefebvre, quoted in Rigby, *Popular Culture in Modern France,* 37.

18. Richard Pells, *Not Like Us: How Europeans Have Loved, Hated, and Transformed American Culture since World War II* (New York: Basic Books, 1997), 240.

19. Ibid., 241.

20. Rigby, *Popular Culture in Modern France,* 2.

21. Quoted in Rigby, *Popular Culture in Modern France,* 3.

22. Malcolm Cook, ed., *French Culture since 1945* (London and New York: Longman, 1993), 305.

23. Malcolm Cook, "Introduction," in *French Culture since 1945,* cites Mitterand, *Ici et Maintenant,* recording that in Socialist municipalities the culture budget approached 12%.

24. Cook, *French Culture since 1945,* 3. Cook cites Louis Dollot, *Culturelle individuelle et culture de masse* (Paris: PUF, 1974).

25. Bourdieu, quoted in Rigby, *Popular Culture in Modern France,* 161.

26. Rigby, *Popular Culture in Modern France,* 163, quoting D. Pinto, "La conversion de l'intelligentsia," in *L'amérique dans les têtes. Un siècle de fascinations et d'aversions,* ed. D. Lacorne et al. (Paris, Hachette, 1986), 124–136.

27. Rigby, *Popular Culture in Modern France,* 164, 123.

28. Jill Forbes, "The Rise of Audio-Visual Culture," in *French Cultural Studies: An Introduction*, ed. Jill Forbes and Michael Kelly (New York: Oxford University Press, 1995), 261.

29. See Carrie Tarr, *Reframing Difference: Beur and Banlieue Filmmaking in France* (Manchester: Manchester University Press, 2005).

30. Forbes, "The Rise of Audio-Visual Culture," 260.

31. Ibid.

32. Ibid. 234.

33. Ibid., 233, 234, 235.

34. Ibid., 258, quoting *Tel Quel* USA issue, 1977. No page number or author given.

35. Ibid., 262, no reference given.

36. Derderian, *North Africans in Contemporary France,* 15.

37. Ibid., 178,174: "Ethnic minority political and cultural actions are certainly related. Accounts of the associational movement necessarily make reference to militant theater or rock music projects that provided an important formative experience while helping activists to articulate enduring and influential view-points.... Cultural expression has been and remains important in denouncing discriminatory policies, condemning all forms of racial intolerance, challenging stereotypes, and offering more complex and nuanced accounts of ethnic minority populations. By attempting to bring about a greater degree of understanding cultural actors have done much to improve the prospects for mutual recognition. Yet when looking at the realm of culture I have also tried to note the difficulties involved in breaking silences" (174).

38. Ibid., 175.

39. Alec Hargreaves, "The Contribution of North of Sub-Saharan African Immigrant Minorities to the Redefinition of Contemporary French Culture," in *Francophone Postcolonial Studies: A Critical Introduction,* ed. Charles Forsdick and David Murphy (London: Arnold, 2003), 146.

40. Ibid., 148.

41. Ibid., 150.

42. Ibid., 153–154.

43. Ibid.

44. My use of this formulation, a "republic of culture" takes into account the political history of the term *République* and the current valorization of the adjective *républicain*, for example, in the *Parti Socialiste* platform for the 2012 presidential election. The platform describes the republic as "our common patrimony" and calls for a "reaffirmation of our Republican identity" and a "reconnecting to the promise of Republicanism" (Section III, p. 43). Republican values, such as the institution of secularism and public education, attributed to Jules Ferry's government in the Third Republic, are now seen as positive by the majority of the French. But a left-wing critique of François Hollande's visit to Ferry's statue on his first day in office in May 2012 pointed out that Ferry's legacy includes what is now broadly seen as a negative record of colonial administration. My use of the term *republic* is meant to conjure up these debates, about a French "idea" of a nation, organized in part around language and around culture, and its ideological high and low points. See http://www.parti-socialiste.fr/static/projet2012_integrale.pdf

45. Winifred Woodhull, "Postcolonial thought and culture in Francophone North Africa," in Forsdick and Murphy, *Francophone Postcolonial Studies,* 211–220.

46. Etienne Balibar, "Uprisings in the Banlieues," *Constellations* 14, no. 1 (2007), 47. (First published November 2006 in *Lignes*.)

47. Ibid., 49, 61. See also "Nicolas Sarkozy continue de vilipender "racailles et voyous" *Le Monde* 11 novembre 2005.

48. Ibid., 51.

49. Ibid., 59, 57, 60.

50. Ibid., 51.

51. Ibid., 52.

52. Ibid., 61–62.

53. Ibid., 62., 63.

54. Ibid., 63.

55. Ibid., 65.

56. Ibid., 64, 65, 66.

57. See http://www.hiphopcitoyens.com. "Hip Hop Citoyens va aussi continuer à apporter son expertise et son savoir-faire dans l'organisation de manifestations Hip Hop qui concernent les jeunes franciliens. Association de promotion des cultures urbaines et de médiation en direction de la jeunesse, Hip Hop Citoyens travaille depuis plusieurs années pour favoriser l'accès des jeunes à la citoyenneté par la culture. Si 'Paris Hip Hop: la quinzaine du Hip Hop' reste le point d'orgue de notre action, nous développons de nouveaux axes tournés vers un meilleur accompagnement des jeunes porteurs de projets issus de la culture Hip Hop. Face au manque d'investissement institutionnel et privé, il est important que nous restions mobilisés pour faire entendre la voix de toute une partie de la jeunesse française et d'un mouvement artistique si prolifique. Il s'agit aussi de faire vivre la culture Hip Hop à la française dans le reste du monde par l'échange et la mise en place de projets internationaux."

58. Etienne Balibar, "Historical Dilemmas of Democracy and Their Contemporary Relevance for Citizenship," *Rethinking Marxism* 20, no. 4 (October 2008), 523.

59. Aimé Césaire, "An Interview with Aimé Césaire, Conducted by René Depestre," in *Discourse on Colonialism*, trans. Joan Pinkham (New York: Monthly Review Press, 2000), 88.

60. http://www.nytimes.com/2008/06/17/arts/17abroad.htm

61. These remarks made in a conversation with the author in New Orleans, June 2010, are borne out by the work of Alec Hargreaves on minorities in France, to be discussed at length in chapter 3.

62. In a January 2011 interview in which he appeared with Tariq Ramadan on Al Jazeera television, Slavoj Zizek argued that the so-called Arab Spring revolutions showed that thinking about difference that had gone under the label of "multiculturalism" had been incorrect and linked to the thinking of the "clash of civilisations" promoted by Huntington. In fact, Zizek argued, the struggle for democracy that he saw enacted in Tunisia and Egypt showed how *similar* these other cultures were to Western democracies. *Multiculturalism*, in his definition, was a weak label that—while claiming to respect cultural differences—in fact reified difference where there wasn't any. This argument resembles that of Jean-Loup Amselle, presented earlier and also discussed in chapter 3.

63. Interview in *Le Parisien*, November 3, 2005: "je suis hip hoptimiste! Arrêtons de voir le mal partout. Toutes ces personnes d'ethnies différentes qui vivent ensemble dans les quartiers sont lameilleure raison d'y croire. J'ai grandi à Sarcelles, dans le quartier juif avec des Maghrébins, des Indiens, des Africains. On a chacun nos traditions, mais on se parle tous, on vit sur le même palier. Et le mélange se fait naturellement. "

64. Interview in *Le Parisien*, November 3, 2005: "pourquoi la France ne reconnnaît-elle pas ses responsabilités pour les colonies? le jour où on apprend ce qui s'est

réellement passé, on se sent trahi....Pourtant, je vous assure que les fils d'immigrés se sentent bien en France...on y a mangé, on y a grandi, on aime ce pays. Mais on aimerait qu'on nous le rende."

65. Quite different from first-generation immigrants studied, for example, in Arjun Appadurai's exploration of the experience of modernity across nations or the transnationals arising from the end of "national characters" discussed in Emily Apter's 1999 *Continental Drift*, here I am identifying, via Balibar, but in the dances themselves, a different kind of nationality, identity, and modernity.

66. Balibar, "Historical Dilemmas," 525, referring to Rawls, 1999.

67. Andrew Parker and Eve Kosofsky Sedgwick, "Introduction," in *Performativity and Performance*, ed. Parker and Sedgwick (New York: Routledge, 1995), 2.

68. Joseph Roach, "Culture and Performance," in Parker and Sedgwick, *Performativity and Performance,* 60.

69. Ibid.

70. Judith Butler, *Excitable Speech: A Politics of the Performative* (New York: Routledge, 1997).

71. Judith Butler, "Preface," in *Gender Trouble: Feminism and the Subversion of Identity* (New York: Routledge, 1999), xv.

72. Along with "Play—the capacity to experiment with one's surroundings as a form of problem-solving" and nine other skills, in Henry Jenkins with Kate Clinton, Ravi Purushotma, Alice J. Robison, and Margaret Weigel, "Confronting the Challenges of Participatory Culture: Media Education for the 21st Century," an occasional paper on digital media and learning (Chicago: MacArthur Foundation, n.d.), 4. See also Henry Jenkins, *Convergence Culture: Where Old and New Media Collide* (New York: New York University Press, 2006).

73. Chris Salter, *Entangled: Technology and the Transformation of Performance* (Cambridge, MA: MIT Press, 2010), 352.

74. Ibid., 352, quoting Nathalie Depraz, Francisco Varela, and Pierre Vermersch, eds., *On Becoming Aware: A Pragmatics of Experiencing* (Amsterdam: John Benjamins Publishing Company, 2003).

75. Ibid., xxv, citing Dwight Conquergood, "Performance Studies: Interventions and Radical Research," in *The Performance Studies Reader*, ed. Henry Bial (London: Routledge, 2002), 312.

76. Ibid., xxvi.

77. Ibid., xxvii. For Salter, what is most important is how "performance as a mode of being in the world radically differs from *representational* forms of knowledge." For representation, his definition depends on a split between the representation (image/text/code) and the referent. In theater, he argues via Aristotle that mimesis suggests that "the thing or act on the theatrical stage stands in for or represents someone that is not present but that we nevertheless should identify with through an act of empathy" (xxvi). Via Artaud, however, he argues for a theater not of representation but of "life itself, in all of its unstable, shifting materiality" (xxvi).

78. Ibid., 349.

79. Ibid. xxvii.

80. Ibid., xxvii, quoting Barad, "Posthuman Performativity: Towards an Understanding of How Matter comes to Matter," *Signs: Journal of Women in Culture and Society* 28, no. 3, 801–831. Salter's work echoes a philosophical approach and a poetic approach to performance, elaborated through Guattari's critique of both mechanist and vitalist understandings of the machinic, and redefining the machine as

"the apparatus that has...the ability to engender new forms of subjectivity and experience, making marks in and on the world" (xxxiii). It also relies on science and technology studies' "actor-network" theory developed by Latour and Callon, as well as Barad's "agential realism."

81. See my *Dancing Machines: Choreographies of the Age of Mechanical Reproduction* (Stanford: Stanford University Press, 2003), 194, for discussion of this concept by Donna Haraway.

82. Rancière, *Dissensus*, 190.

CHAPTER 2

1. Bill T. Jones, interviewed in P. A. Skantze, "Dancing Away toward Home: An Interview with Bill T. Jones about Dancing in Contemporary Europe," in Heike Raphael-Hernandez, ed., *Blackening Europe: The African American Presence* (New York: Routledge, 2004).

2. In *Dancing Machines*, chapter 6, "Submitting to the Machine," I argue that Josephine Baker's dancing both mocked and mimed an industrial productivity that was put in place in scientific management. The argument about the "recuperation" of hip hop dancers can be understood in similar terms. These dancers are performing forms that are radically new, even contestatory. Yet they are also gaining major stages and audiences through French cultural funding structures.

3. Dominique Rabaté, *Le Chaudron fêlé: Écarts de la littérature* (Paris: José Corti, 2006), 13.

4. Judith Butler, *Excitable Speech: A Politics of the Performative* (New York: Routledge, 1997), 141.

5. Molly Ann Rothenberg, *The Excessive Subject: A New Theory of Social Change* (Cambridge, UK: Polity Press, 2010), 104, 107, 110.

6. Ibid., 106. Rothenberg shows that Butler sees bodily agency as a way to remediate the founding loss described in psychoanalysis through foreclosure. But Butler understands foreclosure as protecting the subject, counter to psychoanalysis' definition of foreclosure as the cause of psychosis. "In principle, then, for Butler, the loss can be remedied—by an appropriation of speech acts that will lead to the opening of previously 'closed' contexts, resulting in the inclusion of the politically oppressed. Psychoanalysis has a name for the position Butler adopts: the neurotic" (112).

7. Diana Fuss, *Essentially Speaking: Feminism, Nature and Difference* (New York: Routledge, 1989), 61, 62. Irigaray argues for a radical difference of women "from the start" (Fuss cites the formulation "no event makes us women"from Irigaray's *This Sex Which Is Not One*) identified with an essentialism that, Fuss writes, might not be reactionary, reductive, ahistorical, or apolitical *ipso facto* (55).

8. Luce Irigaray, "Why Cultivate Difference? Toward a Culture of Two Subjects," *Paragraph* 25 no. 3 (November 2002), 79–90.

9. Of an estimated 200 million French speakers, only 65 million are "French," according to *The New York Times,* May 25, 2010, 21.

10. Julia Kristeva, *Nations Without Nationalism*, trans. Leon S. Roudiez (New York: Columbia University Press, 1993).

11. "Francographic" writing has been defined by Katarzyna Pieprzak and Magali Compagnon in their edited volume, *Land and Landscape in Francographic Literature: Remapping Uncertain Territories* (Newcastle: Cambridge Scholars Publishing, 2007).

12. Philippe Mourrat, Chef de projet à l'Etablissement public de la Villette, Directeur des Rencontres des cultures urbaines, quoted in "Le Hip hop est-il récupérable par l'´Etat?" *Mouvements* 11 (Septembre-Octobre 2000), 67.

13. Robert Stam and Ella Shohat, "French Intellectuals and the U.S. Culture Wars," *Black Renaissance Noir* 2001, 112.

14. Ibid.

15. Ibid., 113.

16. See, for example, Joseph Roach, *Cities of the Dead: Circum-Atlantic Performance* (New York: Columbia, 1996), on the ghostliness or haunting of contemporary popular forms by disembodied forgotten African forms.

17. Pierre Bourdieu and Loic Wacquant, "On the Cunning of Imperialist Reason," in *Theory, Culture and Society* 16 (1999), 51.

18. At one roundtable during the *Rencontres* at la Villette 2000, discussion suggested some historical confusion among the speakers and the public regarding the specifics of segregation in the United States.

19. Steve Cannon, "Paname City Rapping: B-Boys in the Banlieues and Beyond," in Hargreaves and McKinney, *Post-Colonial Cultures in France* (New York: Routledge, 1997) 161–162.

20. The word *black* is listed in the *Dictionnaire bilingue de l'argot d'aujourd'hui; Bilingual Dictionary of Today's Slang* (Paris: Presses Pocket, 1996), 364, as a standard, nonslang term for a "black person."

21. Olivier Bourderionnet, "A 'Picture-Perfect' Banlieue Artist: Abd Al Malik or the Perils of a Conciliatory Rap Discourse," *French Cultural Studies* 22, no. 2 (May 2011), 151–161. Bourderionnet emphasizes the same kind of contradictions in the popularity of Adb El Malik that I have found in hip hop dance and argues that in the face of the existence of preestablished genres and audiences for popular music, Abd el Malik "comes across as gently subversive and echoes France's struggle to reconcile its attachment to tradition and its need to adapt to a changing society."

22. Prévos, André. "The Evolution of French Rap Music and Hip Hop Culture in the 1980s and 1990s," *The French Review* 69.5 (1996): 713–25.

23. Mark Antony Neal, lecture at Tulane University, October 2008. See M. A. Neal, *What the Music Said: Black Popular Music and Black Public Culture* (New York: Routledge, 1999).

24. John McWhorter, *All About the Beat: Why Hip Hop Can't Save Black America* (New York: Gotham Books, 2008), 24, 25, 28–29.

25. Because French rap groups such as NTM do use explicit language, the French public cannot be assumed to be naive about hip hop lyrics; yet the same suspension of judgment seems directed toward rap lyrics in English as to Anglophone rock and roll. Songs by Lou Reed or David Bowie containing explicit references to drugs and sex can be heard regularly in their original versions on the soundtrack of the Monoprix stores. It appears that although English is now spoken across the European Union (as the official language of European Union) and in France, there remains a certain freedom in this domain that is unusual in US and UK public culture.

26. In classes where the teachers give the names of the steps and insist on their importance in the professional practice of hip hop, English names are almost always used; other names seem to have been invented in French as the steps themselves may have been. These are discussed later.

27. See, for example, Marie-Christine Vernay, *La Danse Hip Hop* (Gallimard: Cité de la Musique, n.d.) in the series *Carnets de Danse,* which includes modern, jazz, and classical dance manuals for children. This book, priced at approximately 15 euros, includes a music CD commissioned from Franck II Louise and helps the children who can afford it not only learn the steps but also choose their clothing, organize hip hop dance parties, and speak the lingo.

28. Cannon, "Paname City Rapping," 164.

29. Ibid., 161–162.

30. Bourdieu and Wacquant, "On the Cunning of Imperialist Reason," 49. Underlining the differences between the US and French situations, Bourdieu and Wacquant speak of the French use of the term exclusion to describe the marginalized equivalent of the American "underclass." Although not ghettoized to the same extent as in America, and in an infrastructure far from its American counterpart, the French "underclass" is for Bordieu and Wacquant "a fictional group, produced on paper by the classifying principles of those scholars, journalists and related experts in the management of the (black urban) poor who share in the belief in its existence because it is well-suited to give renewed scientific legitimacy to some and a politically and commercially profitable theme to mine for the others."

31. Claudine Moise, *Danseurs du Défi* (Montpellier: Indigènes, 1999). 88. In the texts on sale at the book exhibit as part of the la Villette festival, ranging from children's how-to manuals to scholarly studies of the movement, the lexicons almost always included in the books uniformly list "posse" as an unmarked term of collectivity.

32. See, for example, André J. Prévos, "Le Business du Rap en France," *The French Review* 74, no. 5 (April 2001), 900–921.

33. "Dix Ans, dix Coups de Coeur," *Suresnes Cités Danse, Le Monde*, i.

34. Although Rennie Harris was first signed by the Parc de la Villette, the Suresnes Cités Danse festival presented his *Rome and Jules* in January 2001. Other US companies using hip hop movement vocabulary or dancers by the 1990s included those of New York choreographers Maya Claire Garrison, Jane Comfort, and Ralph Lemon.

35. Conversation with Olivier Sergent, "administrateur" (manager for the company) for Melting Spot, at la Villette *Rencontres Urbaines*, 2000.

36. Christine Coudun, "La companie Black-blanc-beur: du désir au besoin," in *Rue des Usines* 31–32, *La Hip hop Danse; de la rue à la scène,* (Winter 1996), 50.

37. Stéphanie Nataf, "Ce que je crois, par Stéphanie Nataf," *Le* Monde, January 11, 2002, 27.

38. See Roberta Shapiro, "La Danse a l'Envers," in *Le Goût des belles choses; ethnologie de la relation esthétique*. Mission à l'ethnologie Cahier 19. (Paris: Editions de la Maison des sciences de l'homme, 2004), 195–215.

39. Jean-Loup Amselle, *Branchements: Anthropologie de l'universalité des cultures* (Paris: Flammarion, 2005) 13–14. Amselle is referring here to Rene Etiemble, *Parlez-vous franglais?* (Paris: Gallimard, 1964).

40. Jean-Loup Amselle, Vers un multiculturalisme français: L'empire de la coutume (Paris: Flammarion, 2001) (translated as Affirmative Exclusion: Cultural Pluralism and the Rule of Custom in France by Jane Marie Todd).

41. Jean-Loup Amselle, *l'Ethnicisation de la France* (Paris: Nouvelles Editions Lignes, 2011), 13.

42. *Ibid.*, 23–24

43. *Ibid.*, 30, 31.

44. *Ibid.*, 34.

45. See J. P. Thorm, *Faire kiffer les anges*, documentary, 1996.

46. Roberta Shapiro, "The Aesthetics of Institutionalization: Breakdancing in France," *The Journal of Arts Management, Law, and Society* 33, no. 4 (Winter 2004), 316–335.

47. Ibid., 317. The following quotes are from pages 317 and 318 in this article.

48. Shapiro's work identifies an aesthetic vocabulary for hip hop dance reviews as early as 1992; Kauffmann describes "institutional interest" in these choreographies beginning in 1993. Philippe Mourrat, in an interview with the author, declared that a self-conscious discourse about a choreographic language for *la danse urbaine* dated from 1999.

49. Shapiro, "The Aesthetics of Institutionalization," 328, also cites Isabelle Kauffmann, "Bataclan, trocadéro, Opéra Bastille. Le travail chorégraphique hip hop: Entre inspiration underground et aspiration carriériste," (unpublished), 2003. Chapter 3 will discuss Kauffmann's 2007 thesis, *Génération du hip hop. Danser au défi des assignations*, doctoral dissertation (University of Nantes, 2007), which describes the changing status of French hip hop from a "popular" (working-class) dance to a *danse "savante"*—but significantly, not through more sophisticated techniques but by a "partial institutionalization and a larger diffusion in theaters with a bourgeois public."

50. Hugues Bazin, *La Culture Hip Hop* (Paris: Desclée de Brouwer), 1995.

51. Halifu Osumare, *The Africanist Aesthetic in Global Hip Hop: Power Moves* (New York: Palgrave Macmillan, 2007), 19.

52. Max Silverman, *Facing Postmodernity* (London and New York: Routledge, 1999), 97, citing D. Loosely.

53. Roberta Shapiro and Marie-Christine Bureau, "Un nouveau monde de l'art? Le hip hop en France et aux Etats-Unis," *Sociologie de l'art* 13 (2000).

54. In articles published in the 1990s, Loic Wacquant underlined the noncomparability of US urban ghettos and the French suburban cités where hip hop reigns. Loic J. D. Wacquant, "Pour en finir avec le mythe des 'cités-ghettos'; les différences entre la France et les Etats-Unis," in *Les Annales de la recherche urbaine* (Paris: Centre de recherche d'urbanisme, September 1992), 20–30. For Wacquant, the "underclass" is a nonexistent group created by journalists and academics in the United States to hide current conditions of crisis and the failure of social programs for the urban poor. See also Loic J. D. Wacquant, "l'underclass urbaine dans l'imaginaire social et scientifique américain," in *L'exclusion: l'état des savoirs* (Paris: La Découverte, 1996), 248–262.

55. O. Meyer, Suresnes Cités Danse 12ème édition, janvier-fevrier 2004. "Ferment et brassages. Le hip hop a été le ferment initial de Suresnes Cités Danse. Mais loin de chercher à enfermer cette manifestation du corps urbain dans le 'catalogue' des produits socio-culturels, j'ai tenu à en faire rejaillir les énergies dans un espace de création ouvert à d'autres vents. L'édition 2004 témoigne de cette volonté de décloisonnement, en frayant 'un voyage dans d'autres pays, d'autres univers' (Brésil, Inde, Cameroun ou Italie)…Façon de rappeler que la 'cité,' si elle rassemble au sein d'espaces délimités, est aujourd'hui comme hier un lieu de brassages, où s'exprime la belle diversité du cosmopolitisme. C'est bien ce raccourci que tente Suresnes Cités Danse: du territoire de chacun à l'universel."

56. Rencontres Nationales de Danses Urbaines du 23–28 avril 1996, Cité de la Musique, 12.

57. Silverman, *Facing Postmodernity,* chapter 4: Cultural Debates. In light of this argument, we might see this positioning of hip hop as part of the cultural patrimony, in part to answer critics like Finkelkraut and Fumaroli.

58. "Des mots, des textes, des paroles peuvent-elles être le moteur d'une pièce chorégraphique? A travers cette création nous revisitons les plus belles chansons et dansons sur les plus beaux textes du repertoire de la chanson française. La danse se laisse guider par d'illustres paroliers et interprètes, ceux là même qui ont bercé la jeunesse de nos parents et grands parents. Brel, Piaf, Brassens sont nos sources d'inspiration. 'Paname' est l'hommage de la génération hip hop à celle de ses ainés, et à nos racines qui sont résolument francophones. C'est un pont entre plusieurs générations, une réappropriation urbaine des classiques de la chanson française" (*Paname* press materials).

59. Michel Caserta, director, Eleventh Biennale de danse en Val-de-Marne (8 mars-6 avril 2001). "Contrairement aux thématiques qui ont animé les précedentes 'Biennale' cette edition 2001 fait appel à un ensemble de pays regroupés par un intérêt commun, la langue française, c'est à dire un espace qu'on appelle francophone...moins sur un thématique que sur la possiblité de travailler avec des pays du Magreb, d'Afrique noire, avec la Belgique, la suisse, le Quebec....Il s'agit davantage d'un partage d' intérêts que de l'élaboration d'un thème commun à tous. Cette approche donne une plus grande dynamique dans les échanges, les points de vue. C'est aussi une ouverture vers les pays lointains avec l'attirance qu'ils peuvent susciter.Un voyage au delà de nos rivages, à la rencontre d'une grande richesse des art et des cultures."

60. Michel Germa, président du conseil general, Val-de-Marne. "En choisissant avec la 11è biennale de faire connaître la danse de pays francophones différents, une nouvelle fois elle privilegie la confrontation, le dialogue, l'échange avec d'autres cultures, au plus haut niveau. C'est une démarche tournée vers la construction d'un développement solidaire des hommes, vers la satisfaction de leur besoin de vivre leurs corps, de connaître les autres, de s'épanouir dans la fraternité, la liberté et la paix.Enfin, je ne saurais conclure sans appeler à la vigilance et à l'action de chacun pour obtenir de l'Etat des moyens financiers qui favorisent notamment la création et sa confrontation avec un large public."

61. Stéphanie Nataf, interview with the author, St. Gaudens, France, July 16, 2010. This description develops the themes presented in an earlier interview, Stéphanie Nataf, "Ce que je crois, par Stéphanie Nataf," *Le Monde*, January 11, 2002, 27. "Notre danse est une sorte de médicament qui peut faire du bien, un bien qu'elle nous a apporté." [Our dance is a kind of medicine that can have good effects, the same good effects that it brought to us.']

62. Giorgio Agamben, "Notes sur le geste," "As being-in-language is not something that can be announced/articulated in propositions, gesture in its essence is always the gesture of not finding oneself in language, always a 'gag' in the full sense of the term, that indicates literally the gag that closes one's mouth to block language and then the gag improvised by the actor to alleviate a memory lapse or the impossibility of speech." This text will be discussed further in chapter 5.

CHAPTER 3

1. "Top French Schools Asked to Diversify, Fear for Standards," *The New York Times,* June 30, 2010, http://www.nytimes.com/2010/07/01/world/europe/01ecoles. html?pagewanted=1&_r=1&hp quoting Oualid Fakkir, 23, who is graduating with a master's in finance.

2. "In February the Conférence des Grandes Écoles, under considerable pressure, signed on to a 'Charter of Equal Opportunity' with the government committing the schools to try to reach the 30 percent goal before 2012 or risk losing some financing. But how to get there remains a point of contention. There is a serious question about how to measure diversity in a country where every citizen is presumed equal and there are no official statistics based on race, religion or ethnicity. A goal cannot be called a 'quota,' which has an odor of the United States and affirmative action. Instead, there is the presumption here that poorer citizens will be more diverse, containing a much larger percentage of Muslims, blacks and second-generation immigrants. The minister of higher education at the time, Valérie Pécresse, argued that French who grow up in a poor neighborhood have the same difficulties regardless of ethnicity. But the government is examining whether the current test depends too much on familiarity with French history and culture. 'We're thinking about the socially discriminatory character, or not, of these tests,' Ms. Pécresse said. 'I want the same *concours* for everyone, but I don't exclude that the tests of the *concours* evolve, with the objective of a great social opening and a better measure of young people's intelligence.'" http://www.nytimes.com/2010/07/01/world/europe/01ecoles.html?pagewanted=1&_r=1&hp

3. A group of French intellectuals, refusing to join in the debate which they found dangerous, and proposing that it be recast in different terms, signed and circulated a text "Towards a real debate" that was made available on the website www.rue89.com, translated by Dominic Thomas.

4. See, for example, Felipe Smith, *American Body Politics: Race, Gender, and Black Literary Renaissance* (Athens: Georgia University Press, 1998).

5. Website of the French Cultural Services, New York, www.frenchculture.org. This information was posted at the time of the festival in 2008.

6. Ibid.

7. In the field of French studies, Alec Hargreaves's work has emphasized the multicultural elements in North African immigration into France.

8. *De la Cité au Ciné*, Envoyé Spécial, television program France 2, aired on TV5 MONDE, 3/28/11.

9. Ginette Vincendeau, "Designs on the *Banlieue*; Mathieu Kassovitz' *La Haine* (1995)," in *French Film: Texts and Contexts,* ed. Susan Hayward and Ginette Vincendeau (London: Routledge, 2000), 321.

10. Vincendeau, 322.

11. Max Silverman, *Deconstructing the Nation: Immigration, Racism and Citizenship in Modern France* (London: Routledge, 1992), 4.

12. Robert Stam and Ella Shohat, "French Intellectuals and the U.S. Culture Wars," *Black Renaissance Noir* 2001, 106–107. Others have argued that multiple models and differences are necessarily present and incorporated into an ideology of assimilation.

13. Silverman, *Deconstructing the Nation,* 5, 8.

14. Herrick Chapman and Laura L. Frader, eds., *Race in France: Interdisciplinary Perspectives on the Politics of Difference* (New York: Berghahn, 2004), 14.

15. Ibid. 6.

16. Ibid. 7.

17. Stephen Jay Gould, *The Mismeasure of Man* (New York: Norton, 1996).

18. Jean-Loup Amselle, *Affirmative Exclusion: Cultural Pluralism and the Rule of Custom in France,* trans. Jane Marie Todd (Ithaca, NY: Cornell University Press, 2003), 6.

19. Ibid., xiii.
20. Ibid., xiv, xv.
21. Alec Hargreaves, "Veiled Truths: Discourses of Ethnicity in Contemporary France," in Roland Hsu, ed. *Ethnic Europe: Mobility, Identity, and Conflict in a Globalized World* (Stanford: Stanford University Press, 2010), 83–103.
22. Ibid.
23. Emmanuelle Saada, "Race and Sociological Reason in the Republic," *International Sociology* 17 (2002), 361, 365, 385.
24. Saada, "Race and Sociological Reason in the Republic," 365: "The exportation of the civic model to the French colonies (as part of the 'civilizing mission') plays an important role in these canonical approaches as evidence of the strength of the French commitment to its principles.... [T]he metis decrees, however, do not lend much support to this account, and indicate—to the contrary—that colonial citizenship was predicated more on blood ties than on political and cultural participation."
25. Saada, "Race and Sociological Reason in the Republic," 362. She also refers the reader to Brubaker and Cooper, 2000.
26. Duana Fullwily, quoted in *Harvard Magazine*, May–June 2008, 63, 65.
27. Spencer Wells, director of National Geographic Society-IBM nonprofit Genographic Project, quoted in *Harvard Magazine*, May–June 2008, 64.
28. Quoted in *Harvard Magazine*, May–June 2008, 65.
29. Slavoj Zizek, *Welcome to the Desert of the Real* (London: Verso, 2002) .
30. Elizabeth Mudimbe-Boyi, ed., *Remembering Africa* (Portsmouth, NH: Heinemann, 2002), xiv.
31. Bogumil Jewsiewicki writes movingly of a dance performed by painter Vincent Nkulu and Mufwankolo at the Lumbumbashi Museum, Congo, during a concert/storytelling by Edouard Masengo, to a song popular in the bars in the 1960s. Jewsiewicki quotes John Middleton's comment that in certain contexts, the Lugbara dance because "verbal statements alone could be too crude": "The Dance among the Lugbara," in Society and the Dance, ed. Paul Spencer (CUP, 1985), 180, in Elizabeth Mudimbe-Boyi, *Remembering Africa,* 179.
32. Mary Pratt, in Mudimbe-Boyi, *Remembering Africa.*
33. Ronnie Scharfmann, "Nubile (in) Morocco," in Mudimbe-Boyi, *Remembering Africa*, 310.
34. Scharfmann, in another article, displays this beautifully: reading Marie Chauvet's *Amour Colere Folie*, she writes, "Each time that I reread it, I approach it with feelings of intense fear, rage, impotence, claustrophobia, and disgust, but also with fascination, pity, and admiration. It also happens that I avoid this text, forget what I have read even as I reread it, or I no longer assimilate what I am in the process of reading because it is too terrifying." She identifies her reaction to the novel as "behavioral variants of denial" or "post-traumatic stress disorder" ("The Discourse of Violence in *Amour, colère et folie*," *Postcolonial Subjects; Francophone Women Writers,* 230–231). What interests me here is the difference between a critical approach to texts and a less critical or less complex approach to dance.
35. Christopher Miller, *Nationalists and Nomads; Essays on Francophone Literature and Culture* (Chicago: University of Chicago Press, 1999).
36. Program, Parc de la Villette, *Rencontres 2000:* "une pièce qui remonte aux sources de la conquête du Nouveau Monde pour mieux en interroger les fondements"; [hip hop and capoeira are] "deux mouvements artistiques liés à une forte recherche identitaire."

CHAPTER 4

1. Paul Krugman, "French Connections," *International Herald Tribune,* July 24, 2007, 9.
2. Jean-Noël Jeanneney, *Quand Google defie l'Europe* (Paris: Mille et Une Nuits/FayardJ, 2005). Jeanneney's response to the Google project describes the French National Library's own efforts to digitize its collections, not hostility toward the technology.
3. It is possible, for example, for one to use the public section of the BNF and listen to music or read a periodica, without having to apply for the researcher's card that limits access to the library collection. (Whether people do use it, and whether there really is free access, is another matter.) The BNF online, Gallica, has made many scanned texts from the archive available to the public with an Internet connection. The architecture and planning of the new library focused as much on this public access as on the archival, national history and heritage housed there.
4. Bernard Stiegler, *Prendre Soin: de la jeunesse et des generations* (Paris: Flammarion, 2008).
5. See, for example, Virilio, *L'Art du Moteur* (Paris: Galilée, 1993).
6. See my *Dancing Machines: Choreographies of the Age of Mechanical Reproduction* (Stanford: Stanford University Press, 2003), chapter 2: "Choreocinema."
7. Vanessa Schwartz, *It's so French! Hollywood, Paris, and the Making of Cosmopolitan Film Culture* (Chicago: University of Chicago Press, 2007), 2, 7.
8. Schwartz, *It's so French!,* 4.
9. Schwartz, *It's so French!,* 4–9.
10. Schwartz, *It's so French!,* 7.
11. Ginette Vincendeau, "Designs on the *Banlieue*; Mathieu Kassovitz' *La Haine* (1995)," in French Film: Texts and Contexts, ed. Susan Hayward and Ginette Vincendeau (London: Routledge, 2000), 320, 311.
12. Ginette Vincendeau, "Designs on the *Banlieue*" 316, 324.
13. Mireille Rosello, "*Georgette!* De Farida Belghoul: Television et departenance," *L'Esprit Createur* XXXIII, no. 2 (Summer 1993), 37.
14. Marie-Christine Vernay, *La Danse Hip Hop* (Paris: Cité de la Musique Carnets de Danse, 1998), 43.
15. Philip Auslander, "Afterword: Is there Life after *Liveness*?" in *Performance and Technology: Practices of Virtual Embodiment and Interactivity,* ed. Susan Broadhurst and Josephine Machon (New York: Palgrave, 2006), 194.
16. Auslander, "Afterword," 196.
17. While in the United States these programs tend to be associated with cutting-edge development in the private sector, in Europe they tend to be associated with research at universities and labs under sponsorship. One might conclude—generalizing broadly—that in the United States the market links popular culture to new media (or produces new media instantly for a popular market), whereas in Europe, in the past decades, new media are often produced or deployed in supported cultural or institutional contexts.
18. Chris Salter, *Entangled: Technology and the Transformation of Performance* (Cambridge, MA: MIT Press, 2010).
19. Salter, Entangled, xxi.
20. Salter, Entangled, xxi.
21. Broadhurst and Machon, *Performance and Technology,* xvi.
22. Laura Marks, *The Skin of the Film: Intercultural Cinema, Embodiment, and the Senses* (Durham, NC: Duke University Press, 2000), 138, 2.

CHAPTER 5

1. In the United States, the Cambodia Genocide Project founded at Yale University and under the direction of Gregory Stanton has opened the forum for discussion of what families affected by it have called "what actually happened." Work is now being published in English on families' experiences and ignorance of the massacres. See, for example, Loung Ung, *First They Killed My Father: A Daughter of Cambodia Remembers* ((New York: Harper Collins. 2000), and *Lucky Child.: A Daughter of Cambodia Reunites with the Sister She Left Behind* (New York: Harper Collins, 2005).

2. Jan Bremmer and Herman Roodenburg, eds., *A Cultural History of Gesture* (Ithaca, NY: Cornell, 1991), 11.

3. Ibid., 5–6.

4. In *Dance Pathologies,* I suggested reading Dora's opening and closing of her reticule, read by Freud as symptomatic, as a more conscious and richer gesture, like a dance. For Freud, the case of Dora stages movement (gesture) as a substitute for language when language can't say everything or when a person can't use it. I want also to consider movement not as a default but as a choice to go beyond the limits of language.

5. Hélène Cixous, "Le droit de légende," introduction to the *Prise de l'école de Madhubai* in *Théâtre: Portrait de Dora—La Prise de l'école de Madhubai* (Paris: des femmes, 2007).

6. Cixous, "De la scène de l'inconscient à la scène de l'Histoire: Chemin d'une écriture," in *Hélène Cixous, chemins d'une écriture.* Sous la direction de Francoise van Rossum-Guyon et Myriam Diaz-Diocaretz (PUV, Saint-Denis, 1990/Rodopi), 19.

7. Ibid., 24.

8. Ibid. (translation modified).

9. Ibid., 141.

10. Cixous, "First Names of No One," in *The Helene Cixous Reader,* ed. Susan Sellers (New York: Routledge, 1994), 33.

11. Cixous, "De la scène," 32.

12. Ibid., 28.

13. Ibid., 28–29.

14. Ibid., 33

15. Ibid., 34.

16. Alan Riding, "How Dances Defied Death in Cambodia," *The New York Times,* November 10, 1999.

17. Ibid.

18. Ibid.

19. Cixous, *Rootprints: Memory and Life Writing,* interview with Mareille Calle-Gruber (London: Routledge, 1997), 61.

20. Ibid., 60.

21. Giorgio Agamben, *Moyens sans Fins: notes sur la politique* (Paris: Rivages, 1995), 75.

22. Ibid., 76.

23. Ibid., 80.

24. Ibid., 63.

25. Ibid., 68.

26. Ibid., 69.

27. Ibid., 70–1.

28. Ibid.

29. Interview with the author, May 8, 2008, la Villette, Paris.

30. "The Blogger King; King Sihanouk Announces His Abdication—Online," Economist.com, http://www.economist.com, August 19, 2004. The King's website was http://www.norodomsihanouk.info.

CHAPTER 6

1. bell hooks, *Art on My Mind: Visual Politics* (New York: New Press, 1995), and *Outlaw Culture: Resisting Representations* (New York: Routledge, 1994). Nelson George, *Hip Hop America* (New York: Viking, 1998). Tricia Rose, *Black Noise: Rap Music and Black Culture in Contemporary America* (Hanover: Wesleyan University Press, 1994). Robert Stam and Ella Shohat, "French Intellectuals and the U.S. Culture Wars," *Black Renaissance/Renaissance Noir* 2001.

2. Susan Ossman (dir.), *Mimesis; Imiter, représenter, circuler. Hermes* no. 22. (Paris: CNRS Editions, 1998); Homi Bhabha, "Of Mimicry and Man: The Ambivalence of Colonial Discourse" *October 28* (Spring 1984), 125–133. Michael Taussig, *Mimesis and Alterity: A Particular History of the Senses* (New York: Routledge, 1993); Arjun Appadurai, *Modernity at Large: Cultural Dimensions of Globalization* (Minneapolis: University of Minnesota Press, 1996).

3. Aristotle defines tragedy and comedy according to the class of people they imitate: "the difference between tragedy and comedy coincides exactly with the master-difference: namely the one tends to imitate people better, the other one people worse, than the average." Aristotle, *Poetics* (Ann Arbor: University of Michigan Press, 1970), 18. In chapter 35 of *The Republic*, preceding his critique of drama, Plato defines the artist as one who "represents things" imitating, at a third remove, the thing in its "true nature." Plato, *The Republic* (New York: Oxford University Press, 1977), 327–328; painting is a "representation of a semblance" and the poets' work is "nothing more than semblances," "at the third remove from reality." Such imitation has been cast as negative not only following Plato's critique of drama as appealing to the emotions rather than the higher faculties but also in the Christian antitheatrical tradition. See Jonas Barish, *The Anti-Theatrical Prejudice* (Berkeley: University of California Press, 1981). Elin Diamond, *Unmaking Mimesis: Essays on Feminism and Theater* (New York: Routledge, 1997), exploring feminist and Brechtian theater practice, seconds a reading of The *Republic* attributed to Philippe Lacoue-Labarthe: emphasizing that the problematic of mimesis is "not a 'problematic of the lie' of the simulacrum, but instead involves the subject—and 'the feminization' of that subject. Ultimately mimesis has little to do with a mirror held up to nature or reality—the aesthetic of realism—but rather suggests—if we follow Platonic anxiety to its limits—a trick mirror that doubles (makes feminine) in the act of reflection" (vi). It should be noted, however, that Lacoue-Labarthe's text (Philippe Lacoue-Labarthe, "Typographie," in *Mimésis des articulations* [Paris: Aubier-Flammarion, 1975]) reads Plato through Nietzsche. For Bernard Pautrat, writing in the same volume, Brechtian theater practice invents a "mimésis sans identification (ou presque)" via distancing. (Pautrat, "Politique en scène: Brecht," in *Mimésis des articulations*). For Girard (Girard, *Shakespeare: les feux de l'envie* [Paris: Grasset, 1990]), the mimesis of the drama is a reflection of a mimesis at work in all human societies, a "mimetic desire" that brings individuals into violent conflict with generative potential. The violence unleashed through mimetic competition is at the origin of the forms of ritual sacrifice that, for Girard, found tragedy and comedy. While the violence in the world of rap music and hip hop

in the United States suggests to some of its critics a pattern of ritual killing and cultural formation like those studied by Girard, the situation in France presents a different pattern.

4. Walter Benjamin, "On the Mimetic Faculty," in *Reflections* (New York: Harcourt, Brace, Jovanovich, 1978), 333–336.

5. Barbara Browning, *Samba: Resistance in Motion* (Bloomington: Indiana University Press, 1995).

6. Philippe Lacoue-Labarthe, "Typographie."

7. Jacques Rancière, *Le Destin des images* (Paris: La Fabrique, 2003).

8. Marcel Mauss, *Techniques, Technology and Civilisation,* ed. and with an introduction by Nathan Schlanger (New York: Durkheim Press/Berghahn Books, 2006), 77–95. This essay in English is reproduced from the 1973 Ben Brewster translation.

9. Roberta Shapiro, "La Danse a l'Envers," in *Le Goût des belles choses; ethnologie de la relation esthétique*. Mission à l'ethnologie Cahier 19. (Paris: Editions de la Maison des sciences de l'homme, 2004).

10. André Leroi-Gourhan, *Le Geste et la parole* II: *La memoire et les rythmes* (Paris: Albin Michel, 1964), 60, 261.

11. Alain Corbin, "Cris et Chuchotements" dans *L'histoire de la vie privée* sous la direction de Philippe Ariès et Georges Duby (4. *De la Révolution à la Grande Guerre*) (Paris: Seuil, 1999), 558.

12. Ibid., 560. The reference is to the Vigarello text cited earlier—"le redressement."

13. Ibid., 561–562.

14. Leroi-Gourhan, *Le Geste et la parole* I: *Techniques et language* (Paris: Albin Michel, 1964), 211.

15. Leroi-Gourhan, *Le Geste et la parole* II, 259.

16. Ibid., 259.

17. Leroi-Gourhan, *Le Geste et la parole I, 208.*

18. Ibid., 88–89.

19. Ibid., 209.

20. Ibid., 210.

21. Ibid., 210, 211. "La rythmicité figurative sonore et gesticulatoire est probablement sortie au fil du deroulement géologique, comme le langage, synchroniquement avec le développement des techniques."

22. Ibid., 260.

23. Leroi-Gourhan, II, 79 and II, Chapter XI.

24. Leroi-Gourhan, II, 29.

25. Leroi-Gourhan, II, 31; I, 59; I, 62.

26. Leroi-Gourhan, II, 35.

27. Leroi-Gourhan II, 262; II, 60.

28. Leroi-Gourhan II, 262–263.

29. Leroi-Gourhan II, 266; II, 268.

30. Carrie Noland, *Agency and Embodiment: Performing Gestures/Producing Culture* (Cambridge, MA: Harvard University Press, 2009).

31. Leroi-Gourhan, II, 79.

32. Leroi-Gourhan, *Le Geste et la parole* II, 88–89.

33. Ibid., 92.

34. Michel de Certeau, *l'Invention du quotidien; 1. Arts de faire* (Paris: Gallimard, 1990), 154, 152.

35. De Certeau, 196.

36. De Certeau, 247, 253.

37. De Certeau, referring to Detienne, 123.
38. De Certeau, from the jacket copy, no page; (second quote) XLIII.
39. De Certeau, 75.
40. De Certeau, 77, summarizes and comments on Foucault.
41. De Certeau, 79, and 90–96.
42. De Certeau, 102–103.
43. De Certeau, 99.
44. De Certeau, 90. For de Certeau, both Foucault's and Bourdieu's analyses (models, hypotheses) "faire parler" (97) a savoir-faire that is somehow blocked (ignorant, disavowed, invisible)—"Pullulement de ce qui ne parle pas ou ne parle pas encore (98)"—that then is offered up to the scientist's analysis. *Les arts de faire* goes so far as to suggest that Bourdieu's analysis is itself an example of "docte ignorance," ultimately unable to say what it knows (96), adopting the "tradition populaire" of affirming the contrary in the habitus: "Il affirmera, avec l'habitus, le contraire de ce qu'il sait—tactique populaire traditionnelle—et cette protection (homage rendu a l'autorite de la reason) lui vaudra la possibilite scientifique d'observer ces tactiques en des lieux soigneusement circonscrits" (96). And he will describe Foucault as the "danseur déguisé en archiviste," negotiating each step of research as an *art de faire* like the tightrope dancing defined by Kant. De Certeau: the Foucault quote, 122, and the Kant reference, 114.
45. De Certeau, 111–112.
46. Dance class with "Gabriel," CIDJ Dance Center, February 3, 2001.
47. The *depliant* for the space listing activities notes that the company "Etha Dam" *(State of Mind)* also rehearses here.
48. The language of the battle has been used by very different kinds of dancers; one Cunningham dancer described to me how: "I could dance circles around anybody at that time . . . ," and in New York modern dancers were part of musical theater and dance competitions, tap and other popular forms. The transition "up" to concert stages follows that of other US forms in France.
49. This interview was published in my article "Le hip hop. Une autre revolution," *Terrain 44* (2005), 57–70. "Est-ce que tes frères et soeurs, ta famille, aiment bien que tu fais du hip hop? Elle dit que ses parents ne savent pas. Je demande: tu leur as dit simplement que tu suis un cours de danse? Non, dit-elle. Ils ne savent pas. Ils sont tres strictes, ils seraient contre. Mon père. . . . dit-elle . . . ils sont tres strictes. Je lui demande, c'est pour des raisons religieuses? Elle dit, "oui. Je lui dis, si tu leur expliques bien que c'est important pour toi, pourquoi tu le fais, ce que cela te rapporte? Aïcha dit, "oui, comme un espace où tu peux . . . t'exprimer." Reprinted here with permission.
50. Isabelle Kauffmann, *Génération du hip hop. Danser au défi des assignations* (doctoral dissertation, University of Nantes, Maison des Sciences de l'Homme, 2007).
51. In her title, Kauffmann uses the word *assignations*, which has a juridical meaning in French: allocation or assignation, a writ, or a summons. I have translated as "designations" for lack of a better equivalent here.
52. Kauffmann, *Génération du hip hop.*

CONCLUSION

1. *Aéroports de Paris*, No. 32 Juillet-Aout, 2008; Actualités, 68.
2. Silverman cites and discusses Baudrillard's *A l'ombre des majorités silencieuses, ou la fin du social* (Paris, Grasset, 1981) in Silverman, *Facing Postmodernity*, (London and New York: Routledge, 1999), 145.

3. In *Liveness*, Philip Auslander argues that the very definition of "live" performance must be rethought.
4. René Girard and Michel Serres, *Le Tragique et la Pitié* (Le Pommier, 2007).
5. Simon Schaffer, "Babbage's Dancer and the Impresarios of Mechanism," in *Cultural Babbage: Technology, Time, and Invention*, ed. F. Spufford and J. Uglow (London: Faber and Faber, 1996).
6. Simon Singh, The Code Book: The Science of Secrecy from Ancient Egypt to Quantum Cryptography (New York: Random House Anchor Books, 2000).

INDEX